Studies in the Philosophy of Wittgenstein

International Library of Philosophy
and Scientific Method

EDITOR: TED HONDERICH

For list of books in the series see back endpaper.

Studies in the Philosophy of Wittgenstein

Edited by

PETER WINCH

LONDON
ROUTLEDGE & KEGAN PAUL
NEW YORK : HUMANITIES PRESS

First published 1969
by Routledge & Kegan Paul Limited
Broadway House, 68–74 Carter Lane
London, EC4V 5EL
Reprinted 1971

Printed in Great Britain
by Unwin Brothers Limited
The Gresham Press, Old Woking, Surrey, England
A member of the Staples Printing Group

ISBN 0 7100 6393 8

CONTENTS

INTRODUCTION: THE UNITY OF WITTGENSTEIN'S PHILOSOPHY

Peter Winch

THE essays in this volume are all new. Contributors were selected with a view to providing a fairly representative range of Wittgenstein's philosophical interests but, once selected, they were left entirely free to write on what most interested them. There is, therefore, no claim to any systematic 'covering of the ground' and, inevitably, some of Wittgenstein's most central preoccupations are independently discussed by various individual contributors. This, I think, is in the spirit of Wittgenstein's method, particularly in his later works, of passing over the same point again and again from different directions, thus building up a picture of its complex relations to other points of philosophical interest.

I shall try, in this Introduction, to give some account of the development of Wittgenstein's treatment of certain central issues, relating these issues, where I can, to the points discussed by the other contributors. One of my main aims will be to combat the widespread view, which seems to me disastrously mistaken, that we are dealing with two different philosophers: 'the earlier Wittgenstein' and 'the later Wittgenstein'; hence my subtitle 'the Unity of Wittgenstein's Philosophy'. Of course, when I speak here of 'unity', I by no means wish to imply that we have to do with a single 'system' of philosophy (like Spinoza's, say), stretching from the *Tractatus* to and beyond *Philosophical Investigations*. On the one hand the ideal of such a philosophical system was always an object of criticism for Wittgenstein even at the time of the *Tractatus*, but more explicitly so, and for different though related reasons, in his later writings. And on the other hand it would be quite absurd to deny that the philosophy of, say, *Philosophical Investigations*, is in obvious and fundamental conflict with that of the *Tractatus*. Indeed, the earlier sections at least of *Philosophical Investigations* are an explicit criticism of the point of view underlying the earlier work. Moreover, progressively as its argument develops, it concerns itself in more and more detail with topics in epistemology and the philosophy of mind which are either not dealt with at all in the *Tractatus* or at most receive passing mention there.

But if we are impressed by this last fact in the wrong way, we are in great danger of not seeing the wood for the trees. Many contemporary philosophers, I think, implicitly accept Russell's view that Wittgenstein just abandoned his early interest in the nature of logic to concentrate on (what Russell held to be) the easier task of describing the use of certain expressions in ordinary language.[1] This view completely misunderstands the point and nature of these 'descriptions', which were intended as contributions to the discussion of the very same problems as had exercised Wittgenstein in the *Tractatus*: problems about the nature of logic, the relation of logic to language, and the application of logic in language to reality. It was precisely Wittgenstein's insight into the deficiencies of his treatment of these problems in the *Tractatus* that led him to see that the problems about logic require for their understanding a treatment of very diverse-seeming philosophical problems. This turns upside down his view in the *Tractatus* that, once the central logical problems had been settled, the dissipation of other philosophical difficulties would in principle have been dissipated at one blow, so that all that would remain to be done would be a sort of mopping-up operation. In contrast with this view, the problem about the nature of logic is itself seen as under constant and developing treatment in *all* the later philosophical discussions. This applies even to Wittgenstein's treatment of such apparently diverse

---

[1] It is noteworthy for instance, that in the bibliography to *Philosophical Logic*, edited by P. F. Strawson (Oxford University Press, 1967) the only work by Wittgenstein listed is *Tractatus Logico-Philosophicus*—as if Wittgenstein's other works were not concerned with philosophical logic.

questions as the nature of Freud's contribution to psychology and of Frazer's social anthropology.

Let me first try to sketch how these problems about logic, language and reality presented themselves to Wittgenstein in the *Tractatus*, problems dealt with in the contributions by Miss Ishiguro, Mr. Rhees and Professor Shwayder. They are all contained in the central question, 'What is a proposition?', a question which is discussed in the light of a number of particular puzzles, some of the more important of which are as follows. There is, first, a puzzle about the relation which holds between a proposition and a fact in virtue of which we say that a proposition 'states' a fact. What makes this perplexing is that a proposition does not have to be true in order to be meaningful. A proposition must already stand in a relation to reality if it means something (i.e. if it really is a proposition at all); to understand the proposition is to know what fact it states to obtain—and the question whether that fact really does obtain is a further one. Because a proposition may be false, its meaningfulness cannot consist in any relation in which it stands to an actually obtaining fact (at least not the fact that it *states* to obtain—for perhaps there is no such fact). If one then tries to say that the meaning of a false proposition consists in its relation to the fact stated by its negation, one is then confronted with the hardly less perplexing problem of the nature of negative propositions: do these state negative facts? And what are these supposed to be, given that the world is everything that *is* the case? How can one reconcile the dictum that the world is everything that is the case with the view that a proposition essentially involves a relation to the world and with the requirement that a proposition may be meaningful and yet false?

The question of how propositions are related to their negations is a special case of the question of what relations hold between a proposition and other propositions—the relations which enable us to infer one proposition from others. It would be tempting to say that this is the question: What is logic? But this might misleadingly suggest that the nature of logic has only become an issue at *this* stage; whereas it is vital to our understanding of Wittgenstein to see that the nature of logic is already being inquired into in Wittgenstein's treatment of the puzzle about the relation between propositions and facts. This point can perhaps be expressed in the form of another problem: What is the relation between a proposition's ability to state a fact and its ability to stand in logical relations to other propositions? Now Wittgenstein thought (and quite rightly) that there must *be* such a relation; that it is not merely a contingent matter that a proposition can combine these two functions; that unless propositions had logical relations with each other they would not state facts (i.e. would not be propositions) and unless they stated facts, they would not have logical relations with other propositions. It is this last point which Wittgenstein is pursuing, though from a different point of view, when he later discusses the importance of the fact that symbols which occur in the context of mathematical calculations also have a 'civil status' (cf. Shwayder's contribution) and that, if this were not the case, their manipulation according to syntactical rules would not constitute 'calculation' or 'proof'.

Shwayder says that 'Wittgenstein's philosophy was Kantian from beginning to end'. Whether or not we accept this extreme view, there is still perhaps illumination to be won from comparing Wittgenstein's problem in the *Tractatus* with the difficulty Kant felt over Hume. Hume had tried to account for the formation of concepts psychologically: 'impressions', by means of some psychological mechanism, give rise to 'ideas'. His account of purely logical 'relations between ideas' is quite separate from this account of the formation of ideas; it appears as just a brute fact that ideas, thus formed from impressions, *do* stand in logical relations. Hence Hume's scepticism about the power of logic to further our understanding of the real world. Now Kant's difficulties over synthetic *a priori* judgements led him to the view that logical considerations must be involved at the outset in the fact that judgements say something about the empirical world. Judgements must have a logical structure (expounded by Kant in accordance with Aristotle's table of categories), not merely if inferences are to be possible from one judgement to another, but also if they are to say anything at all. The rôle which Kant ascribed to synthetic *a priori* judgements in this connexion is closely related both to Wittgenstein's conception of the 'elementary propositions' in the *Tractatus* and also to the rôle he ascribed to 'paradigms' in his later writings.

Wittgenstein in the *Tractatus* held that words in a language are capable of referring to objects in the world only in so far as they are possible components of propositions, a view carefully discussed by Miss Ishiguro. 'Only propositions have sense; only in the nexus of a proposition does a name have meaning' (3.3). The proposition has a logical structure which is identical with the structure of the fact which it states. The possession by the proposition of this structure shows the possibility of a fact with the same structure. Indeed a propositional sign is itself a fact (3.14) and the sign is used 'as a projection of a possible situation. The method of projection is to think of the sense[1] of the proposition' (3.11). So: '*That* is how a picture is attached to reality; it reaches right out to it' (2.1511). A name and the object to which it refers exist in the same 'logical space'; the name also exists in the same logical space as the other names with which it may significantly combine in propositions; and the object exists in the same logical space as the other objects with which it may combine in facts. Logical space determines what combinations of names (i.e. what propositions) are possible *and also* what combinations of objects (i.e. what facts) are possible.

Now one way of understanding how the kind of discussion that is carried on in *Philosophical Investigations* and the later writings is related to the *Tractatus* would be to look at some difficulties in the *Tractatus* notion of 'structure' and 'logical space'. What sense are we to attach to the word 'logical' here? (For it is clear that the notion of 'structure', as applied to elementary propositions is also thought of as in some sense a 'logical' notion.) When Wittgenstein comes to speak in the *Tractatus* about inference from one proposition to another, all the weight of the discussion seems to rest on the notion of truth-functional relations. Wherever there is inference there is truth-functional complexity; but since elementary propositions are not truth-functionally complex, 'one elementary proposition cannot be deduced from another' (5.134). Wittgenstein gives 'structure' an important rôle in his account of inference.

5.13   When the truth of one proposition follows from the truth of others, we can see this from the structure of the propositions.

5.131   If the truth of one proposition follows from the truth of others, this finds expression in relations in which the forms of the propositions stand to one another: nor is it necessary for us to set up these relations between them, by combining

---

[1] Perhaps the German here is better rendered: 'to think the sense'.

them with one another in a single proposition; on the contrary, the relations are internal, and their existence is an immediate result of the existence of the propositions.

'Structure' here can surely *only* mean 'truth-functional structure'. But an elementary proposition is also said to have a 'structure'; and it is hard to see how this could be a truth-functional structure. So it looks as though the 'logic' involved in the logical structure of elementary propositions must be different from that involved in truth-functional logic. But this of course *cannot* be Wittgenstein's view, since one of the points he insists on most fiercely in the *Tractatus* is the unity of logic: 'there can *never* be surprises in logic' (6.1251). There is, it is true, the following remark, which Wittgenstein gives a prominent place in his scheme of numeration: 'A proposition is a truth-function of elementary propositions. (An elementary proposition is a truth-function of itself.)' (5). I take the significance of the parenthesis to be that it is no contingent matter that elementary propositions can have truth-functional operations performed on them; it already belongs to their nature as propositions that this should be possible. No doubt this is important, but it still provides us with no account of what we are to understand by 'logic' in the expression, 'the logical structure of elementary propositions' or in talk about the 'logical space' in which objects and their names have their being. The difficulty here is closely connected with that which was one of the main factors in inducing Wittgenstein to move away from the *Tractatus* notion of elementary propositions. In his Aristotelian Society paper on 'Logical Form' he is preoccupied with the fact that certain propositions about colours (which might be taken as natural candidates for the status of elementary propositions, if analysed just a little further) are *not* logically independent of each other. Further, the logical relations which such propositions do have to each other seem to depend, not on truth-functional notions, but rather on the *nature of colour*. This brings me to my next point.

The following passage in the *Tractatus* illustrates the conception of logical space.

2.0131   A spatial object must be situated in infinite space. (A spatial point is an argument place.)

A speck in the visual field, though it need not be red,

> must have some colour: it is, so to speak, surrounded by
> colour-space. Notes must have *some* pitch, objects of the
> sense of touch *some* degree of hardness, and so on.

Thus, we shall have to say, the ways in which the word 'red', say,
can be combined with other words so as to express significant
propositions, is determined by colour-space. I can say 'This book
is red', but not 'This number is red'. But is this determined by
logic, or by the nature of colour, books, number? Now it seems
clear that Wittgenstein must say it is a logical matter, the field
of logic being the field of the distinction between what can and
what cannot intelligibly be said. Yet Wittgenstein also wants to
distinguish what belongs to logic from what belongs to, say,
the nature of space, the nature of colour, the nature of material
objects.

> 2.181   A picture whose pictorial form is logical form is called a
> logical picture.
>
> 2.182   Every picture is *at the same time* a logical one. (On the other
> hand, not every picture is, for example, a spatial one.)

So what makes a picture a logical picture is what it has in common
with any picture: i.e., what it is about it which makes it a picture
at all. And yet, surely, what makes it true that 'every note must
have *some* pitch' is not what propositions about notes have in
common with every other proposition, but rather what makes them
propositions *about notes*. The difficulty may be expressed in the
form of the following question. How, in respect of relations to
logic, is what makes something a proposition connected with
what makes it a proposition about a particular category of
object?—The difficulty has analogies with that which Kant felt
about the *application* of the categories and which he attempted to
overcome with his doctrine of Schematism.

According to the *Tractatus* the structure of propositions is
revealed by analysis. Non-elementary propositions will be analysed by having their truth-functional structure made clear. If
the analysis is 'complete' we shall be left with a number of
elementary propositions, not themselves susceptible of further
truth-functional analysis. These elementary propositions will consist of names immediately 'concatenated' with each other. The
concatenation of names will itself exhibit a structure, though not

a truth-functional structure. One thing which is common to the truth-functional structure of non-elementary propositions and to the non-truth-functional structure of elementary propositions is that in neither case shall we be able to *say* what this structure is. With regard to non-elementary propositions this point is made in 5.13 and 5.131, quoted above. With regard to elementary propositions the point is involved in the fundamental *Tractatus* doctrine, which Miss Ishiguro rightly distinguishes sharply from Russell's logical atomism, that 'only in the nexus of a proposition does a name have meaning' (3.3). The point here is that one cannot further analyse an elementary proposition by splitting it up into its component names.

Now what, so I have been arguing, disturbs the *prima facie* coherent unity of this doctrine is just the ambiguity of the word 'structure' as applied to elementary and non-elementary propositions respectively. And what makes this a serious difficulty is just that the structure of elementary propositions must be a *logical* structure. This is clear in general from the fact that the notion of structure is introduced in this context to mark the distinction between collections of names which do, and those which do not, say something, express significant propositions. It would certainly be intolerable to exclude from logic such a vitally important sector of the distinction between sense and nonsense. But it is also clear that this notion of the structure of elementary propositions invades the field of truth-functional logic. It affects our understanding of quantification, for example, in that we have to understand what are and what are not possible values of 'x' in functions like 'x is red', if we are to understand the sense of propositions like '($\exists$x) (x is red)'. It is also relevant to the 'paradoxes of material implication', which arise because, if we think in exclusively truth-functional terms, we are unable to distinguish expressions of the form 'p$\supset$q' which do make sense from those which do not.

The central rôle which the notion of a language game, or form of life, plays in Wittgenstein's later writings enables him to overcome this difficulty. Just as the signs used in mathematical calculations also have a 'civil status', so truth-functional relations between propositions are not just exhibited in the things we do with marks on pieces of paper. They are exhibited in the various kinds of human activity which, *given the appropriate social context,* count as 'accepting a proposition as true', 'inferring one proposition from another', 'making a supposition', 'choosing between alternatives', and so on. In this connexion we may recall Russell's view (in the *Inquiry into Meaning and Truth*) that 'or' represents a feeling of indecision. Though this is wrong as it stands, it suggests what is right: that the word 'or' would not mean what it does apart from such actions as deciding between alternatives, choosing, offering alternatives, and so on. What distinguishes these truth-functional notions and justifies us in giving them a central place in logic is their all-pervasive character. They are not peculiar to any particular language-game but enter into practically all areas of human activity. Does it ever make sense, for instance, to speak of a language game which involves no conception of negation? Apart from other considerations, what would become of the distinction between a correct and an incorrect move in the game unless there were the possibility of correcting mistakes? 'No, that is *not* how it is done. Like this.' We must remember here, of course, that the manifestations of these fundamental logical operations will be very various. Contrast, for example, choosing between two pieces of cake and choosing between marrying and becoming a monk. But it is even more important to remember that these ('truth-functional') operations could not exist independently of those other operations by which, for example, we identify the *kinds* of objects we are talking about; because, unless we could be said to be talking *about* things of a definite kind, we could not either be said to be, e.g. choosing between, considering together, rejecting things of a definite kind. And here we are dealing with the kind of issue which made Wittgenstein, in the *Tractatus*, speak of the 'structure' of elementary propositions and of the 'logical space' in which objects exist. His treatment of 'Five red apples' (*Philosophical Investigations*, I, § 1) already shows how these issues can be understood in terms of the operations involved in language games. Thus, paradoxically and yet characteristically, the unity of logic is saved precisely because of a much less formal kind of discussion of what logic is.

Consider the following passage from the *Tractatus*.

2.024   Substance is what subsists independently of what is the case.

2.025   It is form and content.

9

2.0251   Space, time and colour (being coloured) are forms of objects.

2.026   There must be objects, if the world is to have unalterable form.

2.027   Objects, the unalterable, and the subsistent are one and the same.

2.0271   Objects are what is unalterable and subsistent; their configuration is what is changing and unstable.

2.0272   The configuration of objects produces states of affairs.

The demand that the world should have an unalterable form (*'eine feste Form'*) is identical with the demand that propositions must have a determinate sense, if it is to be possible to say anything at all. What exactly is this demand? Consider it in relation to the remark I have already cited from 3.11: 'The method of projection is to think the sense of the proposition.' The point surely is that, in so far as we have to do only with a *propositional sign*, what *proposition* is in question is still not determinate. For any sign can be variously interpreted. I *could* take an arrow with its head pointing to the left as meaning that I should turn right, or that I should stop and dig a hole, or break into song. Moreover, if what I call 'interpreting the sign' consists in producing a further sign, exactly the same difficulty arises for the interpretation of the further sign which I produce. How is this proliferation of interpretations to be halted? Only, it appeared to Wittgenstein at the time of the *Tractatus*, by reaching an interpretation which is not susceptible of further interpretation. This is the idea which is expressed in *The Blue Book* (p. 34). 'What one wishes to say is: "Every sign is capable of interpretation; but the *meaning* mustn't be capable of interpretation. It is the last interpretation."' The elementary propositions of the *Tractatus* were intended to fill this rôle. No further analysis (interpretation) of them is possible. They just consist of names in *immediate* mutual concatenation; these names are *immediately* correlated with objects, which again are in *immediate* mutual concatenation. My italicization of *'immediate'* in that last sentence is supposed to express that we are concerned here with indissoluble, internal relations. Everything here is *'fest'*. In *Zettel*, § 297, Wittgenstein obviously refers back to this *Tractatus* viewpoint when he imagines someone saying: 'How do I manage always to use a word correctly—i.e. significantly; do I keep on consulting a grammar? No; the fact that I mean something—the thing I mean, prevents me from talking nonsense.'

Let us look at the matter from a slightly different direction. What happens when A says something to B, where A means what he says and B understands what A means to say? Well, on the surface, A utters certain sounds and makes certain gestures and B responds by making further sounds, and gestures and doing certain acts. But of course all this could have happened and yet A might not have meant what he said nor B have understood it. Suppose we now introduce mention of the fact that the sounds uttered by A are used by him, and understood by B as being used by A, in accordance with certain rules. Of course, we have begged a great many of the most important questions already in saying this, for we need to make clear what is involved in following a rule and, in doing this, we shall be faced with all the difficulties about infinite multiplicity of possible interpretations which have already been alluded to. But suppose we are satisfied that all these difficulties have been overcome, perhaps on the lines of the discussions in *The Blue and Brown Books* and the earlier parts of *Philosophical Investigations*, is there still not cause for uneasiness? For do we not now seem to be saying that communicating with each other simply consists in our following certain conventions in our dealings with each other? And then what has become of the idea that to say something is to stand in a relation to some independent reality? We seem to be in a position not essentially different from that of a Protagoras or a Gorgias. There is no reality; and if there were, no man could come to know it; and even if a man could come to know it, he could not communicate what he knew to anyone else.

I have harped on these difficulties in order to make clear why the idea of an 'inner process', in connexion with notions like thinking, understanding, meaning and intending, runs in such an obsessional way through all Wittgenstein's later writings. We are constantly under the temptation to think that there *must* be such a process if there is ever to be such a thing at all as thinking about something, or saying that something is the case. And this temptation is the very same temptation as that which led Wittgenstein to talk about 'elementary propositions' in the *Tractatus*. If there is a definite process which *is* 'understanding', then its occurrence will guarantee that understanding has taken place, that no **further** 'interpretation' is called for. If there is an elementary proposition then its existence guarantees that something definite has been said; it stands alone and does not need the support of anything else in the form of other words or other symbolic expressions to ensure that it says something. It shows the possibility of the state of affairs which it describes directly, by the fact that its component names are immediately correlated with objects.

If we want, then, to understand the force of Wittgenstein's arguments against the various forms of the idea of an inner process, we must understand the force of his reasons for coming to reject the *Tractatus* requirement that there should be elementary propositions. Rush Rhees has said (in discussion) that Wittgenstein once remarked that what was wrong with his conception of elementary propositions in the *Tractatus* is that he had confused the 'method of projection' with the 'lines of projection'.[1] I suppose he meant something like the following. At first sight it looks as though one could represent the relations between an elementary proposition and a *Sachverhalt* in the following diagrammatic way:

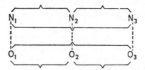

where N_{1-3} represent names combined in a proposition and O_{1-3} objects combined in a *Sachverhalt* and where the dotted lines represent the correlation of the names with the objects. This is a diagram which the *Tractatus* suggests although, of course, the *Tractatus* also urges that such a representation must be without sense in that it attempts to say what can only be shown, or attempts to picture something about a picture which must be revealed in the picture. This objection is very like the objection made later in the *Tractatus* (5.6331) to representing the visual field thus:

Just as our representation of the visual field cannot include the eye which sees, so our representation of the elementary proposition cannot include the objects with which the names in the proposition are correlated. *That* the names are correlated with objects must show itself in the proposition itself. We cannot get beyond the elementary proposition. In the same way we can see that Rouault's 'Three Judges' is a picture of three men simply by looking at the picture. And ultimately we *can* only see this in the picture. We may be helped to read the picture by putting it alongside other things, but doing this latter is not going to guarantee that we do see the three men there. We shall either see this or not—*in* the picture.

Wittgenstein's discussion of the hidden complexities in the notion of 'ostensive definition' in, e.g., *Philosophical Investigations*, I, §§ 26–37 is directed to essentially the same point. Suppose we say that an ostensive definition establishes a correlation between a name and an object. Perhaps we think that, as it were, a string has been attached to the name at one end and to the object at the other end, or that, as it were, a label has been attached to an object. But what has this, by itself, achieved? Suppose I have a desk and attach various labels to it, as follows: 'medium brown', 'oval', 'desk', 'item of furniture', 'late Victorian', etc., etc. Any of these labels could be called 'naming an object', but the mere fact that I have carried out this operation, *considered in isolation*, says nothing. I have got to understand how the label is being used, its grammar; otherwise I just don't know what has been labelled. In other words, the *lines* of projection don't do what is required of them; they only function in the context of a *method* of projection. If I do suppose that the lines of projection carry all the weight in establishing the correlation between name and object, then it will appear to me that I have got to have the object clearly in view before I can draw the lines. But once I see that it is the method of projection which is important, then I can say that 'the object drops out of consideration as irrelevant' (*Philosophical Investigations*, I, § 293). That is, the Tractarian objects are quite unnecessary, an idle wheel, the intrusion of which is masking the true workings of the mechanism. And so Wittgenstein is able to reply to the suggestion he quotes in *Zettel*, § 297 (cited above, pages 10–11): ' "I mean something by the words" here means: I *know* that I can apply them.' All that is necessary for me to be able to say something is that the words I use should be applied in accordance with their grammar.

Once we have seen this, however, we are in a position to carry much further the *Tractatus* objections to the idea that we might be able to *say* how names are interrelated in an elementary proposition and how they are correlated with objects. These same objections can now be levelled at the idea that it would be possible to formulate the elementary propositions themselves. For an elementary proposition is one in which the connexion of names with each other and with their objects is immediately 'shown'. And what has just been said amounts to the assertion that there can be no such proposition. These connexions are displayed, not in the proposition itself, but in what *surrounds* it, in the grammar according to which the words in it are applied. Expressing the matter thus enables us to make two further points: (i) concerning the nature of Wittgenstein's later objections to the idea that thinking is a special sort of process; (ii) concerning his distinction between what can be said and what can only be shown and the way in which this distinction persists, in transmuted form, from the *Tractatus* through to his last writings.

(i) In just the same way as no 'labelling' operation could *by itself*, outside the context of an established grammar, establish any connexion between name and object; and in just the same way as no formulated proposition could *by itself* display the structure of a *Sachverhalt*; just so could no process *by itself* constitute thinking something, meaning something, understanding something. Here too it is what surrounds the process, not the process itself (given that there is one at all), which enables us to say that someone has understood something, means something, understands something. To adapt an example of Professor Geach's: if someone says that 'Everybody loves some girl' does not entail 'There is some girl whom everybody loves', then this may, in appropriate circumstances, be enough to convince us that he has grasped the nature of a certain fallacy. But of course in other circumstances we may have grounds for doubting whether he is taking the second of these propositions in the right way—grounds deriving from *other* things he says and does; and then we shall not be able to say that he understands the fallacy.

(ii) In *Zettel*, § 453, Wittgenstein writes that 'sometimes the voice of a philosophical thought is so soft that the noise of spoken words is enough to drown it'. He is, I believe, expressing here the same sort of thought that led him to say in the *Tractatus* that the important things in philosophy cannot be said but must be shown. If we tried to formulate in words an elementary proposition, we should inevitably find that we had not got what we were looking for. Because any formulated proposition can in principle, in different circumstances, be taken in different ways; whereas an elementary proposition must be one which of itself guarantees how it is to be taken, and no such proposition can be formulated. It is as if we were trying to express in our formulation itself how the formulation is to be taken; and this cannot be done. Once this is clearly seen (and it was not *clearly* seen in the *Tractatus*[1]), the direction of philosophical inquiry has to be different. One no longer searches for an ultimate nugget of sense; instead, one tries to represent quite ordinary utterances in the right light, by gesturing in the right direction. In philosophy 'one says the ordinary thing—with the wrong gesture'.[2] The wrong gesture displays a wrong understanding of the 'dimensions' in which what is said has sense. This phrase—'the wrong dimensions'—is one which recurs constantly in *Zettel* and shows the intimate connexion between Wittgenstein's earlier conception of 'logical space' and his later conception of 'grammar'; while on the other hand the way he speaks later shows a clear awareness of the fact that the geometrical (spatial) overtones of 'logical space' had seriously misled him as to the kind of 'dimensions' that are really in question in philosophy.

Wittgenstein says of his criticisms of Freud[3] that he is engaged in a certain sort of 'persuasion'. The point is connected with what I have just been discussing. It cannot be a matter of 'proving that Freud is wrong' (or right, for that matter). What Wittgenstein does try to do is to make clear the point of view from which the things Freud says look compelling (the nature of their 'charm'). And at the same time he tries to show how the charm may vanish if the point of view is shifted slightly. (His method is essentially the same in his discussions in the philosophy of mathematics.) In other words he is trying to show that the 'dimensions' within

---

[1] Miss Ishiguro's paper is in large part an extended development of this point.
[2] *Zettel*, § 451.
[3] See Dr. Cioffi's contribution.

which Freud tries to locate certain mental phenomena are at least not exhaustive of the dimensions in which those phenomena exist. Of course, there is no guarantee that anyone subjected to this sort of 'persuasion' will cease to find Freud's outlook 'charming', and I do not think that Wittgenstein would have wanted to call a man who did not so cease 'mistaken'. But this does not mean that there are no intellectual standards to be observed in this kind of discussion. If, for instance, someone were to insist on saying that Freud's views were just correct (or incorrect, for that matter) then he would I think be open to the charge of having committed a definite intellectual mistake, of being confused about the nature of the issue. And Wittgenstein's discussions of what is involved in a proposition's having sense throw light on the sort of confusion involved here.

I want now to return to Wittgenstein's reasons for coming to think that the *Tractatus* talk of 'objects' was unnecessary and misleading. In expounding this matter I intentionally used a phrase from the celebrated 'beetle in the box' criticism of the idea that pain is a 'private object' ('the object drops out of consideration as irrelevant').[1] It seems to me that the aptness of this remark in the context of a quite *general* discussion of whether we need 'objects' in order to characterize the distinction between sense and nonsense is suggestive.[2] On the one hand it serves to emphasize the continuity between the logical investigations in the *Tractatus* and the discussions of topics in the philosophy of mind in *Philosophical Investigations* and the other later writings. But on the other hand this particular juxtaposition suggests a possible criticism of Wittgenstein's treatment of sensations.

Let me approach this by considering two alternative ways in which we might express the relation between the *Tractatus* and *Philosophical Investigations*. In very many places it looks as though Wittgenstein's later view about what was wrong with the *Tractatus* is that the mistake lies in the whole attempt to account for language in terms of the relations between proposition and fact, between name and object. This view is supported by the emphasis throughout *Philosophical Investigations* on the innumerability of the *different* uses of language and the wrongheadedness of

---

[1] *Philosophical Investigations*, I, § 293.

[2] Mr. Manser also, in his paper, points to the connexion between Wittgenstein's discussion of pain-utterances and his earlier conception of elementary propositions.

trying to describe them all in terms of a single model. There is certainly nothing wrong with this interpretation in itself, but it may lead to a mistake. It might now seem as though one could just accept the *Tractatus* as perfectly sound considered as an account of one particular sub-section of language: that which concerns the use of language to state factual propositions. What this overlooks, however, is that *Philosophical Investigations* is *also* a protest against the idea that everything which is properly called 'a proposition which states a fact' can be given the same sort of description. What we call 'stating a fact' can take many different forms; we say something about a particular use of language when we say that it consists in the stating of a fact, since we can contrast it with other uses of language which do not consist in this at all. But there will remain much more to be said about the differences between what stating a fact amounts to in one sort of example and what it amounts to in other cases.

This point is connected with the *Tractatus* insistence that 'name', 'object', 'proposition', etc. are formal concepts. When Wittgenstein says, of the beetle in the box: 'the object drops out of consideration as irrelevant', he is, of course, *contrasting* the game he is describing (and, by analogy, the use of pain-language) with *other* language-games in which the object is not irrelevant, where, for instance, opening your box and showing its contents to someone else is indeed a legitimate move in the game. But now, if this is *all* we say, it might look as though the 'reference to the object' in the language-games with which pain-language is being contrasted, is quite unproblematic. Of course, Wittgenstein is quite right when he insists that merely concentrating your attention on your sensation and thinking of a word will not in itself constitute 'giving the sensation a name'. But his discussions make it equally clear that merely concentrating your attention on a table and thinking of a word will not constitute 'giving the table a name'. In each case the talk about 'concentrating your attention on x' tacitly presupposes the grammar of the expression 'x'. And if we wanted to describe the language-games in which we give names to material objects in the same sort of depth as Wittgenstein is here describing the language-game of talking about one's sensations, it would be *equally* important to insist that 'the object drops out of consideration as irrelevant'. The reason for this is, of course, *not* that no object is involved in these language-games, but rather because (to adapt a phrase used by Wittgenstein in a different connexion) *that* part of the grammar of the expressions in question is clear enough. What we need to understand is the context of practices and interests which gives the purely formal conception of an 'object' some definite sense in particular cases.

For this reason it seems to me that it might be a symptom of confusion to insist too vehemently and for too long that 'pain' is not the name of an object. Of course it would be equally confused to insist too vehemently and for too long that 'pain' *is* the name of an object.

What we have to recognize is that there is *no* language-game the philosophically puzzling aspects of which will be illuminated simply by saying that it involves the use of a name to refer to an object.

Both Professor Cook and Mr. Reinhardt discuss in their contributions the confusions involved in thinking of Wittgenstein as any sort of behaviourist. If the point I have just been making is a sound one I think it provides a way of bringing out an important difference between Wittgenstein and Ryle. It seems to me that there are much stronger grounds for calling *The Concept of Mind* behaviouristic than there are for saying this of any of Wittgenstein's writings. One important difference is just the fact that the notion of a 'method of projection' continues to play such an important part in Wittgenstein's thought and this gives to his writings on the philosophy of mind a dimension which Ryle's lack. Without denying any of Wittgenstein's important claims about the grammar of sensation-words, we are, it seems to me, still free to say, if we like: Of course, when I speak about pain I am speaking about something quite different from behaviour of any sort; only, if I am to be clear in what I am talking about, it will not help to concentrate my attention on that peculiar phenomenon that I call 'pain', because it is precisely the features of the situation which make it possible for me to do this which are puzzling me. What I need to do rather is to expose clearly the method of projection in connexion with which alone the word 'pain' has the sense it has. And this is what I am doing when I describe the language-games into which this word enters.

Continuing to talk in terms of a 'method of projection' here has the following merit. It serves to bring out the close connexion—I might say the identity—of the question of what sort of an object pain, for instance, is and the question of what sort of relation exists between the word 'pain' and what it refers to. In the *Tractatus* 'what has to be accepted, the given'[1] is the object, the substance of the world, what is unchangeable and fixed. Given that objects are what they are, a certain mode of projection will be needed if we are to name one and use the name in propositions. But in *Philosophical Investigations* the order of priority is reversed. What sort of object pain is is determined by the way we use the word 'pain': *in* that use we see the kind of relation between name and object that is here in question and there is nothing more to say about the object than we can say in our descriptions of the use of the word. This last is the doctrine of the *Tractatus* too, but the big difference in *Philosophical Investigations* lies in the kind of 'description' that is looked for. Instead of looking for the elementary propositions which underlie our ordinary use of pain-language, we try to display the unexpectedly complex relations which hold between the quite ordinary ways in which we speak and act in common discourse. 'What has to be accepted, the given, is—one might say—forms of life.' (*Philosophical Investigations*, II, xi.) The shift in point of view is quite slight, but decisive. It does not involve a complete abandonment of everything that had been said in the *Tractatus*, but rather a rearrangement of it, a setting of it in a wider context. We have to look, not for what lies hidden *beneath* our normal ways of talking, but for what is hidden *in* our normal ways of talking. 'In philosophy one is in constant danger of producing a myth of symbolism, or a myth of mental processes. Instead of simply saying what anyone knows and must admit.' (*Zettel*, § 211.)

---

[1] This phrase of Wittgenstein's comes, of course, from *Philosophical Investigations*, not from the *Tractatus*.

I

USE AND REFERENCE
OF NAMES

Hidé Ishiguro

PEOPLE have often contrasted the picture theory of meaning of the *Tractatus* with the use theory of meaning of the *Philosophical Investigations*. Many have also argued that the picture theory of meaning is based on the concept of 'naming', since in the picture theory language catches on to reality through names which stand for objects. This has led people to talk as if the use theory of meaning was an expression of Wittgenstein's later rejection of his *Tractatus* theory. I believe that talk of such contrast is highly misleading, and that it arises out of a misunderstanding of the *Tractatus* view of what it is for a name to refer to (*bedeuten*) an object. This misunderstanding is also responsible for the false and widely held belief that Wittgenstein's theory of meaning and language renders conceptual change impossible and disables social criticism. It seems to me to be a truism that a word or a symbol cannot have the rôle of referring to a fixed object without having a fixed use. How could there be a philosophical doctrine of expressions and the objects to which they referred which was not at the same time a theory about the use of those expressions? No interesting philosophical question about the meaning of such expressions can be based on a contrast between 'naming' and 'use'. The interesting question, I think, is whether the meaning of a name can be secured independently of its use in propositions by some method which links it to an object, as many, including Russell, have thought, or whether the identity of the object referred to is only settled by the use of the name in a set of propositions. If the latter holds, then the problem of the object a name denotes *is* the problem of the use of the name.

Contrary to widespread belief,[1] Wittgenstein rejected the former view throughout his writings and tried to work out various versions of the second. So far as this question is concerned, the main difference between the *Tractatus* and the *Philosophical Investigations* is not the presence or absence of the 'use' concept but that the *Tractatus* concept of 'use' is much less comprehensive than in the *Investigations*. That is to say, in the *Tractatus* Wittgenstein is interested in the problem of the rôle expressions play in a language, which he considers only in relation to the truth-stating purpose of language. He is not concerned with the various other things people may do by using such expressions—such as beseeching, promising, and so on.

The aim of this paper is twofold. The first is to examine and assess the view that it is only by determining the use of a name that one can determine its reference and to do so through an investigation of the reasons given in the *Tractatus* for this thesis. The second is to propose a new way of understanding the *Tractatus* theory of names, objects, and the relationship of referring which holds between them. This proposal follows from the first investigation. I will try to show that the *Tractatus* view of the logical independence of elementary propositions makes it impossible for 'objects' to have the criteria of identity we normally ascribe to particulars. The concept of a simple object in the *Tractatus* is that of an instantiation of an irreducible predicate where the question of individuation of different instantiations of the same predicate cannot arise. The 'objects' of the *Tractatus* are not particular entities in any normal sense, but entities invoked to fit into a semantic theory, so, when Wittgenstein later rejected the independence of elementary propositions, he was able to get rid of this peculiar notion of objects as well without altering his theory of names or reference in any fundamental manner.

---

[1] As an example of this view, which I think is misleading, see Max Black, *A Companion to Wittgenstein's Tractatus*, pp. 114–15, 'Wittgenstein considers the question of how the meaning of names can be communicated. His disturbing answer is that it is impossible to explain a name's meaning explicitly; the only way to convey the meaning is to use the name in a proposition, thereby presupposing that the meaning is already understood. On this view, the achievement of common reference by speaker and hearer becomes mysterious.'

What then is Wittgenstein's theory of names? The key to the *Tractatus* view of the relation of objects and Names[1] is expressed in the controversial 3.3, which says 'Only propositions have sense (*Sinn*); only in the nexus of the proposition does a Name have reference (*Bedeutung*).' It is well known that 'Name' is a technical word in the *Tractatus*. Not only can Names not be analysed further by any definitions, but the objects to which they refer are simple and cannot be given by a definite description. Like Russell and Quine, the Wittgenstein of the *Tractatus* thought that most of what we call proper names can be analysed further and can be treated logically as definite descriptions (3.24). Real Names cannot occur explicitly in ordinary, non-elementary propositions.[2] What 3.3 expresses is a general thesis about expressions and the objects they designate, which plainly derives from Frege's *Foundations of Arithmetic*, which does not advance such views about names. We will see that Wittgenstein's notion of simple objects made him take this view even more seriously. One cannot look for the references of Names independently of their use in propositions.

It was in the context of his attempt in the *Foundations of Arithmetic* to explain his claim that numbers were objects rather than concepts, and that number words had objective reference (*Bedeutung*) and referred to objects, that Frege wrote 'Only in a proposition have words really a reference (*Bedeutung*). . . . It is enough if the proposition taken as a whole has a sense (*Sinn*); it is this that confers on its parts also their content' (§ 60, repeated in § 62). One cannot refute the claim that numerals have objective reference just by saying that we cannot imagine numbers. Numbers are obviously not spatial objects. One cannot imagine, nor for that matter point to them—something which is specially evident if one thinks of the number zero or a million. Not only can we not picture or point to such numbers, we cannot even picture a million objects of whatever kind as distinct from a million and one of them, nor point to zero things. This might lead people to conclude that number words do not refer to anything. What Frege says in reply to such objections holds not only for number words but for all words. There are material objects we

---

[1] I will write *Name* with a capital to indicate the technical sense the word has in the *Tractatus*—a name which cannot be further analysed by definitions.

[2] *Tractatus* 4.23. 'The name occurs in the proposition only in the context of the elementary proposition.'

cannot point to or imagine, e.g. an elementary particle. Frege's claim is that reference cannot be determined independently of how we settle and understand the sense of a proposition in which the word occurs. To understand this is nothing more nor less than to know the truth-conditions of these propositions. This is a view which Wittgenstein accepted completely. Throughout his later works, Wittgenstein discusses the temptation to look in the wrong direction for a mark which would tell us why a word refers to a certain object. We look for mental processes that go on as we utter the words rather than the rule governing the use of the words that we can come to grasp. And similarly in the *Tractatus* Wittgenstein is anxious to stress that we cannot see how the name refers to an object except by understanding the rôle it plays in propositions. Although the *Foundations of Arithmetic* was written eight years before Frege distinguished the sense (*Sinn*) and reference (*Bedeutung*) of expressions,[1] and the word '*Bedeutung*' is used here in a very general way, it seems nevertheless that Frege is using '*Bedeutung*' in these passages to mean what he later meant by reference; in the sense in which the expressions '$\frac{6}{3}$' and '2' have the same '*Bedeutung*' and refer to the same number even if the manner in which each is presented is different. Throughout the *Tractatus* Wittgenstein makes a distinction between *Sinn* and *Bedeutung* in a manner roughly corresponding to Frege's later works, and it seems clear that when Wittgenstein repeated this maxim of Frege's *Foundations of Arithmetic* in *Tractatus* 3.3 and 3.314 he took '*Bedeutung*' in the sense of 'reference'.[2] He uses

[1] 'Über Sinn und Bedeutung', 1892, *Zeitschrift für Philos. u. philos. Kritik*. It is clear from a letter Frege wrote to Peano in 1896, where he still makes the point about words having '*Bedeutung*' and '*Sinn*' only in the context of a proposition in ordinary language, that he maintained the maxim 'Only ask for the "*Bedeutung*" of a word when it is used in a proposition' even after he made the '*Sinn*' and '*Bedeutung*' distinction.

[2] Unless we distinguish Wittgenstein's use of '*Bedeutung*' and '*Sinn*' carefully, and take the former as 'reference', as Miss Anscombe rightly says in *Introduction to Wittgenstein's Tractatus*, we will not be able to make sense of the following claims. 3.331, where he criticizes Russell's formulation of the Theory of Types because Russell had to mention the '*Bedeutung*' of the sign when establishing the rules for them. Wittgenstein is referring to Russell's talk about individuals, or classes, or classes of classes which different kinds of signs 'denote' and which Russell calls 'terms' of propositions, and not to meanings of signs in any ordinary sense.

4.126, that the sign which distinguishes a formal concept is a characteristic feature of all symbols whose '*Bedeutungen*' fall under the concept. Wittgenstein is here talking about the way in which e.g. we express that the signs refer to objects, by using 'a' 'b' 'c' ... as signs, or that the signs refer to functions by using '*bedeuten*' and '*vertreten*' (stand for) and '*nennen*' (name) inter-changeably in the *Tractatus* (3.221) and distinguishes them from '*bezeichnen*' (to signify) which is used much more widely and loosely to cover all relations between expressions or signs and what they mean. For example, a sign '*bezeichnet*' via the signs which occur in its definition (3.261). A variable '*bezeichnet*' the formal concept (4.127) and propositions held to be true are propositions which are '*bezeichnet*' with the assertion sign in Frege's logic (4.442). In none of these cases do the expressions '*bedeuten*' or refer. Later in the *Philosophical Investigations*, § 49, where Wittgenstein again refers to Frege's passage, this time explicitly, he makes it clear that he takes '*bedeuten*' in the sense of 'name' as distinct from 'describe'.

It is a fundamental difference between Wittgenstein's and Russell's position that Wittgenstein holds that no expression, not even a name which cannot be further analysed, can be said to have reference out of the context of propositions. It is *not* a part of the *Tractatus* theory that if a symbol is logically simple and cannot be further analysed then it can be secured a reference independently of and prior to its occurrence in a proposition, which for Wittgenstein is a 'propositional sign in its projective relation to the world' (3.12). Unlike Frege, Wittgenstein does not even think in terms of saturated and unsaturated sense, or complete and in-complete parts of thought. The only basic distinction he makes is between the way in which defined signs signify and undefined signs signify. In general the *Tractatus* talks of sense only with regard to propositions. The sense of a proposition is the thought which it expresses. All that sense amounts to for constituent expressions is their use. That is to say, they play a part in making up propositions which have sense. We therefore 'cannot give a sign the wrong

---

'f' 'g' 'h' as signs—i.e. the references of different kinds of symbol fall under different concepts.

5.02, where Wittgenstein criticizes Frege's theory about the '*Bedeutung*' of pro-positions—it is clear that he is talking about Frege's view that propositions refer to truth-values, and not about Frege's view of the sense of propositions.

Again, we will fail to see the point of one of the important theses of the *Tractatus* that logical constants do not stand for anything (and have no reference), unless we make the *Sinn/Bedeutung* distinction. Of course logical constants have sense in that they have a use and become constituent signs of complex propositions, which have a sense—but Wittgenstein wants to say that unlike names or predicates (even re-lational predicates) they do not refer to anything. ' . . . nothing in reality corresponds to the sign "∼".' (4.0621).

sense',[1] since the sense a sign has is nothing more than the rôle it has been assigned in language. We know the use of such signs, and as 4.03 says, must use old expressions to communicate a new sense. Names and predicates can be said to have the rôle of referring when they occur in propositions. Names refer to objects, and predicates (whether monadic or relational) refer to what holds of the objects. Strictly speaking one can do without predicate expressions in any subject predicate proposition, since one can always express the predicates that are true of objects by the ordered concatenation or pattern of the Names of the objects.[2] A name then has a reference only in the sense that we know how to use the name in sentences to refer to an object about which we can say true or false things. Thus, although it makes sense to talk of the object which a name refers to without using the name in any particular proposition, this is so only because we know in *general* the kind of propositions in which the name can occur. We do this by thinking of the class of propositions obtained by treating the name as a constant and treating the other expressions which make up the proposition as variables (3.312).

Is this view of Wittgenstein a defensible one, or is it 'clearly wrong' as e.g. Professor Geach argues in his *Reference and Generality*?[3] I think we will gain insight into the point Wittgenstein is making by comparing it with some of Russell's views. It is perfectly true that one can use a name by itself, e.g. in the vocative to hail a person as Geach writes, but the fact that we can use names in such ways seems to me to depend on names obtaining the references they do have by their use in propositions, as Frege and Wittgenstein claimed.

Russell's notion of 'meaning' seems in his earlier works to carry many Meinongian or Bradleian undertones. In his article 'On Denoting',[4] Russell assumes that an expression used as a

---

[1] 5.4732.

[2] Even in the case where there is only one object involved, as in 'A is red', one can have a convention whereby one expresses that an object is red by writing the name of the object sideways. Then the above proposition could be expressed as '∀'.

[3] *Reference and Generality*, first edition, pp. 25–6. After reading this paper in manuscript form, Professor Geach has kindly shown me his revised version of the same passage, written for the second edition due to come out in Autumn 1968. He makes clear that even when names are used independently, e.g. to call someone, or on labels, the use is not independent of the language system to which the names belong.   [4] 'On Denoting', *Mind*, 1905.

grammatical subject in the verbal expression of a proposition does not have any meaning by itself unless its meaning, which he equates with the object denoted, figures intact in a proper analysis of the proposition. Thus for Russell not only do words like 'everything', 'nothing' and 'something' have no independent meaning; phrases such as 'a man' or even 'the king of France' have no meaning. These are called incomplete symbols.[1] For Russell, to say of a word that it has meaning by itself is tantamount to saying that the meaning of the word *is* an object such that if we express a proposition using the word, the proposition will be about the object. 'John Smith is fat' would express a proposition about John Smith if the meaning of the phrase 'John Smith' is the man John Smith.

Thus, although Russell in this article refers to Frege's '*Sinn*' as meaning, and '*Bedeutung*' as denotation, Russell's own notion of the meaning of an expression is quite different from Frege's notion of '*Sinn*'. If anything it is closer to Frege's '*Bedeutung*'. The very phrases which for Frege have '*Sinn*' but no denotation like 'the least convergent series' or 'the king of France', have in Russell's view no meaning on their own. But in what sense could the meaning of a word ever be the object referred to? At a pinch one might say that the meaning of 'Karl Marx' is that it is the name of the man Karl Marx, but hardly that the meaning *is* the man. The *Tractatus* is right when it says that I can only speak *about* objects. I cannot express (*aussprechen*) them (3.221).

In the *Tractatus* words or signs have their use, i.e. their fixed rôle in logical syntax, and when used in propositions many of them refer to objects, or properties that are true of objects, but they do not have a sense or meaning which they express in addition to this. Signs which refer to objects (as distinct from properties or relations which are true of objects) are called names.[2] Quine says that to be is to be a value of a variable. Similarly the *Tractatus* says that to be an object (thing, entity, etc.) is to be a value of a variable name (4.1272). To be an object, or a function, or a fact, is not a classification of things in the sense in which to be solid or to be

---

[1] 'By an "incomplete" symbol we mean a symbol which is not supposed to have any meaning in isolation, but is only defined in certain contexts. In ordinary mathematics, for example $\frac{d}{dx}$ and $\int_a^b$ are incomplete symbols.... Such symbols have what may be called a "definition in use". This distinguishes such symbols from what we may call proper names.' (*Principia Mathematica*, p. 66.)

[2] *vide* 4.24, 4.1211.

coloured or to be moving is. It is a purely logical notion, as it was for Frege, which the *Tractatus* calls a 'formal concept'. We cannot properly ask in isolation whether John is an object or whether a colour is an object, or relations are objects. Nor is the question whether 'objects' are physical things or mental objects appropriate. If we forget the fact that only the absolutely simple are to be called objects in the strict sense, and allow ourselves the relative or 'shifting' use of the word 'object', as Wittgenstein does in 4.123, the proposition 'that table is red' is about the object table, the proposition 'John is the father of Paul' is about the objects John and Paul, and the proposition 'that colour is darker than this' is about the objects colours, and 'being a father is an asymmetric relation' is about the object 'being a father'.

But then what is the logical criterion of an expression being a name? How does one establish that an expression, say 'a', is a name of an object? Not by someone pointing to something and uttering 'a'. One would not know whether 'a' is being used to describe, to name, to count. Even if one could somehow make it clear that 'a' is being used as a name rather than a predicate or as a sentence, one would not have settled what was being named by pointing. Is it the place? The material thing? The surface? An aspect? Or what is it? Russell wrote as if names get attached to their bearers by the speaker's intention. According to him, at any given moment there are certain things of which a man is 'aware', which are 'before his mind'. 'If I describe these objects, I may of course describe them wrongly: hence I cannot with certainty communicate to another what are the things of which I am aware. But if I speak to myself, and denote them by what may be called "proper names" rather than by descriptive words, I cannot be in error. So long as the names which I use really are names at the moment, i.e. are naming things to me, so long the things must be objects of which I am aware, since otherwise the words would be meaningless sounds, not names of things.' ('On the Nature of Acquaintance', 1914.) Such a private act would not for Wittgenstein make a sound into a name of an object although a man can privately commit himself to a consecutive use of an expression, and thereby give an object a name for his own purpose. The aspect or the surface of the thing which is before my mind has shape, colours, as well, and it is only the consecutive use of the name that will establish which of all those things I did name. I cannot therefore 'communicate to another what are the things of which I am aware' by uttering the sounds. The *Tractatus* view is that if one uses names in propositions and one understands the syntactical rôle they play, then the proposition would not have a definite sense *unless* the names obtained a definite reference. This means that *if* people take 'f(a)', 'g(a,b)' as stating a definite state of affairs,[1] *then* they do see that 'a' 'b' are used to refer to the objects which the proposition is about. ('g(a,b)' will express a state of affairs involving two not three objects.)[2] In the case of ordinary proper names we identify the bearer by a definite description or indicate the kind of thing we are talking about and use a demonstrative to point out which one of that kind we mean. But if the objects cannot be identified by a definite description, nor be picked out by pointing, since they are 'independent of what is the case', how can one see that the word or sign refers to a fixed object?

This is done according to *Tractatus* 3.263 by 'elucidations'. An elucidation does not give a definite description of the object denoted by a Name—as this is claimed to be impossible—nor is it a definition of the Name. Elucidations are propositions in which the Names are used rather than mentioned. I take it that in making an elucidation we are to assert the propositions containing the Name. When we catch on and understand what is asserted, we have grasped what the proposition is *about* and we know what the object is which is referred to by the Name. For example, in Peano's axioms, O, number and successor are treated as primitive signs—i.e. they are *not* defined in terms of other terms. In Peano's axioms these signs are used, so that one can come to see the mutual

---

[1] Wittgenstein misleadingly talks of propositions *describing* states-of-affairs, and of propositions *representing* states-of-affairs—instead of saying as he should that propositions *state* states-of-affairs.

[2] It has been a standing controversy whether predicates or properties are included in the objects of the *Tractatus* or not. It is true that if properties do not count as objects it is difficult to see how in the state of affairs expressed by 'fa', 'objects fit into one another like the links of a chain' as they are said to do in states of affairs in 2.03. But not only do other passages of the *Tractatus* go against the view that predicates are objects; it seems to me to be a central thesis of the *Tractatus* that subject-predicate propositions, i.e. propositions in which properties are ascribed to objects, can be expressed as a function of the objects. It is better to acknowledge the difficulty Wittgenstein has in explaining the limiting case of a state of affairs in which there is only one object involved, than to render the thesis empty (see note 2, p. 41). As Strawson has argued, the word 'about' may be unable to carry the burden of distinguishing objects and properties mentioned in a proposition. Wittgenstein nevertheless thought, with Frege, that if 'fa' is a proposition, we have an intuitive grasp of the difference between the roles of 'f' and 'a'.

relationship of the references of these signs. When we understand what Peano's axioms say, we have already identified, O, the successor of O, the successor of the successor of O, and so on. Miss Anscombe, who has so correctly dissociated the *Tractatus* from the empiricist epistemologies and reductionisms with which it has often been wrongly identified, seems to be mistaken when she writes that although 'Wittgenstein pretended that epistemology had nothing to do with the foundations of logic and the theory of meaning, with which he was concerned, the passage about the "elucidation" of names, where he says that one must be "acquainted" with their objects, gives him the lie'.[1] 3.263 is no more committed to any particular theory of epistemology than any other part of the *Tractatus*. 3.263 says 'The references (*Bedeutungen*) of primitive signs can be accounted for by means of elucidations. Elucidations are propositions that contain the primitive signs. So these propositions will only be able to be understood if the references of the signs are already known (*bekannt*).'

Wittgenstein is not saying in the last sentence that we must already be acquainted with what the primitive sign refers to by itself, and that it is only because of this that we understand propositions containing these signs. Such an interpretation will make the claims made by these three sentences completely circular and unilluminating. Surely Wittgenstein is here claiming that when one comes to understand these elucidations, one is already identifying what the primitive signs which occur in them refer to. Identifying the reference of the primitive signs, and understanding the elucidations are not two separate epistemological steps because the identity of the references of names and the sense of the elucidations are not *logically* separable. This identification need not be done in the presence of the object. Even when the object is a perceptible one it need not be present. The object may not even be a perceptible one at all. This is obviously the case with ordinary names. We can grasp the identity of the person named 'Pablo Picasso' without ever having perceived him. We can learn what 'π' refers to and know that it is an unterminating decimal although we cannot perceive numbers, and although any decimal expansion we have seen expressing π would have been of finite length. Why should the situation change with

[1] G. E. M. Anscombe, *An Introduction to Wittgenstein's Tractatus*, p. 28.

names of simple objects? Russell believed that if we understand what a word 'means', we should either be able to describe it or be acquainted with it (in an empirical sense). We can only learn the meaning of a logically proper name by being acquainted with the object and linking the name to the object in the presence of it. But there is no reason to believe that Wittgenstein, who did not require that Names have reference or 'meaning' independently of this use in propositions, shared this view. Just as what is described by a complex symbol can be all kinds of things, so the reference of Names may be all sorts of objects. The identification of an object need not have anything to do with having a sensory experience of the object or being able to point to the object. The word *'bekannt'* used by Wittgenstein need not mean 'acquainted' in the sense in which something is given to the senses. I think that it means 'acquainted' in the sense in which we may be said to be acquainted with a foreign language (as in *'die Sprache ist ihm bekannt'*) or with literary works. When Russell wrote in *Mysticism and Logic*, page 219, that 'Every proposition which we can understand must be composed wholly of constituents with which we are acquainted' he did mean 'acquainted' in a special empiricist sense. Whereas the *Tractatus* 3.263 is saying that one cannot understand a proposition without understanding what the proposition is about. Thus although we need not have come across the objects referred to by the Names used in a proposition before, if we do come to understand the sense of the proposition then at that moment we already know what the Names refer to.

If the elucidations contradict each other, and no consistent use of the Names which occur in them has been specified, then the Names have not been successfully given the rôle of referring to an object. Thus 3.328 says 'if a sign is without use, it is without reference'. Again if two Names have exactly the same use—and one can always be substituted for the other, then, the two signs refer to the same object. 5.47321 explains why this is. 'Occam's maxim is, of course, not an arbitrary rule, nor one that is justified by its success in practice; its point is that unnecessary units in a sign-language do not refer to anything. Signs that serve one purpose are logically equivalent, and signs that serve none have, logically speaking, no reference.'

In the *Tractatus* one does not decide that one can substitute one expression for another expression *because* they refer to the same object. If two names are used in such a way that one can be substituted for the other, *then* the names *do* refer to the same object. Thus 4.241 says ' "a = b" means that the sign "b" can be substituted for the sign "a" ', and 4.242 adds that expressions of the form 'a = b' are mere devices to show the rôle of the signs and state nothing about the reference of the signs 'a' and 'b'. (Strictly speaking, the equation does tell you that the object referred to has these two names.) An equation (or any so-called identity statement) is, according to the *Tractatus*, a way of *showing* something about two sets of signs or expressions, i.e. that they are used to refer to the same object. It is not an assertion *about* the object referred to by the expressions. 'It is impossible to assert the identity of the reference of two expressions. For in order to assert anything about their reference, I must know what their reference is without knowing whether the expressions refer to the same thing or not.'[1] In other words, one can show that expressions refer to the same object, but one cannot informatively say of the reference of expressions that they are one and the same. This is because 'to say of two things that they are identical is nonsense, and to say of one thing that it is identical with itself is to say nothing at all'.[2]

The *Tractatus* view is, it seems, very close to what the often misunderstood Leibnizian principle *'eadem sunt quorum unum alteri potest substitui salva veritate'*, asserts. Leibniz was laying down the criterion of identity of terms—(which are concepts expressed by words or phrases, and not the objects which fall under the concepts,[3] whereas for the early Russell terms were the objects). Terms (not things) t_1 and t_2 are to be considered identical if t_1 can be interchanged for t_2 in every proposition in which it occurs without affecting the truth-value of the proposition. That is to say, two expressions are to be treated as expressing the same concept if one can be replaced by the other *salva veritate*. Similarly in the *Tractatus* it is not that we know that two words name the same object and then conclude that they are allowed to be interchanged.

---

[1] 6.2322 Wittgenstein simplifies the problem by supposing that either one knows the reference of both expressions, or knows neither; which is wrong.

[2] 5.5303.

[3] '... sive Termino sive notioni' p. 85. 'Per *Terminum* non intelligo nomen sed conceptum seu id quod nomine significatur, possis et dicere notionem, ideam.' p. 243. '... et ita distinguendum erit inter Terminum et Rem seu Ens' p. 393. *Opuscules et Fragments Inedits de Leibniz*, edits par Couturat 1903. Leibniz is confused at times in other works as to whether terms are concepts expressed by words, or whether they are verbal expressions of concepts.

Rather, if we treat all the propositions where one expression is substituted for the other as having the same truth-value as the original proposition, then we are *using* the two expressions as having the same reference. It goes without saying that equations containing the expressions are not to be treated as one of these propositions, since, according to Wittgenstein, they are not proper propositions at all.

It might be thought that in order to decide that 'ϕa' and 'ϕb' have the same truth-value, I have either already to know that *a* and *b* are one and the same object, or else know that 'a' and 'b' have the same sense or express the same concept in some independent way —perhaps by definition (a common concern of Leibniz and of Frege in his *Begriffsschrift*). If the former is true, then substitutivity does not provide any criterion of identity of reference, and if the latter is true, then, as Frege writes in his *Grundlagen*, § 67, 'all identities would then amount simply to this, that whatever is given to us in the same way is to be reckoned as the same . . . a principle so obvious and so sterile as not to be worth stating'. Whereas, as Frege goes on to say, identity claims are not sterile precisely in that we are able to recognize something as the same again even though it is given in a different way.

For the *Tractatus* the second alternative is ruled out because a Name is a simple symbol which is not defined via other signs. The sign itself is completely conventional and displays no logical structure. But why does not the first alternative hold? It is more difficult and more important to see why it does not hold and why the objection as a whole falls down.

In order to do this let us forget about simple objects for a moment, and examine what it is in ordinary contexts to know that *a* and *b* are the same object. It often happens that two people are using expressions believing that they are referring to the same thing or person and then suddenly realize that as a matter of fact they were talking about different things. For example A is talking about the point *a* meaning the tiny dot—or tiny black spot on the paper, and B is using 'the point *a*' to mean the geometrical position of the spot, which itself has no colour. Asked to point to the object they are referring to, they both point to the same area of the paper before them. Asked to fix their minds on the object they are thinking about, they would both fix their attention on the particular locus on the paper in which, as a matter of fact, the black spot is. But they come to realize that they are talking about different things when one person claims that *a* is black, for example, and the other person disagrees, because he is talking about something which cannot have any colour.

When such disagreement arises, how do they settle the question whether they are disagreeing about what is true of one and the same object or whether they are talking about different objects? And how do they decide whether they are talking about different kinds of objects, or about different particulars of the same kind? This is not a clear-cut question. But it seems that there must be some set of propositions about any object whose truth has to be agreed by anyone who is talking about an object of that kind, or at least a set of coherent attitudes or reactions to the object which are shared by anyone referring to it, which might be expressed by others as a belief in the truth of a certain set of propositions. For example, if 'm' is used to refer to a natural number, a person has to know how to go on counting and how to manipulate numbers in certain ways. He must in some way have a criterion of re-identifying the same number when he encounters it again and know how numbers differ from other kinds of objects even if he cannot formulate verbally the claim that m is either O or a successor of another number. If 'a' is used as a name of a geo-metrical point, the person must be able to work with points in all sorts of ways without being taken in about the physical features of the dot which shows the point; even if the person does not know Euclid's first definition. Similarly with any empirical object. If 'a' is used as a name of an individual cell, the person would need to have grasped a certain network of theories which enables him to trace or reidentify cells through their changes.

I suspect that the 'elucidations' of the *Tractatus* are a set of propositions of this kind. The elucidations make us see what the object is by showing its internal properties.[1] By making us grasp the kind of object which is in question they make us see in what sort of state of affairs the object *could* occur. What kind of proposi-tions the elucidations are depends on the nature of the particular object in question. Whatever kind of propositions elucidations are, if it is only by grasping the truth of the elucidations that we understand what objects we are talking about, then it cannot be

---

[1] 2.01231 'If I am to know an object, though I need not know its external proper-ties, I must know all its internal properties.'

the case that we have to know that 'a' and 'b' refer to the same object *before* we can decide of *any* 'ϕa' and 'ϕb' that they have the same truth-value. The objection raised against the *Tractatus* view that expressions have the same reference if we treat them as having the same use collapses. That is why, if we take the *Tractatus* view that Names cannot be further analysed seriously, then as Wittgenstein says, an identity claim cannot be about the objects which Names stand for, but is a way of showing how Names are to be used.

In the case of ordinary names, we cannot identify the reference merely by grasping what kind of object it is. We will have to know that the object is that particular rather than another one of a given kind. I will try to show later that in the case of the simple objects of the *Tractatus* the question how one can distinguish an object of one kind from another object of the same kind cannot be properly raised. To summarize what we have seen up to now about the relation of the use of names and the identity of their reference: (i) We settle the identity of the object referred to by a name by coming to understand the sense, i.e. the truth-conditions of the proposition in which the names occur. (ii) Two names refer to the same object if the names are mutually substitutable in all propositions in which they occur without affecting the truth-value of the propositions. (iii) In order to be able to do this and understand that the truth-conditions of propositions containing name 'a' or 'b', we have already to agree about the *truth* (not just the truth-conditions) of a certain sufficiency of propositions in which 'a' and 'b' occur. Thus the identity of the object referred to by a name cannot be settled prior to or independently of the sense of the propositions in which they are used, and agreement about the truth of some of these propositions.

I will now examine some of the consequences of this *Tractatus* view of meaning. The *Tractatus* view entails that it is the use of the Name which gives you the identity of the object rather than vice versa. We cannot give a name a meaning and use *by* linking it to an object unless the object is already identified by the use of other names or definite descriptions. If the object is already identified as the bearer of another name, the problem of the name and object is still there unsolved. If the object can be identified by a description we can learn the reference and use of a name by correlating it to the object picked out by the definite description, as indeed we normally do. The *Tractatus* mistakenly assumes that in such cases we are correlating a name with a definite description rather than with the object which falls under the description—and therefore refuses to consider the correlated symbol as a name in a logical sense. As Wittgenstein was to realize later, even if a complex could only be given by its description,[1] it does not of course follow that one cannot refer to the complex by a name. The *Tractatus* theory of names is basically correct, however, in so far as it is a refutation of views which assume that a name is like a piece of label which we tag on to an object which we can already identify. A label serves a purpose because we usually write names—*which already have a use*—on the label. The labelling by itself does not establish the use of the label. If a label is pasted on a bottle, one does not even know whether the label is correlated with the owner of the bottle, the contents of the bottle, the bottle itself, or a particular property, e.g. poisonous, of the contents. Russell seems to have assumed that logically proper names were like *token* labels since he talks as if by uttering 'this' in the presence of 'what one is acquainted with at the moment', or 'what one sees at a given moment', you give the word 'this' a meaning and turn it into a name. The word 'this', at the moment, he claims stands for an actual object of sense and is therefore a logically proper name.[2]

But what kind of a name is 'this'? In the *Tractatus* catching onto the use of a Name *is* grasping the identity of the reference of the Name. When we establish the use of a Name we establish the reference of all token signs of a given type when the signs are used in propositions. As Wittgenstein wrote in *Notes on Logic*, 'names are not things but classes'. Each token sign of 'this' or 'A' is a different token sign or thing from another 'this' or 'A', but the use or sense is attached to the whole class of signs or expressions of the same type. Thus 'A' is the same sign as 'A',[3] and likewise 'this' is the same Name (if it is a Name at all) as 'this'. If the meaning of 'this' changes for Russell on every occasion of its use, then as he also believes that *the* meaning of a name is a particular, every token 'this' ought to be a different name, not the same ambiguous proper name as Russell claims. Names would not then be a class of similar word tokens with an identical use as they

---

[1] 3.24.   [2] 'Philosophy of Logical Atomism' in *Logic and Knowledge*, p. 201
[3] 3.203.

are for the *Tractatus*. The same argument applies to Russell's notion of ordinary proper names. Russell thought that each person can attach a different definite description to the same ordinary proper name at different times. We may then ask him why should the name be considered the same one if various tokens of it are used with diverse meanings. On the other hand if we try to defend Russell's stated position and claim that every logically proper name is an ambiguous proper name and claim that 'this' is always one and the same name which somehow gets a different meaning every time it is used, then we have to assume that the word already has some general meaning which tells us why a different particular object is meant by the word on each occasion of its use. This general meaning would be something like 'the object the speaker is pointing to' or 'the object in front of me'. (Russell was to argue this later in his discussion of 'egocentric particular'.) This again would make the word 'this' quite different from any *Tractatus* Name since the word 'this' would then have to be replaceable by these descriptions. It could not then be a primitive sign.[1]

In the *Notebooks*, Wittgenstein wrote 'What seems to be given us *a priori* is the concept: this—Identical with the concept of the object.'[2] And indeed if one does not take objects as necessarily and absolutely simple, but as things which we *treat* as simples by referring to them and saying this about them (as Wittgenstein did here), then indeed if we are in a position to refer to an object by a name or definite description we can always refer to it by using the expression 'this'. For every entity that we can individuate can be referred to as 'this' or 'that', regardless of whether the object is present or absent, or given or not given to the senses. Once we have a way of identifying the number 2, for example, we can refer to it and say 'this is smaller than 3'. If we can pick out a particular shape from other shapes we can say things about it like 'This is

[1] In *Philosophical Investigations*, §§ 38, 39, 45, Wittgenstein gives a detailed criticism of the theory that the word 'this' is a name. This might be taken as a refutation of his own view in the *Tractatus* since he is arguing in these pages against the view that there must be simple objects which can only be named, which was claimed in the *Tractatus* as well as in Russell's *Philosophy of Logical Atomism*. It is clear that he is criticizing Russell's theory when he talks of the 'conception of naming as an occult process' and of the 'philosopher who tries to bring out the relation between name and thing by staring at an object in front of him and repeating a name or even the word "this" seven times'. Such views were never a part of the *Tractatus*.

[2] *Notebooks*, 16, 5. 1915.

asymmetrical'. It does *not* follow, however, that the word 'this' is a name. No more than it follows from the claim 'to be an object is to be a value of a name variable' that the variables of quantification are names. The first consequence then of the *Tractatus* view of Names is that a Name is not like an individual tag or a paper label. A Name is a class of similar token expressions, each of which is used in propositions to refer to the *same* object. It is not like a pronoun or like a Russellian logically proper name. It is at least more like an ordinary proper name than it is like any pronoun.

The second consequence I want to discuss of the *Tractatus* view of Names is a feature which distinguishes them from normal proper names; that Names refer to simples and that complexes cannot be named but only described. This is based on a false assimilation in the *Tractatus* of the relation of propositions and the facts they express and the relation between an expression and a complex object which it signifies.

As I have already said, there is no reason why we cannot name a complex object which we can also identify by a description. Nor need the name be a mere abbreviation of the description. This wrong view comes, I think, from a combination of a correct insight Wittgenstein had about the impossibility of naming facts with his general talk about 'complexes', which failed to distinguish between facts and complex objects which we can specify extensionally and which are 'things'. There are facts that are true of complex objects, but the object, however complex it may be, is not a fact. I will begin by defending the view that not only facts but states of affairs cannot be named. Although facts (*Tatsachen*) are what the world consists of (1.1), their identity is too intimately dependent on language or thoughts expressed by some projective method for them to be treated extensionally. A proposition, whether true or false, describes an atomic state of affairs (*Sachverhalt*), and if the proposition is true and the atomic state of affairs obtains we identify a fact. Suppose two cubes a and b are in front of me. If the following propositions: 'a is bigger than b', 'a is to the right of b', 'a is of a darker red than b', 'there are two cubes', 'there are 12 square surfaces', 'there are 16 vertices', are all true, then they all express different facts. None of these propositions is logically equivalent to any of the others, and thus according to the *Tractatus* they do not have the same sense.

The facts described by the propositions cannot be said to be identical simply because they concern one and the same arrangement of two material objects. There are as many elements in the fact described as there are referred to in the proposition, i.e. as there are articulated by the proposition. And if we follow the *Tractatus* view the properties or relations which are ascribed to these elements must, I believe, be considered intensionally: a point I will discuss later on. Thus although one can raise the question whether a fact expressed by one proposition is the same or different from that expressed by another (by a discussion of the logical equivalence relationship etc.), one cannot say of a verbally unidentified fact, f_1, unexpressed by *any* projectional method, whether it has n elements, or whether it is the same as fact f_2, because as yet we have not settled the identity of the 'it' that we are talking about. Pointing, or naming, or even naming all the elements of the fact we have in mind, will not identify the fact. There may be an indefinite number of facts involving the same elements. Thus as 5.5423 says, if we have a figure on the page which can be seen in two ways as a cube we are seeing two different facts. In this case we are looking at the same drawing, and we have distinguished the same number of lines but we can see two different facts represented, depending on how we supply the rules of projection. It is because of their referentially opaque nature that states of affairs can be described but not named (3.144). If I use names or simple signs to talk about states of affairs—as when I use letters like p or q to mean 'a is to the right of b' or 'a is bigger than b', then 'p' or 'q' are abbreviations of the sentences, and not names of the states of affairs. Similarly, if I decide to call the fact that Rome is to the north of Naples 'Ivan', 'Ivan' will be, as it were, the code name of the proposition 'Rome is to the north of Naples', since it is only via the proposition (expressed verbally, or by some sign or diagram, with its rule of representation) that I can specify the fact. As Wittgenstein says, propositions can describe states of affairs because they are articulate. We understand what the proposition describes by understanding the constituents (4.024). And by constituents, Wittgenstein means (unlike the early Russell) the words, or the signs, or the pictorial elements which make up the propositional sign. That is why he also claims that a proposition is a function of the expressions contained in it (3.318). This is what the picture theory of meaning comes to.

The Wittgenstein of the *Tractatus* (like Russell) is, however, wrong to talk about all complex objects in the same way as he does about facts. For although the identity of a fact cannot be settled except by settling the identity of the proposition which describes it, the identity of complex objects such as General de Gaulle does not depend on our articulating any one particular description. It is of course true, as we have seen, that the question of identity of objects cannot be raised unless we see what kinds of propositions about them make sense and we cannot do this unless we agree about the truth of some propositions. But, as has been correctly argued by many recent writers on this subject, there is no one individuating description which has to be equated to the names or presupposed by all who refer to General de Gaulle or Istanbul. Thus, even if, Russell says, what appears to be a proper name of a complex object could be replaced by a definite description of the form '$(\imath x)\ \phi\ x$' *salva veritate*, it is not the case that the complex object can be identified only by this particular definite description. One need not analyse it into any particular existential proposition, and therefore one need not understand the constituents (which, in the case of Wittgenstein, are the constituent expressions or signs) of any particular proposition. Therefore 3.24 is wrong when it says 'A proposition about a complex stands in an internal relation to a proposition about a constituent of the complex'. Even if we were to call an object which can be given by some complex description 'a complex' it does not follow that all of the descriptions which identify it stand in an internal relation to the complex. Thus it does not follow either—so long as analysis of propositions involves replacing the proper names of complex objects by definite descriptions—that 'A proposition has one and only one complete analysis' as 3.25 says. For, if many of the definite descriptions which pick up one and the same complex object such as General de Gaulle do not even have a semantic or logical relationship to each other, there is no reason to think that, if we replace ordinary proper names by different definite descriptions, the end stage of the complete analysis would necessarily be the same. This would be so *only* if one assumes, as Leibniz did for example, that an ordinary proper name of a (complex) object is an abbreviation of the sum of all the predicates which are true of the object. This means that if 'a sign that has a definition signifies via the signs that serve to define it' (3.261), then an ordinary proper name cannot be treated as a sign which has a definition. A name need not be taken as a function of the constituent expressions of a particular description and, consequently, a proposition containing ordinary names need not be taken as a function of these constituent expressions. It would then not be true *in general* that 'the sense of a truth-function of p is a function of the sense of p' as 5.2341 says. Wittgenstein criticizes Frege for calling a proposition a composite name (3.143); Wittgenstein makes the opposite mistake of treating names of complex objects as propositions.

And here I come to the third and most important consequence, which is that the notions of '*Bedeutung*' (reference) and '*bedeuten*' (refer) are intensional ones in the *Tractatus* and, therefore, that the simple objects whose existence was posited were not so much a kind of metaphysical entity conjured up to support a logical theory as something whose existence adds no extra content to the logical theory. A point I will argue now. It has often been claimed that according to the *Tractatus* the meaning of a Name is its bearer, since 3.203 says that a Name refers to an object and that the object is its reference. And since the *Tractatus* says that an elementary proposition is a concatenation of Names, it has been claimed that *Tractatus* offers an extensional basis of semantics. I do not think that this claim is quite right. Later in the *Philosophical Investigations* Wittgenstein criticized the view which confuses the reference (*Bedeutung*) of a name with its bearer. The reference of the name 'Nothung' is the sword Nothung. If the sword is broken the bearer of the name 'Nothung' no longer exists. If the bearer of a name and the reference of a name are identical, the name should no longer have a reference either. But the sentence 'Nothung has a sharp blade' has sense, and one would want to say that in the proposition 'Nothung' has a reference. As if to avoid the difficulty, the *Tractatus* claimed that ordinary names such as 'Nothung' could not be names in the strict logical sense. I think this shows not that Wittgenstein wrongly identified the notions of bearer and reference in the *Tractatus* but rather that although he was not articulate about this, he had already realized that talk about references of names is not like talk about the bearers of ordinary names. 'Reference' is a semantic category with its peculiar logic. The bearer of the name 'Socrates' no longer exists, but the name has reference. So long as the name plays the rôle of identifying the man that once existed, it will always have reference. Just as references of names are permanent in our language, so according to Wittgenstein objects are unalterable and persistent (*bestehend*) (2.0271). Just as we use the same noun in affirming or denying or questioning, so objects persist independently of what is the case (2.024). These features of the objects, combined with their logical simplicity, in turn imbue Names which refer to them with very peculiar features.

Wittgenstein's belief that Names must be possible if propositions are to have definite sense[1] is based on two logical theories which he holds in the *Tractatus*. One is the view mentioned earlier, which I think is basically right, that propositions about objects, that is to say, propositions in which one ascribes certain properties to objects or says that objects stand in a certain relation to one another, which one might express as 'fx', '$\phi(x.y)$', can in principle be expressed without predicate expressions or relational expressions. As Professor Copi and Miss Anscombe have said, one can express them by a certain pattern or arrangement of the names of the objects. Thus '$\phi(x.y)$' could be expressed $\overset{x}{_y}$, and 'fa' could be expressed '$\mathfrak{v}$' (where 'a' is written upside down). That is to say, in any subject-predicate proposition which we can write as function of the subject names it is essential to have constituents which stand for the subjects but it is not necessary to have a function sign. What particular function of the names it is can be indicated by a specific concatenation of the names of the objects, which is not to be treated as a list of names.[2] So although in normal logical notation we do actually use function signs or relational expressions such as 'f', 'ϕ', or 'R', they are not essential in order to express what they do express.[3] The second theory is that so long as there are defined signs then there must be undefined signs. If not we will have an infinite regress and the

---

[1] 3.23. 'The requirement that simple signs be possible is the requirement that sense be determinate.'

[2] 4.22. See also footnote 2, p. 28. And, similarly, generalized propositions with quantifiers can be expressed without function signs, e.g. by expressing '($\exists y$)y is red' by '($\exists y$) λ', '(x)(y)f(xy)' by '(x)(y)$\overset{x}{_v}$'. And just as we learn the conventional meaning of each different predicate in ordinary language, we can learn the convention of expressing various properties by different patterns of name variables.

[3] 3.1432 'Instead of "The complex sign 'aRb' says that a stands to b in the relation R", we ought to put, "that 'a' stands to 'b' in a certain relation says *that aRb*".'

propositions which we form by using signs which have meaning via definitions will not have a definite sense. As we can express propositions which have definite sense—i.e. definite truth-conditions, these two theories lead Wittgenstein to say that it must be *possible* that there should be irreducible singular terms—i.e. Names. It is because of this that Wittgenstein claims that all propositions are truth-functions of elementary propositions (5). Not only propositions in which truth-functional connectives occur, and which have surface syntactical complexity, but all propositions are derivable from elementary propositions by logical operations.

The requirement of Names in the *Tractatus* might then seem like the claim for the indispensability or irreducibility of 'singular terms' of which one of the most persuasive recent defenders has been P. F. Strawson. I think, however, that, paradoxical as it might seem, Wittgenstein's request for the possibility of Names does not entail the indispensability of 'singular terms'. In her explanation of the *Tractatus* demand for Names, Miss Anscombe has written that Names are required if we are to be able to construct propositions and understand their sense (as we do) without already knowing what is true and what is false. For to understand the sense of a proposition is to understand its truth-conditions, and this means that there must be propositions which are false in only one way, and this is so only if there are Names.[1] That is to say, according to Miss Anscombe, if we have

(1) fA where 'A' is of the form 'the ϕ'

the truth-condition of (1) will involve the truth-condition of

(2) There is an x such that ϕx, and for all y, ϕy only if y = x. (1) can be interpreted as saying fx of this x, and can thus be false in two different ways, namely either when it is not the case that there is only one x which is ϕ, or when there is such an x, but which is not f. But (2) will only be true if

(3) ϕb

for some b where 'b' is a Name (or where 'b' can be paraphrased as 'the ψ' and so on until we arrive at some χc where 'c' cannot be paraphrased any more). And (3) can be false in one way only—when the object b does not have the property ϕ. Thus if propositions do have definite sense and their having sense does not depend on the truth of another proposition, then there must be

[1] G. E. M. Anscombe *Introduction to Wittgenstein's Tractatus*, p. 47.

propositions of the form 'ϕb' where 'b' is a name. But does (1) entail (3) and is Wittgenstein really committed to maintaining this?

It has already been shown that names of complex objects need not be reducible to one particular definite description. But so long as the use of a name of a complex object presupposes the use of some definite description, (1) would seem to entail (2). But why does it entail (3)? There seems to be no logical difficulty in supposing that in the final analysis one realizes that the truth-conditions of (1) involve the truth-condition of (2). And as Miss Anscombe rightly says, this involves understanding that (2) can be false in two different ways, one of which is the falsity of an existential proposition. But we do not have to know the *truth-value* of the existential proposition in order to give a definite sense or truth-conditions to (1). We need only know the *truth-conditions* of the existential proposition. To understand the sense of 'fA', where 'A' is of the form 'the ϕ', is to understand the *sense* of '($\exists$x) ϕx' as well as 'fx'. We must understand what it is for there to be one and only one x which is ϕ (without having to know its truth or falsity), and we must understand what it is for such an x to be f *if* there is such an x. Thus even if our analysis ended at (2) it would not be the case that 'whether a proposition had sense would depend on whether another proposition was true', which 2.0211 says would be true if there were no substances. It would of course not follow that because we stopped our analysis at (2), we have proved that substances do not exist. Wittgenstein clearly claims that there *must* be simple objects in order that propositions have definite sense. But to say that there are objects, and to say that one must arrive at their Names at the end of logical analysis, are two different claims. As far as Names are concerned he writes that they must be *possible*. I will try to show that within the framework of the logical atomism of the *Tractatus* it hardly makes any difference at all whether one claims that final analysis leads to elementary propositions or to existential statements logically equivalent to them. This equivalence itself seems to be maintained by Wittgenstein when he says 'We can describe the world completely by means of fully generalized propositions, i.e. without first correlating any Name with a particular object' (5.526).

Let us examine this question a bit more carefully. 5.47 says quite clearly that 'fa' says the same thing as '($\exists$x) fx . x = a'.

This would suggest that 'fa' could never be equivalent to an existential proposition since it is an existential proposition plus something more: namely the identity claim that x = a. For example, to claim that there is a man who killed Caesar, and that he is Brutus, is quite different from just asserting that there is a man who killed Caesar. And indeed if 'a' is an ordinary proper name, 'fa' always says something more than '($\exists$x) fx'. 'a' plays the rôle of identifying or specifying a particular object which the proposition is about. We read in the *Notebooks* that 'Names are necessary for an assertion that *this* thing possesses *that* property and so on. They link the propositional form with quite definite objects.' It must be remembered however that Names which occur in elementary propositions are different from names like 'Brutus'. The references of Names are simple objects which 'can only be named' and not given by definite descriptions. So in the proposition '[$\exists$x] fx . x = a' where 'a' is a name, a is merely identified as an object which is f. I cannot imagine it excluded from the possibility of combining with others (2.0121)—so in order to know a I must know what it would be for it to be true that g(a.b), h(a.b.c) etc. but not that they are true; and a itself has no material or contingent features which allow me to identify it by a description. Thus to say '($\exists$x) fx . x = a' comes to the same as 'an object is f'. Strawson has argued convincingly that 'the identificatory function of singular terms should be acknowledged . . . , and clearly distinguished from the operation of asserting that there is just one thing answering to certain specifications.'[1] And indeed in 'fa' or '($\exists$x) fx . x = a', one is not asserting that there is just one thing which is f. (In fact, there may be many things that are f.) One *is* talking about a particular object a. But as I have said, so long as 'a' is a Name, the object a in fa has no contingent properties which would enable one to identify it by a definite description. To identify a would be nothing more than identifying an f. And for the *Tractatus*, propositions which have the same truth-conditions have the same sense.

It might be objected that in order for 'fa' even to have sense before it is true or false, there must be an object named by 'a', whereas '($\exists$x) fx' has sense even when it is false—when there is no object. But what is it to require that there must be an object

---

[1] P. F. Strawson 'Singular Terms and Predication', *Journal of Philosophy*, Vol. 58, No. 15, 1961. Reprinted in *Philosophical Logic*, O.U.P., p. 77.

a which might or might not be f? Let us take seriously Wittgenstein's claim in 5.526 that Names can be dispensed with in our description of the world. He argues this point in greater detail in his *Notebooks* of 16 October 1914. 'Yes the world could be completely described by completely general propositions, and hence without using any sort of names or other designating (*bezeichnendes*) signs. And in order to arrive at ordinary language one would only need to introduce names etc. by saying, after an "(∃x)", "and this x is A" and so on.' We realize that in this example since we *introduce* the name 'A' by saying (∃x) fx and this x is A, it would be quite impossible to envisage the A as not having the property f. There is no other criterion for A to be identified as an object. 'A' is here what we call a dummy name. We realize also the truth of the claim, hinted previously, that properties or relations in the *Tractatus* be treated intensionally. The irreducible properties or relations which are ascribed to objects in elementary propositions cannot be identified extensionally as the class of objects which have the property, or which stand in the relation. If it is only via the properties which it has that an object is introduced, the properties in turn cannot be defined by the objects which have them. According to my interpretation, the objects of the *Tractatus* are as far removed as can be from 'bare particulars' which people like Professor Copi have claimed they are. They are necessarily instantiations of some properties, although Wittgenstein cannot say what kind of properties they are instantiations of. He merely tells us that the properties concerned are not material properties like being of a particular colour.

In proofs in elementary geometry we often ascribe dummy names to objects which are assumed to have no properties except those which are ascribed to them in the proofs. For example, we say 'Let a be the centre of the circle C' and go on to deduce the various relations it has to other things. We cannot however go on to suppose that a is not the centre of the circle, for a has no identity other than that of being just that. We may come to decide, after using a dummy name 'a', that 'a' did not secure a reference. But as long as we use 'a' and talk of object 'a' it is the centre of the circle C—and an object necessarily has to have a property other than being an object, since, as the *Tractatus* says, *object* is a formal concept. I hope it is clear that I am not claiming that every proposition of the form 'fa', 'gbc' where 'a', 'b', 'c', are Names, must be true. In the example of the geometrical proof, the proposition 'a is on line L' may well be false. Some elementary propositions are true, some are false (4.25). It seems nevertheless the case that, if some proposition of the form φa is necessarily true in order for us to be able to identify a at all, and, as an elementary proposition of the form φa is claimed to be logically independent of any other elementary proposition, then the condition of the use of the Name 'a' is nothing more than the conditions which enable us to say '(∃x) φx'. It is because of this that Wittgenstein could not, strictly speaking, require that Names exist, but only that Names *be possible*: that we would be able to use Names.

If, as I have argued, Names in the *Tractatus* are like dummy Names, the relationship of *bedeuten* or referring which holds between Names and objects is also of a very special kind, as also is the nature of objects themselves. We have already seen that the identity of an object can be determined only by settling the sense of the propositions in which the Names occur. But the sense of an elementary proposition of the form 'fa' is exactly the same as the sense of a proposition of the form 'fb' where 'f(x)' expresses the same property, and 'a' and 'b' are different Names. Just as in the geometrical proof mentioned earlier, saying 'Let a be the centre of the circle C' is exactly the same as saying 'Let b be the centre of the circle C', if 'a' and 'b' are dummy names. What the dummy names are used to identify are nothing more nor less than an instantiation of the description or predicate which follows. If the conditions of using a dummy name *are* the conditions of saying 'there is a so and so which . . .', then dummy names cannot fail to refer to an object so long as the set of propositions in which they occur make sense. Referring to an object here means that the dummy names have use. When we identify two human beings by their proper names and predicate something of them—as when we say 'Bernard Shaw and Oscar Wilde are Irish', we identify the two men not merely as different Irishmen, and so naturally their names are not interchangeable. Dummy names are interchangeable so long as we interchange them consistently, and so I believe are Names in the *Tractatus*.

I am not claiming that Wittgenstein explicitly thought that his Names behave like dummy names, but only that in effect they are made to do so. The objects Names refer to are entities which have a criterion of identity quite different from those according to which we normally identify and distinguish spatio-temporal objects. However simple a spatio-temporal object is, as a particular it only belongs to this world and not to all possible imaginary worlds as the objects are said to do (2.022). The simplest spatio-temporal objects not only have the possibility of occurring in various states of affairs, but do occur in many. They are instantiations of many properties. The tiny fleck of snow on my palm is made of H_2O; it fell at a particular time in January 1968 in a particular spot in London, etc. etc. Even if one takes the view that there is no logical necessity for the object to have some or most of these properties, and even if one believes that it could have had various other external properties under different circumstances, the fact remains that the object *has* all these external properties. If an object lacks any of the properties that A has, or has any property that A does not have, then it simply is not A: thus no spatio-temporal object of this world identified in the normal way could be a constituent of any other imagined world. The identity of any particular spatio-temporal object is not determined by its 'possibilities'. Many philosophers have therefore been tempted to take the 'objects' of the *Tractatus* as either being properties or sense data. I have already given reasons why predicate expressions are not considered as Names in the *Tractatus*, and thus why the properties or relations (that are true of objects) to which predicate expressions refer when they occur in propositions or which are expressed by a structure of the concatenation of the Names of objects are not to be treated as objects. Sense data theory will not *by itself* provide us with objects which are common to all worlds either. Each token sense datum is not only bound to this world but also to the person who has the experience. If we are referring not to token sense data but to types of sense data, then we are considering properties which are true of certain areas of our visual field, which again are not objects. To suppose either that objects of the *Tractatus* are spatio-temporal things, or that they are sense data, lands us in similar difficulties. To ask what kind of familiar entities correspond to the objects of the *Tractatus* seems to lead us nowhere. The alternative here attempted has been to ask what kind of criterion of identity objects can have to enable them to be 'independent of what is the case' (2.024), and constitute an imaginary world as well as our real one.

As we have seen, the reference of a Name which has as its form the possibility of occurring in various atomic states of affairs is identified nevertheless in an existing atomic state of affairs; i.e. only as an instantiation of a certain property, monadic or relational. At the same time every atomic state of affairs is independent of every other (2.061, 2.062). We can understand what it is for states of affairs to be independent of each other if each state of affairs is described by a general proposition. That there is a red object might be independent of the fact that there is a square object, and so on. But what is it for elementary propositions in which Names occur to be logically independent of each other? If an object A is identified as the reference of 'A' in 'FA', this is so independently of the existence or non-existence of any other atomic state of affairs involving A; independently of whether we are to treat A as the instantiation of any other properties at all. This could not be the case where 'A' is the name of any particular individual. A then is not an object in any extensional sense. If we think of a world different from our own in which the same atomic state of affairs holds as in ours, then one can say in the language of the *Tractatus* that this imaginary world and ours have the same objects. In less eccentric philosophical speech this would be expressed by saying that there are instantiations of the same predicate in the different worlds, or that these different worlds have members of the same set.

The claim, in the *Tractatus* that objects exist should then be understood to mean that there are *instantiations* of certain irreducible properties which for Wittgenstein are different from any material properties. (In understanding, for example, that here is an instantiation of the property red, we also understand that there could here be instantiations of the property being square, being hard and so on.) It is not a claim that there are properties or relations, but nevertheless a claim *about* properties and relations all the same. It is not a claim about the existence of individual concepts in any Leibnizian sense, since any individual concept is a highly complex one including an infinite number of predicates, whereas the claim that objects exist in the *Tractatus* is the assertion that there are instantiations of simple irreducible properties. And it is the combination of the view that the identity of objects referred to by a Name can be determined only by settling the use of the Name, with his view that all elementary propositions must be logically independent of one another that leads him to this position.

My interpretation of the *Tractatus* view of objects may appear to be eccentric. But I would like to end this paper by drawing attention to three important facts which I believe indicate the plausibility of my interpretation. The first is the commentary which Wittgenstein himself gives in the *Philosophical Investigations*, §§ 46–8 about the objects of the *Tractatus*. After writing that the objects of the *Tractatus* are like the simples of the *Theaetetus*, Wittgenstein goes on to give an example of a language-game for which the *Theaetetus* account is valid. The language serves to describe various combinations of squares on a surface which are red, green, white or black. Each coloured square is a simple, and is given the name 'R', 'G', 'W', or 'B', depending on the colour. Each sentence in this language consists of a sequence of these names, e.g. 'RRBGGGRWW', which describes a particular arrangement of the coloured squares. Here we see clearly that every different square of the same colour is given the same name, and is regarded as the same simple. The fact that they are different token squares does not endow them with different names. The names are not claimed by Wittgenstein to correspond to colours, but to *coloured squares*. Yet, different token squares of the same colour have the same names. In other words, the use of a name identifies an instantiation of a property, and does not distinguish between different instantiations of the same properties. This is exactly what I have claimed the Names of the *Tractatus* do. The point I am making is also supported by Waismann's notes of Wittgenstein's comments where it is pointed out how wrong it is to ask whether objects are 'thing-like' or 'property-like'. This is the second point I wish to refer to. Objects, Wittgenstein says here, are elements of presentations (*Darstellungen*). In other words, to say that there are objects is nothing more than to say that there is something described, or presented by a diagram, picture, etc. And to say that there is something described or pictured does not, of course, mean that the thing described or pictured exists.

The third point to which I would like to draw attention is certain areas of Model theory, where, as in the *Tractatus*, some logicians have talked of objects which could be common to different possible worlds. In order to be able to specify a possible world by e.g. a model consisting of an ordered pair $\langle A, R \rangle$ where A is a non-empty set and R is a relation, and a different possible world by another model $\langle A, R' \rangle$ where A is said to be the same non-empty set as in the former and R' a different relation, one has invoked a notion of objects different from our normal notion of particulars. For the objects which are members of the set A have been given an identity which is independent of the relations they satisfy in different worlds. (This peculiarity would not arise if one made the models specify descriptions of possible worlds, rather than the worlds themselves.)

It has been suggested by Stenius, Stegmüller and Hintikka that we might obtain a better understanding of the 'objects' in the *Tractatus* by invoking model theoretical concepts. Although I disagree with various aspects of Stenius's and Stegmüller's views about the *Tractatus*, which amongst other things fail to distinguish between what are to count as properties and objects in a given state of affairs, it seems to me to be correct that the objects of the *Tractatus* which merely determine the possibility of their occurrence in various states-of-affairs have logical features close to those exhibited by those objects in Model theory which can occur in different models.

Let me summarize the main conclusions of this paper. The *Tractatus* does not, as has sometimes been thought, offer an extensional foundation of semantic analysis. The objects of the *Tractatus* are not like things (however simple) in the empirical world which can be individuated extensionally. The concept of a simple object is more like that of an instantiation of an irreducible property. This concept was a logical requisite for the *Tractatus* theory, and followed from the combination of a basically correct theory about names, of a mistaken assimilation of complex things and facts, and of a wrong and unnecessary claim about the independence of elementary propositions. The *Tractatus* theory of Names, which claims that the problem of the identity of the reference of names and the problem of the use of Names in propositions are inseparable, is closely connected with the picture theory of meaning and contains much that is right and illuminating even for those who reject talk about simple objects and mutually independent elementary propositions—as Wittgenstein himself did in his later years.

II

'ONTOLOGY' AND IDENTITY IN THE *TRACTATUS*: À PROPOS OF BLACK'S *COMPANION*

Rush Rhees

'ADEQUATE SYMBOLISM' AND 'ONTOLOGY'

IF we ask what Wittgenstein means by 'adequate symbolism', we shall look to the relation of sign and syntax; for it depends on that. So it is pointless to say, as Black does: we must have some view of what reality is like, before we can ask if the symbolism is adequate to describe it. Black takes this as a reason for his remarks about 'the ontology of the *Tractatus*'. For instance: 'Wittgenstein expects a perspicuous *view* of the nature of logic to have *ontological implications*.' 'Wittgenstein's conception of the nature of language . . . *required a stand on ontological issues*.' 'His ontology (*sic*) *is on the whole suggested by* his views about language.'[1] (My italics throughout.) This is confused, and the remarks about adequate symbolism in the *Tractatus* do not need it.

Since there are signs, there must be a distinction of true and false propositions—a distinction to be decided finally by observation, not by logic. We could say that the *truth* of logical principles is tied to this. When the *Tractatus* says in 6.113 that 'What distinguishes logical propositions is that we can see by the

---

[1] Max Black, *A Companion to Wittgenstein's Tractatus*, Cambridge, 1964, pp. 4, 7 and 8.

symbol alone that they are true', it adds: 'So what is especially important is the fact that the truth or falsity of non-logical propositions *cannot* be seen in the proposition alone.'—In other words, it would have no sense at all to speak of logical propositions unless there were empirical propositions.

Mathematics is not written in tautologies; it is written in equations. But equations would be meaningless unless there were calculation: they get their reality from the general form of logical operation, and so from the internal relations of propositional forms. So we could not treat mathematics as a logical method—we could not see that mathematical proofs are logical proofs—unless *empirical* statements had sense and could be the bases of logical operations.

This is summed up in 4.0312, which expresses the 'Grundgedanke' of the book:

> Die Möglichkeit des Satzes beruht auf dem Prinzip der Vertretung von Gegenständen durch Zeichen.
> Mein Grundgedanke ist, daß die 'logischen Konstanten' nicht vertreten. Daß sich die *Logik* der Tatsachen nicht vertreten läßt.[1]

This is at the foundation of what Wittgenstein has to say about logical analysis—e.g. (in 4.221) 'that in the analysis of propositions we must arrive at elementary propositions, consisting of names directly connected to one another'. He is contrasting this 'unmittelbare Verbindung' of names in elementary propositions with whatever it is that logical constants express. For these appear only in the expression of the results of an operation *on* elementary propositions. You can always transform a proposition containing logical constants into another equivalent to it. But elementary propositions cannot be equivalent to one another.—We can carry out logical operations independently of the truth or the falsity of elementary propositions: independently of what is the case. We can do this *because* of the fundamental difference between elementary propositions and others: i.e., because the logical constants 'do not stand for anything'. Otherwise we could not 'see by the symbol alone' that a calculation or a formal proof was correct.

---

[1] 'The possibility of propositions is based on the principle that objects have signs as their representatives.

'My fundamental idea is that the "logical constants" are not representatives; that there can be no representatives of the logic of facts.'

The *Tractatus* could not begin with a discussion of logical constants and the truth of logical principles. What comes first is the truth or falsity of *material* propositions—in other words *sense*. Without this we could not even speak of *possible* signs.

But to call this 'ontology' is confusing. And to say that the discussions of logic are important because of the ontology which is built on them, is to stand the whole thing on its head. Black quotes the remark in Wittgenstein's 1913 *Notes on Logic*: '/Philosophy/ consists of logic and metaphysics, the former its basis', and Black adds: 'Logic as the *basis* of metaphysics: throughout the book Wittgenstein expects a perspicuous view of the nature of logic to have ontological implications. Logic is important because it leads to metaphysics' (*Companion*, page 4). But the remark he quotes does not say that logic is the basis of metaphysics; it says it is the basis of *philosophy*. And Wittgenstein did not say there or anywhere else that logic has *implications*.

Sentences like 'der Name bedeutet den Gegenstand' (3.203) or 'Der Name vertritt im Satz den Gegenstand' (3.22) belong to the grammar of the words 'name' and 'object' and 'proposition'. The *Notes Dictated to Moore* had said (*Notebooks*, pp. 109, 110): 'In the expression (∃y) . ϕy, one is apt to say this means "There is a *thing* such that . . . ". But in fact we should say "There is a y, such that . . . "; the fact that y symbolizes expressing what we mean. . . . In our language names are *not things*: we don't know what they are: all we know is that they are of a different type from relations, etc., etc.' The *Tractatus* might not put it in just this way, but the main point holds there.

'TOKEN OR TYPE?'

In connexion with 3.203—'A name means an object. The object is its meaning. ("A" is the same sign as "A".)'—Black asks 'Is the propositional sign a token or a type?'; and he goes on: 'When we normally speak of a sentence, we use the word "sentence" in a "type-sense" rather than a "token-sense". . . . That this is the way Wittgenstein himself uses the expression "propositional sign" (which takes over the rôle of "sentence" in his conception) is made quite clear by his remark at 3.203: " 'A' is the same sign as 'A'." If two propositional signs consist of physically similar words respectively attached to the *same* bearers, Wittgenstein counts the two as instances of the same propositional sign.'

But Wittgenstein himself said nothing of the sort: the text says nothing at all about physically similar signs respectively attached to the same bearers.

His remark in the *Notes Dictated to Moore* that 'in our language names are *not things*' says something about the grammar of 'name' and 'thing'; or, as he puts it there, the difference in *logical type*. So, for instance, 'identity' has different rules of syntax when we speak of the identity of a thing and when we speak of the identity of a sign. ' "A" is the same sign as "A" ' expresses—or 'seeks to express'—the identity of a sign. It does not say anything. And it cannot be analysed in terms of 'this scratch here resembles that scratch there'. Perhaps we'd never say 'It's the same sign' unless the scratches did resemble one another, but this is not part of what we *mean* by ' "A" is the same sign as "A" '—'How do you know this is A?' would be as nonsensical as 'How do you know this is white?'.

A mark without syntax is not a sign. And this makes it hard to say what the identity of a sign is.

When Peirce[1] and others write about Types and Tokens they seem to feel that we might analyse the identity of a sign in terms of the identity of a physical object or of an event. But they never manage to: this is plain when Peirce calls a Token an '*instance*' of a Type, and when Ramsey says that 'a *proposition* is a type whose instances consist of all propositional sign tokens which have in common, not a certain appearance, but a certain *sense*'. The 'all'—in 'all propositional sign tokens which . . .'—is bewildering, but since each of these has a sense, it ought to refer to various propositions which are *equivalent* to one another; and if we put it so, we are back where we started: distinguishing type and token has done nothing.—On the other hand, physical similarity between particular scratches cannot be what 'groups tokens together into types', in Peirce's sense of Type; no more than grouping shells or pebbles together would be treating them as Tokens.

Black thinks that Wittgenstein uses 'propositional sign' for a *class* of *token* propositional signs. But what does 'token' add here?

When a printer estimates the number of words on a page he is speaking of physical marks, and it does not matter whether they

---

[1] C. S. Peirce, *Collected Papers*, Vol. IV, §§ 4.537, 4.538, 4.544.

are really words or not. Peirce calls the Token in which a Type is embodied 'an *Instance* of the Type'. But then if I count the instances of various Types on a page I am not counting what the printer counts.

'You cannot make the same scratch twice' could have sense. 'You cannot write the same word twice' could not.

'How can I be sure I am seeing the same token and not a different one? Maybe I am not reading the same copy of the book although I thought I was. Maybe someone had erased that word on that line and printed it again. Etc., etc.' Peirce might have answered, 'All right, you probably can't; and in such cases *it does not matter*.'—I.e., 'Tokens' always means 'Tokens on this page' or '. . . in this copy of this book'—or something of this sort. It is *not* a term for a kind of physical object, like 'scratch'. Ramsey and Black (and Peirce) are not clear about the grammar of it.

If nobody ever said anything, nothing would ever be said. And every time you write a word, you write a word.

But this is just as trivial as it sounds. It does not explain the meaning of 'That's a word'.

If I said 'They are all instances of "word" ', you would probably take me to mean: 'We'd call them all words'. But of course this does not mean 'They are all Tokens of the Type "word" ' in Peirce's sense.

We want to know the syntax of 'sign'. And we think, perhaps, that then we'd know the syntax of *signs*—i.e., what they must have in order to be signs.

Is it not the syntax of words that determines the syntax of 'word'? Unless you *understood* words in their syntax, you would not know what a word is, and you could not use the word 'word'.—If we say this, we do not mean—we *deny*—that the syntax of 'word' is given (or determined) by instances of the Type 'word'.

Black lands in this confusion because he thinks there *is* something by which our grammar is determined—or that this is how the *Tractatus* must be read. This goes with what he says about ontology in his discussion of 'adequate symbolism'.

'THE NAMING RELATION'

We speak in a different sense (1) of a proposition corresponding with reality (this is *Abbildung* or 'projection') and (2) of a name corresponding to what it means or to what is called by it.

When the *Tractatus* says, in 3.3: 'it is only in the connexion of a proposition that a name has meaning', it means that without the picturing or projection in a proposition there would be no correspondence at all. A proposition can describe a state of affairs in a language. Apart from a language it would not be a proposition. In *Tractatus* 5: 'A proposition is a truth-function of elementary propositions.' So the combination of signs in a proposition is not arbitrary.[1] I am committed to the signs I use and the ways I combine them—by the general rule, the syntax of the language. It is through this that the marks and sounds become symbols.

'There might have been a *different* corrrelation (of signs and things).' Alternatives are possible in a language. But a jumble of sounds or scratches would not be an alternative; it would mean nothing to call it one.

'But assigning names is arbitrary—*definitions* are arbitrary.'— What makes it a definition? If I give a name to a colour or a shape I must have distinguished these as I distinguish expressions of a language. And within the language my definition commits me in certain ways, not in others. What the definition establishes—the relation of the name to what it stands for—is not an external relation.

We could say that the rules of multiplication are fixed by definition; in certain algebras these rules mean nothing. Or we might say that 4 is the result of 2×2 by definition; and this would not make the relation of result and multiplication a contingent one.— Words are related to what they say as a result to its calculation.

The *Tractatus* hardly distinguishes naming and calling something by its name. And 3.3 shows that this is not an oversight. 'Nur im Zusammenhange des Satzes hat ein Name Bedeutung.'[2] So we may think that what the word 'red' means is expressed by the sentence 'a is red'.

Someone might say: 'The name must correspond to some

---

[1] Cf. 5.47: ' ... Wo Zusammengesetztheit ist, da ist Argument und Funktion, und wo diese sind, sind bereits alle logischen Konstanten.' Or 4.0141: 'Daß es eine allgemeine Regel gibt ... darin besteht eben die innere Ähnlichkeit dieser scheinbar ganz verschiedenen Gebilde. Und jene Regel ist das Gesetz der Projektion. ...' ('Wherever there is compositeness, argument and function are present, and where these are present, we already have all the logical constants.' 'There is a general rule ... That is what constitutes the inner similarity between these things which seem to be constructed in such entirely different ways. And that rule is the law of projection. ...')

[2] 'Only in the nexus of a proposition does a name have meaning.'

reality. It cannot describe anything if there is nothing which it signifies.' Or suppose I told you: 'I call each of these roses red because each of them *is* red. The word I use corresponds to the colour of the flower.'—But what corresponds is the *sentence*. The *Tractatus* supposed that 'red' determines how I use it.

Wittgenstein rejected this later. It confuses giving a sample and using a sample. I may give a sample—a piece of coloured paper—to explain what I mean by 'vermilion'. Or I may use the sample in place of the word and tell you 'the flowers in that bed are *this* colour'. But I cannot use the sample to explain what colour this *sample* is.

The idea had been that the sample can serve as a 'primary sign'—one which explains itself and cannot be misunderstood. Other signs may be explained by the primary signs; but without the primary signs we'd never know what we were saying. Wittgenstein brought out the confusions in all this. But it showed that the distinction between what a name means and what is called by it is not always simple or easy.

Black knows that the meaning and the bearer of a name are different. But in his remarks on 'difficulties about the naming relation' he seems to think that *arbitrary* means *contingent* and that this means *empirical*. On page 116 he says: 'It is only *contingently* the case that the elements of [the propositional sign] F have the bearers that are attached to them, *since it is perfectly conceivable that F might have had a different sense.*' I have put the last clause in italics, for this does *not* show that: 'F says (so and so)' is an empirical proposition.

If the meanings of names are arbitrarily fixed, this does not mean that the sense of a *sentence* is arbitrarily fixed. What fixes the meaning of a name is a rule. But if someone says 'an arbitrary rule is a contingent proposition', he confuses a rule with a generalization.

IDENTITY

What shows that a name now means what it meant then? What shows that this statement speaks of the same thing as that?

4.243: 'Can we understand two names without understanding whether they signify the same thing or two different things?— Can we understand a proposition in which two names occur without knowing whether their meaning is the same or different? ...'

5.53: 'That what is meant is the same I express by using the same sign, and not by using a sign for identity. [und nicht mit Hilfe eines Gleichheitszeichens.] . . .'

Wittgenstein does not ask 'What shows that this is the same sign?'—nor *can* this be asked. Yet Black seems to think the *Tractatus* tries to answer it. He sees that in 5.53–5.534 Wittgenstein wants 'to show that identities are not truth functions of elementary propositions, as genuine propositions are' (*Companion*, page 290), but then he says: 'The basic idea is to show identity of objects, whether identified by names or included in the ranges of given variables *by means of physical similarities* in the signs for such names and such variables.' I have put that phrase in italics.

Wittgenstein's point is that identity is not a function, not a tautology and not a logical principle; also that there is no 'general concept of logical identity' (compare e.g. Tarski's *Introduction*, page 61).

Wittgenstein could call the laws of logic—the modus ponens, say, or double negation—propositions about propositions. The *Tractatus* brings out this relation of tautologies to genuine propositions by writing them both as truth-functions. But $x = y$, or $x = x$, is not a truth-function. This is the main point. The details of *Principia Mathematica*'s definition—'x and y are called identical when every predicative function satisfied by x is also satisfied by y'—are less important.

Principia Mathematica distinguished the '$=$' of definition from the '$=$' in $x = y$ but assumed that here (in $x = y$) it is the same as the sign of equality in mathematics. Wittgenstein called this a confusion.

To arrive at cardinal numbers *Principia Mathematica* treats of Unit Classes and of Cardinal Couples; and so (e.g. *51.232) of 'the class whose only members are x and y'. To express this: if any third term, z, be assumed to belong to the given class, then $z = x . v . z = y$; and *PM* treats this formula as a function. A little later it says, 'the class of all couples of the form $\iota'x \cup \iota'y$ (where $x \neq y$) is the cardinal number 2'—where the sign in the parenthesis does not express mathematical inequality. *Couples*, apparently, are entities correlated in the form $x = a . y = b . v . x = c . y = d . v . . . .$ etc. Here the sign of identity would be used to express logical correlation but not mathematical equality.

For *'only* x and y have a given property' the *Tractatus* gives a notation in 5.5321:

$$(\exists x, y).\phi x.\phi y: \sim (\exists x, y, z).\phi x.\phi y.\phi z.$$

The *Tractatus* does not introduce numbers in this way. But it shows that what *Principia Mathematica* wants to express can be written without the ambiguous z = x.v.z = y. Here it seems to be using the *PM* symbolism. But the apparent variables are different signs from those which *Principia Mathematica* writes the same way; for there the apparent variables seem to have the generality of a concept. The criticism of identity is also a criticism of the *Principia Mathematica* use of quantifiers—which the *Tractatus* has just been discussing.

It seems as if *Principia Mathematica* explains what it is we say about x and y when we call them identical. Just as it seems to say of those things which form a couple that they stand in this (which?) relation to one another. Perhaps Russell thought that unless he did treat x = y as a function he could not write the propositions of arithmetic in logical notation.

Ramsey seemed to accept the criticism of Russell's *definition* of identity. But he wanted to keep x = y as a *function*; so it looks at first as though he had kept the substance of Russell's theory. 'x = y is a function in extension of two variables. Its value is tautology when x and y have the same value, contradiction when x, y have different values.'[1] But these are not functions in Russell's or Frege's sense; so that when Ramsey speaks of 'an apparent variable ϕ_e', for instance, we do not know what he is saying. What he did share with Russell was a confusion about the application of mathematics and the reference to *things*.

He said (page 49) that

Wittgenstein's convention (regarding identity) . . . puts us in a hopeless position as regards classes, because . . . we can no longer use x = y as a propositional function in defining classes. So the only classes with which we are now able to deal are those defined by predicative functions. . . . Mathematics then becomes hopeless because we cannot be sure that there is any class defined by a predicative function whose number is two; for things may all fall into triads which agree in every respect, in which case there would be in our system no unit classes and no two-member classes.

[1] F. P. Ramsey, *The Foundations of Mathematics*, p. 53.

Apparently Ramsey rejects the formulations of *Tractatus* 5.321 on the ground that any such proposition might be false—we cannot be sure that the facts would justify it: 'things may all fall into triads'. And the advantage of (Ramsey's) functions in extension would be that the correlation here is arbitrary; the assertion of such functions does not depend on whether individuals agree or disagree in their properties.

Wittgenstein would say then as he said later: 'The application of mathematics in our language does not say what is true and what is false, but what is sense and what is nonsense.'

ARITHMETIC

Ramsey and Russell wanted to express arithmetic—mathematics— in logical terms: in terms of relations between functions. The *Tractatus* holds that the propositions of mathematics are equations and that these show *the logic of the world* as tautologies do: but they are not tautologies. ('The logic of the world'—roughly, we speak in the same way of *necessity* and of *impossibility* here as in logic.)

Russell's notation for numerical expressions does not show their interconnexion with operations such as addition and multiplication. The *Tractatus* holds that we understand numbers when we see them as features of a formal system or a calculation. 'Die Zahlen treten mit dem Kalkül in die Logik ein.'[1] A correlation between signs on one side and the other of an implication will not provide this; no more than it gives a conception of formal series.—Suppose we showed that it is the expression of an identity. What is there mathematical about this? How does the conception of '. . . and so on' come into it? How is it the expression of a *rule*?

This is a criticism of Russell's view of the *generality* of mathematics and of logic.

Suppose we said that the result of a calculation holds universally. This is of the same form as saying that the development of a given decimal is periodic. It is what Wittgenstein in the *Tractatus* expressed by 'the general term of a formal series' or 'the general form of number'. And, as he remarked later, the 'generality' of $[1, x, x+1]$ cannot be expressed by '$(x).[1, x, x+1]$'. (He was

---

[1] *Philosophische Bemerkungen*, p. 129: 'This is in line with what I once meant when I said: numbers come into logic with the system of calculation.'

speaking of induction and the idea of 'holding for all numbers'.)

We might feel like saying that the general form of operation was the same as the general concept of a formal series—except that there is not really any such concept; it is a form. And we need to keep this distinction especially when we are speaking of generality. The *sign* for an operation is the general sign for a member of a formal series. Take that given in 5.2522: [a, x, O'x]. This is also the general form of *successive application* of an operation. For the general form of operation *is* the general form of its successive application. But it would be misleading to say that this shows 'the kind of generality which an operation has'. We might distinguish more general and more special operations, but this would be something else. It would not be the generality of the *form* (as opposed, say, to the generality of a concept).

'Numbers are exponents of operations.' They are not properties of aggregates, nor properties of the defining properties of aggregates. To say 'the successive applications of an operation form an aggregate' would be nonsense. It would be treating 'repetitions of the operation' as physical events. It would confuse the form, or the possibility, with *my carrying out* the operation. This would be like a confusion of counting in mathematics—counting the roots of an equation or the inner and the outer vertices of a pentagram (Wittgenstein's examples)—and counting outside mathematics: counting the jars on a shelf or the white corpuscles in a blood sample.

We may want to say 'The order of successive application is a *temporal* order: one after another.' This is all right if we remember that it is an order of possibilities—the order in a construction. 'We cannot construct the polygon before the triangle' (Simone Weil).[1] This does not refer to the times of actual happenings.

One reason for speaking of numbers as exponents of an operation was to show that the expressions of arithmetic belong to a system. Otherwise equations would be arbitrary rules of substitution. We should not know where they belonged; i.e., we should not know what to do with them. Black seems confused about this when he speaks of 'the applications of arithmetic to counting' (page 314).

He is more seriously confused in what he says of 6.02. Here

[1] *Leçons de Philosophie* de Simone Weil, présentées par Anne Reynaud, Paris, 1959, p. 65.

(page 314) Black seems to take the successive application of an operation (his phrase 'the self-application of an Ω-operation' is not in the *Tractatus* and is misleading) to be something like the logical addition of a truth-function to itself. $p \vee p = p$; so if the operation were 'v', then O'O'O'a would be the same as O'a. (cf. 5.2521.) Black may have been led to this by the fact that when Wittgenstein begins his definitions or rather constructions of numbers he decides that the sign for the repetition of the same operation shall be an exponent written first as a succession of '+1's'. But this is the '+' of *arithmetical* addition. And whatever difficulties it may carry here, it is not logical addition.

$$p \vee p = p$$
$$1 + 1 \neq 1$$

As the *Tractatus* uses 'operation', it would be nonsense to speak of a logical sum of operations. And although throughout its successive application the operation is the same, this does not mean that the successive application is no different from a single application of it.

Black concludes: 'It would seem that for all m and n greater than zero we must have Ω^{m}'x $= \Omega^{n}$'x. Does it follow that m = n for all positive integers?'—But what does '=' mean in the first of these sentences? If it means 'is the same operation as', then nothing follows about arithmetical equality. If it is the sign of numerical equality, then I have no idea what the whole expression means. (Black's 'for all m and n greater than zero, we must have ...' is nonsense in this context.)

In 6.01 Wittgenstein had said that the general form of operation is 'the most general form of transition from one proposition to another'. The result of any transition of this form would be a proposition, not a number. The general form of operation does enter somehow into the formal series in which numbers are generated, apparently. But the first idea is that numbers are *exponents* of the successive application of an operation—not that they are generated by it. The formal series in which they *are* generated or constructed is a series of *arithmetical* operations.

In 5.2523 the *Tractatus* says: 'Der Begriff der successiven Anwendung der Operation ist äquivalent mit dem Begriff "und so weiter".'[1] The general form of operation is not itself an

'The concept of successive applications of an operation is equivalent to the concept "and so on".'

operation of a formal series. It is what *makes possible* the development of formal series. And it is what makes mathematical *constructions* possible. So that in arithmetic we can calculate, and we do not wonder whether the same calculation will always have the same result. We can see that that is how it goes; just as with a periodic decimal, when we see that the remainder is the same as the dividend we can see that it goes on like that.

In the *Tractatus* number is a formal concept or a *form*. We do not learn the meaning of a form as we learn the meaning of a name or a phrase; and I could not explain a form to you as I might explain a general concept. 'Form' and 'construction' go together; and you can understand a construction that is carried out; just as you can understand a sentence, without having anyone tell you what it is. But we could not *define* a propositional form without being circular (the expression for 'the general form of proposition' contains 'elementary proposition'). Neither can we define numbers, in that sense. I say 'in that sense' because Wittgenstein's constructions in 6.02 are definitions in a different sense.

When we are given a formal series we can 'see that it must go on like that'. This is what underlies recursive proofs and definitions. Wittgenstein gives a formal series of definitions by writing the definitions of 1 and 2 and 3 and then writing '(and so on)'. The series develops by the repetition of ' +1' and in this way it shows not only that every number after 1 includes the number which precedes it, but also that the rules for addition—the associative and the commutative laws, for instance—hold for all natural numbers. This means that Wittgenstein is *assuming* arithmetic in order to define number; but this need not be an objection.

He recognized later that he needed brackets if the succession of +1's was to be a formal series. Suppose /, //, ///, ////, /////, with nothing in the signs suggesting the operation by which we get from one of them to another. These signs would not be terms in a formal series. There would be no general term or rule of the series determining the development of it. 'And so on' would mean nothing. But if we write $1+1+1+1+1$ this is just as formless. Unless we have the brackets $((((1)+1)+1)+1)$ how shall we know to what we are adding the next 1?

If Wittgenstein had used brackets in 6.02 the connexion with the repetition of an operation might have seemed less direct. He may also have thought that the 1's should be written without differences in order to show that the brackets are *justified*—to show how repetition of an operation provides for the use of brackets. In 6.231 he says 'It is a property of "$1+1+1+1$" that it can be construed as "$(1+1)+(1+1)$".' It is as though the grammar of '$+1$' were fundamental for all numerals of the natural numbers. And sometimes when we want to show that it is the same number on each side of the equation, we may feel that to make the demonstration complete we should resolve each numeral into a sum of 1's. This is all right for small numbers. If we write $(1+1)+(1+1+1) = (1+1+1)+(1+1)$ and then drop the brackets we can see that it is the same sign on each side. But if we did this for $18+17 = 17+18$ the substitution of '$1+1+1\ldots$' would clarify nothing. We should have to count the 1's after the brackets were removed and rely on our original equation. This equation ($18+17 = 17+18$) is obvious anyway. So why were we inclined to substitute the $+1$'s? Is it a way of showing the general form of addition? of showing *why* the rules of addition hold for all natural numbers? As though that way of writing numerals would show how arithmetic springs from the general form of operation.

In 1923 Skolem spoke of recursive proof of the associative law for addition, for instance. Is Wittgenstein assuming something of the sort when he writes 'and so on' in his definitions with $+1$? Is he assuming that the general form of operation provides it? A little later he would say he was not. But perhaps when he wrote the *Tractatus* he was not clear about it. I suppose the general form of operation (if we want to speak of it) would come in when we have *given* the recursive proof for $a+(b+2)$, $a+(b+3)$, ... and we see that this is a series of proofs having a particular form—a form which holds for all natural numbers. This is not the form of the *recursive* proof; it is what is *shown* in the recursive proof.—If we speak here of drawing a conclusion, then we draw the conclusion from the particular model: the paradigm transition from $a+(b+1) = (a+b)+1$ to the corresponding rule for $a+(b+2)$, say. We do not base anything on the form of calculation in general. And when I said just now that the general form of operation 'would come in when . . .' this was not correct; it does not come in at all.

Wittgenstein wanted to show a connexion between arithmetic and the possibility of symbolism. What makes it possible for a symbolism to have sense.

He wanted to forestall the idea that an operation might yield a rigmarole of meaningless signs. Later he wrote of *pseudo-operations*—what look like mathematical operations but are not. It is a pseudo-operation if we cannot see in the signs written down the law or the rule of development which determines them; if the development of a decimal, for instance, is not completely determined by a rule of operation which we know at the start. (In what sense would this be a 'development'?) If it were generally like this—if there were no difference between operation and pseudo-operation—we cou¹d not understand any operation. We should not understand the instruction: 'work out the calculation'. The 'so' in 'and so on' would have no meaning.—If this is what 'There is a general form of operation' means, it does not follow that we can ask to have the general form of operation written down. Wittgenstein dropped the whole way of speaking when (in 1929) he gave up speaking of the general form of proposition. But the distinction of operations and truth functions was important in discussing Russell's logical notation for arithmetic. It was perhaps one step towards recognizing that mathematical and logical operations cannot be run together.

III

WITTGENSTEIN ON MATHEMATICS

D. S. Shwayder

WITTGENSTEIN'S philosophy was Kantian from beginning to end. In other ways, too, he never changed. He always wrote in that maddeningly distinctive, bare bones, dramatically epigrammatic style, flashing like some powerful stroboscope, bewildering the intelligence with alternating brilliance and darkness and often causing a complete blur. The foreword to *Philosophische Bemerkungen* is an intense expression of his persistent view that what matters in the world of the mind must be clear and simple (see also *Tractatus*, 5.4541), and his tragedy was that he knew everything in his own life was less clear and simple than he thought it had to be. The progressive spirit of so-called empirical science and the methodological programmes of its philosophy were always alien to his temper (see *Tractatus* 6.372). He favoured the transcendental 'other world' of metaphysics and logic and mathematics over the valueless inexplicable contingencies of science and of common sense (see *Tractatus* 6.13, 6.421, 6.4312). The only kind of explanation that wouldn't prematurely stop short while still giving the appearance of explaining everything would reveal the deepest constant features of our ways of thinking about the world, and he never arrested the Kantian thrust to demonstrate the fundamental categories of thought and experience. But such experiments could be conducted only in the mind itself. So, in his later work, after he had abandoned the ideal of a unified language, he left to philosophy only the task of describing the 'motley' of human thought.

This view of Wittgenstein's thought brings into perspective his revisitations to the philosophy of mathematics, which kept his interest until at least 1944, in the *Tractatus, Philosophische Bemerkungen* and in those writings collected together under the title, 'Remarks on the Foundation of Mathematics' (which, for ease of reference, I hereafter shall refer to respectively as 'T', 'B', and 'R'). As is well known, he came to Cambridge to study the foundations of mathematics with Russell, and the writings of Frege and Russell on the relationship between mathematics and the use of language were the first and the main continuing influence on his thought, later also affected in conversations with Brouwer and Ramsey and by the writings of Hilbert and Goedel. Wittgenstein's results in the philosophy of mathematics were always inconclusive, inadequate to the issues, technically terrible and sometimes even silly, in R as well as in T—in Kreisel's words, '. . . a surprisingly insignificant product of a sparkling mind'.[1] In a later review article on *The Blue and Brown Books*, Kreisel complains that Wittgenstein characteristically failed, when considering mathematics or almost anything, to go beyond fun-poking to a more satisfying, fuller analysis of theoretical problems.[2] But still there is something fascinating about it all, for reasons revealed perhaps by its limited relevance to logic and to the most concrete parts of classical mathematics—geometry, mechanics and arithmetic. I shall argue that according to Wittgenstein successful mathematizing would expose and confirm the conceptual connexions which obtain in our everyday and scientific ways of thinking and talking. Mathematics, like metaphysics, is, according to this, the conceptual investigation of necessary connexions. Despite his occasional declarations to the contrary, Wittgenstein should have seen mathematics and metaphysics as Platonic cousins, both methods for uncramping the mind (see R page 17). He believed in geometry and mechanics because here the relationship of mathematics to our ordinary ways of thinking is

---

[1] G. Kreisel, Review of 'R' in *British Journal of the Philosophy of Science*, 1958, pp. 135–58. Hereafter 'Kreisel [1]'.

[2] 'Wittgenstein's Theory and Practice of Philosophy', *BJPS*, 1960, pp. 238–52, esp. pp. 239ff. I came onto this paper (hereafter 'Kreisel [2]') only after I had written the substance of this paper. From it I got a lead to P. Bernays' 'Comments on Ludwig Wittgenstein's *Remarks on the Foundation of Mathematics*' (*Ratio*, 1959, pp. 1–22) which comes closer to my own views about Wittgenstein's philosophy of mathematics than anything else I have read.

immediately visible. He thought axiomatics and the use of other heavy methodological machinery pernicious. Pure mathematics and speculative metaphysics alike are apt to be swamped in images and in their own meaningless abstractions, and nowhere, he thought, is this more evident than in the development of set theory from the time of Cantor.

In this paper, I wish to present Wittgenstein's philosophy of mathematics, as I read it, with the primary intention of indirectly establishing the fact of a substantial carryover from T to R, a continuity which I also believe is typical of his whole philosophy. I shall hold that Wittgenstein always thought of mathematics as a method or assortment of methods that aims to demonstrate conceptual connexions latent in or imposed upon our ordinary and scientific uses of language. What gives mathematics its meaning and accounts for its necessity is the civil nonmathematical rôles of the concepts investigated. Wittgenstein not surprisingly lays stress on calculation and on what Hilbert-Cohn-Vossen called 'Intuitive Mathematics', on that kind of non-systematic thinking well illustrated by classical thought-experiments typically conducted outside of mathematical theory by methods which are indeed methods of *demonstration* and not logical derivation. Wittgenstein, just as expectedly, deprecates the highly but artificially structured theories of 'pure mathematics', which are mainly directed towards other parts of mathematics itself.

I shall try to break Wittgenstein's position down into a number of connected 'themes', which I shall develop and elaborate with observations and with references to T, B, and R. My indirect argument for the indicated conclusion is just the references which, however, have been collected pretty haphazardly and are meant to be only illustrative and are certainly incomplete. Sometimes the citation of a reference will also constitute implicit interpretation.[1]

---

[1] I confine myself pretty much to the three books mentioned. When drafting this paper, I did not have the unauthorized 'Math Notes' which circulated widely in the 1950s, though I have been glad to find useful quotations from them in my thesis on T. I believe those notes have been superseded by R. Also, because of unavailability, I made no systematic use of the 'Notes on Logic', 'Moore's Notebooks' and Wittgenstein's journals. So far as the *Philosophical Investigations* is concerned, I have relied on my retained general impression occasionally confirmed by notes on my thesis. References to B and R will be given simply with those initials followed by page numbers.

My secondary intention is to offer an alternative to Mr. Dummett's well-known but widely disbelieved interpretation of R.[1] I agree with Dummett that mathematics cannot tolerate anyone's assumed privilege to stipulate when an assertion is justified, but that is not a criticism of Wittgenstein. My colleagues, Chihara, and Stroud, are right to take Dummett to task for making Wittgenstein out to be a conventionalist in that silly sense.[2] They see that Wittgenstein was out to make logical compulsion intelligible and not to advance claims for some high Carnapian game of language relativity. Kreisel observed that Wittgenstein's disbelief in mathematical objects is not a disbelief in mathematical objectivity ([1], page 138, n. 1). Chihara goes so far as to suggest that Wittgenstein's 'constructive view of mathematics' is consistent with the 'realist's discovery view' (*op. cit.*, page 34), and if forced to a choice I would rather call Wittgenstein a 'Platonist' than a 'conventionalist'. My main theme below will be that Wittgenstein held that mathematics is derivative from the civil use of language and (as Chihara points out, *op. cit.*, page 26, n. 17) that he agreed with Frege that it is this civil application which gives mathematics its meaning. Mathematics unfolds the properties of familiar notions. I would understand if someone described Wittgenstein's philosophy of mathematics as 'transcendental Platonism' or (if you wish) 'conceptualism', for Wittgenstein thought that mathematics at its most characteristic is the conceptual investigation of (other) 'language games'. Something like this is his alternative to the other standard 'philosophies'. Formalism wrongly strips mathematical concepts of their civil rôle, but is right in recognizing that 'mathematics must fend for itself' [T: 5.473; R: 67 twice]; 'psychologism' and 'empiricism' preserve meaningfulness at cost of replacing the necessities of mathematics with the contingent background of thought; and Platonism rescues necessity only by indulging in the worst kind of theology and alchemy. But 'transcendental Platonism' and 'conceptualism' are wrong also, because Wittgenstein throughout stood firm in his opinion that the kind of mathematics that matters is not a body of doctrine or a theory but rather a record of man's

---

[1] 'Wittgenstein's Philosophy of Mathematics', *Phil. Rev.*, 1959, pp. 324–48.
[2] See C. Chihara, 'Mathematical Discovery and Concept Formation', *Phil. Rev.*, 1963, pp. 17–34; B. Stroud, 'Wittgenstein and Logical Necessity', *Phil. Rev.*, 1965, pp. 504–18.

successful efforts to make explicit what is essential in our forms of thought. Mathematics is a difficult kind of reflective, intuitive 'nonobservational' knowledge. Conventional fiats are as much, and no more, part of this as self-interpretation is part of our knowledge of our own intentions.

In presenting and arguing for this interpretation, I shall mostly limit myself to what Kreisel distinguished as questions in 'general philosophy' in contrast with questions in the 'philosophy of mathematics', *viz.*, to questions concerning the relation of mathematics to 'life' in contrast with questions raised by specific mathematical investigations, for which my incompetence is enormous. My policy goes well with Wittgenstein's reluctance to deny anything and with his declared desire to leave mathematical results as they are [R: 104, 157, 174; see also Dummett, *op. cit.*, page 325], if not with his conclusions about the nature of mathematics which I already have suggested intimate a resemblance with metaphysics. For all that, Wittgenstein's early use of truth-tables was a small but historically consequential contribution to mathematical logic itself, and he certainly did often appear to be denying things. I gladly defer to the authority of the mathematicians who say that Wittgenstein didn't grasp the mathematical significance of the results he interpreted and that his specific observations are useful only to those who, in their mathematical innocence, are apt to make horrendous misconstructions. My own judgement is that the useful part of what Wittgenstein has to say about true but unprovable propositions in R [50 *et. seq.*] has since been better said by others and surely does not show much sensitivity to the subtleties of the mathematical questions at issue. I shall, however, say something about Wittgenstein's views on real numbers and consistency.

The bulk of what follows will be a review of recurrent themes in Wittgenstein's philosophy of mathematics. I begin with some general historical remarks and finish with a perfunctory assessment and with an attempt to impart a sense of the plausibility of Wittgenstein's ideas.

SOME BACKGROUND

Perhaps the most distinctive and revolutionary feature of Frege's and Russell's logistical programmes for pure mathematics was the declared aim of anchoring mathematics to the bedrock of nonmathematical thought and language. Logic and mathematics are, according to this view, responsible to the familiar activities of inferring, counting, measuring, and ultimately are theories of the propositions which formulate everyday facts. Both thinkers found it necessary to lay down a number of original and still influential theories about language by which their logical theories were secured. Frege put special emphasis on the distinction between the alleged *Bedeutungen* of proper names and function names (so-called). Of his other key distinctions, that between *Sinn* and *Bedeutung* was essential but only occasionally visible in the system of the *Grundgesetze*, and that between 'content' and 'judgement', though highly visible was insufficiently elaborated. Russell, with greater abandon and less coherence, purported to erect the whole structure of logic and mathematics on the so-called Vicious Circle Principle which first and foremost was a principle about language in its 'civil', nonmathematical appearances.

Wittgenstein found much to provoke him in these theories of language taken simply in themselves. More importantly for our purposes, he thought that the whole logistical programme foundered on a misconception about the relation between mathematics and language. The misconception involved the assumption that mathematics with logic could be arranged as an autonomous theory eligible for systematic recasting as a deductive discipline. The systems of the *Grundgesetze* and *PM* seemed to Wittgenstein like Muscovite monuments to this mistake, against which he polemicized at length across the pages of T. Among the more dramatic symptoms that something was wrong were the contradiction and the ultimate incoherence of the theory of types as a theory of language (see esp. vol. II of *PM*, prefatory statement), and the occurrence among the fundamentals of poorly understood and apparently contingent propositions. Wittgenstein exploited all these difficulties to the full, together with such borrowed positive points of doctrine as Russell's affirmed belief that the theory of types is a theory of symbolism and Frege's argument that we cannot formulate the crucial distinction between function and object. But the main difficulty simply was that neither Frege nor Russell were able to say precisely what they thought the ultimate relation between mathematics and language really was. The logistical method frustrated the logistical intent. Both men finally were driven to the idea that the laws of logic are extremely general propositions, perhaps about the world at large (Russell), perhaps about what we ought to take as true (Frege), or (mysteriously) about a domain of things preferable to the denizens of traditional mathematics only for being more evidently factitious. Wittgenstein for a time concurred with the thesis that logical propositions are very general propositions, but later, taking his cue from the way Frege explained and justified his axioms, argued that the truths of logic are not universal propositions about language or about anything at all, but rather reflections of how we use language. Proof, in this conception, becomes 'demonstration' in the original sense—we exhibit how things are in our language—and not the logical derivation of propositions. Notoriously, the resulting doctrine was excessively rigid in its exaggerated demand that demonstration in the sense of 'showing how it is' is the only recourse available to one who would wish to comprehend better the foundations of thought and the nature of necessity.

This theory of mathematics carried over almost intact into Wittgenstein's 'middle', 'verificationist' period, of which B is up to now the main published record. The extreme position on 'showing' and even the details are preserved. There were some additions and some changes of interest. In general philosophy, he was showing an advancing interest in issues of scepticism and in the problem of privacy in particular. The 1929 article on logical form witnessed a significant alteration of detail though not in principle in the T idea that language is a unified structure with a unified logic which could be comprehended at a shot. His reputed conversations with Brouwer may have confirmed his tendencies towards 'intuitionism' in mathematics and encouraged him to ask us to consider how one could verify statements about (e.g.) real numbers, where only arithmetic and recursive methods generally were acceptable procedures. (See B: 174ff.) In B, Wittgenstein showed a much greater interest than appears in T in the actual ideas of modern mathematics, chiefly the modern conceptions of the infinite and of real numbers and in the theology of *Mengenlehre*. He makes continual but novel application of the idea of 'rules for going on', only dimly prefigured in the Tractarian appeal to operations. In the second *Anhang*, which is a record of conversations with Schlick and Waismann, he turned his argumentative weapons against the philosophy of Hilbert and the emerging doctrine of metamathematics, polemicizing stridently against the philosophy which underlay the concern with consistency and against the alleged importance of Goedel's incompleteness theorem.

These interests and critical tendencies persist into the writings collected together as R in which (I argue) Wittgenstein's Tractarian doctrine also survives, softened somewhat by his dawning recognition of the varieties of language and consequent stress on the 'motley of mathematics'. The chief change, I believe, is that finally he relaxed his rigid insistence that necessities in no way can depend upon the mere contingencies of the human situation. Wittgenstein was finally able to find something like a foundation for mathematics in the natural history of man.

Theme 1.[1] WE MAY BEGIN BY OBSERVING THAT WITTGENSTEIN TOOK AS HIS PRIMARY EXAMPLES OF AUTHENTIC LIVING MATHEMATICS THEORY OF INFERENCE [obvious in T, B, and R alike, but notice that he became progressively less permissive about logic and more relentless in his criticisms of its claims],

CALCULATION,

Kreisel observed that Wittgenstein was concerned with the neglected question of elementary computations. [Also see: Bernays, *op. cit.*, p. 11.] *In T he called his method of arriving at tautologies calculation, thus assimilating the theory of inference and logical truth to arithmetic* [T: 6.1203, 6.126]. *He thought that mathematics was nothing else but the method of substituting into equations, also described as calculation* [T: 6.2331, 6.24].

One can suppose that he had something like trigonometry in mind. [B: 177, 180f.]

> (The theory as presented is probably incoherent if only because the equations in question would not involve mathematical symbols but rather ordinary names.)

His only example contains numerals [6.231, 6.241], and his theory of numbers charitably can be seen as equivalent

---

[1] I shall employ this format:

MAJOR STATEMENT OF THEME
>   *Development*
>   Discussion   [References]
>   (Further discussion)
Rungs sometimes will be skipped.

to the Peano scheme for introducing arithmetical operations.

Stress on calculation and on number systems continues into B [throughout],

It is significant that he appears to adhere still to the theory of the T [132f., 142f.].

and R [e.g., 88f.], *where he observes the connexion with counting* [5f., 28]. *It also is evident that his maxim that process and result are equivalent is nowhere more plausible than for calculation.*

GEOMETRY,

which he likens to calculation [T: 2.0131, 3.032, 6.35; B: 152, 216f.; R: 16ff., 77],

TOPOLOGY [R: 174f.; also see knot-untying example, B: 184],

KINEMATICS,

Wittgenstein was fascinated by gears and simple mechanisms. These are among his favourite examples of proofs by diagrams, where the picture defines the connexions and conveys the sense of rigidity and compulsion [R: 35–9, 119f., 127f.], *and also excellent illustrations of the way in which an actual movement can be taken as a 'demonstration of what is essential'* [R: 25f., 139, 195f.];

AND, DERIVATIVELY, MEASUREMENT,

In both B and R, Wittgenstein frequently appeals to measurement to illustrate internal relations among concepts and the imposition of controls [e.g., R: 27f.; 159f.; 173f., 194];

MECHANICS,

Especially in the T [4.041, 6.321–6.3611, 6.3751]. *There also are a few stray examples in B, especially in the first Anhang and in R* [e.g., 136f.].

AND, FINALLY, IN LATER WRITINGS, THE KIND OF DEMONSTRATION OR GEDANKENEXPERIMENT BY WHICH PHYSICISTS GET US TO COMPREHEND THE PRINCIPLES OF PHYSICS. [See references above under 'kinematics' where a diagram or an actual working mechanism is used as a proof.]

WITTGENSTEIN CONSPICUOUSLY NEGLECTS CLASSICAL DEMONSTRATIONS IN ANALYSIS WHICH CANNOT BE ACHIEVED EITHER BY MERELY EXHIBITING A FIGURE OR BY MAKING A FORMAL CALCULATION. [See Bernays, *op. cit.*, p. 2.]

Theme 2. LOGIC AND MATHEMATICS ARE METHODS FOR THE 'TRANSCENDENTAL' DEMONSTRATION OF THE LOGICAL, ESSENTIAL

PROPERTIES OF OUR 'CIVIL' (NONMATHEMATICAL) WAYS OF THINKING AND TALKING ABOUT THE WORLD.

(For the kind of thing he first had in mind, see T: 6.12, 6.121; B: 142f. He uses 'logical' throughout T in this sense, effectively equivalent to 'internal', 'formal', 'necessary', and 'essential', all of which, especially 'internal', recur frequently in B and R. He employed the highly Kantian 'transcendental' at T: 6.13. For interpretation of what it means, see below.)

The task of mathematics is to demonstrate what it makes sense to say, by showing how to apply a rule; by laying down tracks in language [R: 12, 77f., 80];

by putting ordinary concepts characteristically having a nonmathematical use into memorable relations [R: 25f.].

'What makes people accept a proof is that they use words as language' [R: 44]; 'It is essential to mathematics that its signs are also employed in mufti' [R: 133]; 'Concepts which occur in "necessary" propositions must also occur in non-necessary ones' [R: 153]. This idea of the 'civil' occurrence of mathematical concepts, which is a recurrent one in R [also 8, 41, 79], echoes the Tractarian thought that logic and mathematics must be 'in touch' with reality via their 'application' [T: 2.15121, 5.557]. What makes the game mathematics is the 'application' to ordinary propositions [B: 131, 135, 143; R: 133]; 'Logic gets its whole sense simply from its presumed application to propositions' [R: 118, 133], e.g., through the ordinary sentences which occur in tautologies,

(Tautologies while senseless are not nonsense, but rather limiting, degenerate propositions—not schemata [T: 4.4611, 4.466, 5.143, 6.112, 6.121; also R: 79])

and the ordinary names which occur in the equations of mathematics [T: 6.22, 6.23, 6.2341; B: 143];

(But Wittgenstein himself later observed that, since he left no place for identity statements, these equations are not even degenerate propositions [B: 142].)

it is seen in Wittgenstein's insistence that ideas like those of the numbers which are submitted to mathematical investigation are dependent on concepts [B: 123; R: 150],

(In the T numbers were connected essentially with the rules

by which propositions were generated, but the idea was not worked out [T: 6.02, 6.03].)

and is part of what he sometimes had in mind when he spoke of 'use' [R: 3f.]. The general conception of language is the only mathematical primitive [T: 5.472], language itself is the reality beyond [R: 6, 39, 80] and supplies the necessary intuition upon which mathematics depends [T: 5.4731, 6.233]. The manner in which logical properties of language are demonstratively reflected is well illustrated by Wittgenstein's use of truth-functional analysis, borrowed from Frege [T: 4.431], and which suggests what has since come to be called 'semantics'.

Proof thus conceived serves to reveal the essential 'internal' properties and relations of concepts, e.g., relations of logical consequence or the dependence of measurement on counting. The enterprise presupposes conventions to be sure and perhaps other facts as well, but these are facts which enable our civil nonmathematical ways of talking,

The need for conventions and the dependence of mathematics on 'forms of life' is a persistent theme in R [e.g., 94 *et. seq.*] but was anticipated already in T [3.342, 4.1121]—the employment of 'thought' broadly hints that logic presupposes psychical facts.

from which the mathematics is derivative—mathematics is 'postulated' with the language, and not conversely [T: 6.1233; R: 43f., 159].

Here is where Wittgenstein parted company with Frege and Russell. While agreeing with them in insisting on the fact of *a* relation between mathematics and civil language and in the thought that application is what gives mathematics its meaning, he thought that they had failed to apprehend this dependence with sufficient clarity or constancy [B: 137; R: 41, 78], in supposing that logic could supply laws of truth to language [T: 5.132, 5.4733; see Frege, *Grundgesetze* v. I, xvi; also in his late article 'Der Gedanke', translated and reprinted in *Mind*, 1956, pp. 289–311, esp. p. 289] with resulting confusions about truth and meaning [T: 4.431, 6.111].

(Actually, Wittgenstein's later unsettled way of speaking about mathematical proofs changing concepts [for which see pp. 81f. below] sometimes sounds suspiciously like what Frege had proposed.)

Following Wittgenstein's own usage, call these 'civil' conceptual activities the 'application' of mathematics; to repeat, the application is what gives 'meaning' to mathematics [B: 201; R: 118, 147f., 172, 186].

(Also [B: 229], where he says that application is the criterion of reality in mathematics. Only here 'application' may mean something like 'effectively computable', and illustrates Wittgenstein's occasional willingness to count in 'internal applications', within mathematics itself. He is very careless about this crucial distinction upon which the distinction between pure and applied mathematics depends.)

An immediate consequence of this is that the traditional distinction between pure and applied mathematics is not valid.

The logic of T is like the plain formal 'nonmathematical' logic of the earlier teaching tradition imparted in direct connexion with examples and thought to be evident in the very understanding of language. [See T: 5.13, 6.12, 6.1221.]

(Also [R: 186], which I interpret to mean that concepts which are introduced for exclusive application within mathematics itself, such as $2^{\aleph_0}$, are apt to be footless and very easily thought about in the wrong way. Their meaning too depends upon distant relations to nonmathematical activities like measurement.)

We cannot 'give' mathematics an application or interpretation either by appending explanations on the side [T: 5.452] *or, more formally, by assigning objects to names and classes to predicates or by 'interpreting' variables,*

(See B: 327 where he appears to challenge the Hilbertian distinction between game and theory.)

for the application cannot be called into question, hence cannot be stipulated or anything of the kind. The application must fend for itself [B: 130f.; R: 67 and T: 5.473, but here observe without the important 'Anwendung']. *Mathematical truths are essentially self-applicable* [e.g. B: 130ff., R: 176].

The 'internal' features of language and thought are typically demonstrated in arguments of a kind which have been called 'transcendental'.

The truth of what is shown is guaranteed by the sense of the formulation, and the proof is less an indication of truth than of what it makes sense to say [T: 3.04, 6.2322; B: 144, 170,

200f.; R: 77, 80]. These internal, formal features are given with the objects to which they apply, and their presence cannot meaningfully be doubted or denied because they are presupposed in the very formulation of the doubt.

(This is a familiar theme in philosophy. Wittgenstein probably found his precedents in the turn of the century *furor* over the contradiction and in Russell's unavailing attempt to formulate the Vicious Circle Principle, which still left him in the situation where he could not make meaningful misascriptions or true denials of types, as well as in the Moore-Russell doctrine of 'undefinables', explained as ideas that would be presupposed in any attempted definition.)

In the T, Wittgenstein also held, 'It would be as nonsensical to ascribe a formal property to a proposition as to deny it a formal property' [4.124].

(For which, again, he had the precedent of Russell's admission that we cannot say an object is not of a type other than it is and also of Frege's conclusion that we cannot say that a function is a function.)

Wittgenstein put that by saying it would involve us in an illicit attempt to transcend the limits of thought and language [T: 2.174, 4.041, 4.121, 5.61, 6.45–7]. *The same idea carries over into B where Wittgenstein held that you can neither deny nor assert fundamental principles and presuppositions or definitions* [B: 172, 120, 193, 330]. *Though Wittgenstein later repudiated the 'transcendental metaphysics' of 'possibilities' and of the 'ideal' which so naturally attends these arguments* [e.g., *Investigations*, I, §§ 89–105; R: 6, 22f.], *something similar remains in the important thought that the fundamental agreements in the ways in which we act and the fundamental facts of human nature which constitute the environment in which our concepts are formed and upon which our mathematics reposes are also the 'limits of empiricism'* [R: 121, 171, 176].

Reductio proofs conceived of as deductions are especially suspect on this view, for they would appear to depart from meaningless assumptions [B: 190; R: 147, 177]. They perhaps could be redeemed were we able to rid ourselves of the idea that mathematical demonstration is logical derivation.

It always was part of Wittgenstein's view of the dependence of mathe-

matics on civil language that mathematical results should not be thought of as empirical or empirical-like statements [for development of this, see theme 4 below], *and that we should resist every inclination to suppose that mathematical propositions have their own subject-matter— a domain of 'mathematical objects'—for this can only be an obscuring and pernicious pretence. Hence, the Tractarian polemic against 'logical objects'* [4.0312, 5.4 *et. seq.*], *later extended against the claims of Mengenlehre.* [See Theme 6 below.] *The only logical primitive, again, is language itself. Also, logistical systematization, if ever appropriate, would be appropriate only to empirical theories.* [For development, see Theme 8 below.] *Indeed, mathematical results are not properly to be regarded as propositions at all for, like the laws of logic, they '. . . show what we do with propositions, as opposed to expressing opinions and convictions'* ['Math Notes'], *and what we do with propositions is brought out in the mathematical demonstrations themselves and not in the supposed conclusions of logical derivations.* [For development, see Themes 8 and 9 below.]

Theme 3. MATHEMATICAL PROOF IS AN INSTRUMENT OF CONCEPTUAL CONTROL
    An 'instrument of language' [R: 78, 80, 165]
USED TO DETERMINE WHAT IT MAKES SENSE TO SAY OR WHAT IS POSSIBLE. [See above and B: 140; R: 116.] WHEN SUCCESSFULLY EMPLOYED, IT RESULTS IN THE UNFOLDING [R: 24, 30] OR FIXATION [B: 201], 249; R: 80, 127, 195f.] OF WHAT WE TAKE TO BE ESSENTIAL [R: 12f., 30, 163].
In explaining how this comes about, Wittgenstein appeals to a bewildering variety of analogies and technical notions.

      (He always was careless about terminology, and sometimes regretted it [R: 163, 188, 195, in connexion with 'concept'].)
      'logic'
      (Especially prominent in T, where the word usually was employed to cover everything having to do with the *a priori* determination of the essential 'internal' features of language, but sometimes more narrowly confined to the method of tautologies and contradictions [e.g., 6.22].)
      'internal' [throughout T, B and R]
      'grammar' [B: 129f., 135, 186, 188, 309; R: 40, 77f., 119]
      'syntax' [T: 3.327, 3.33, 3.344, 6.124; B: 143, 178, 189, 216]
      'forms'

(of language, thought, often identified with 'possibilities' [T throughout; B: 178])

'dictionary', 'definitions' and 'what we call' [B: 135, 194; R: 28, 76, 174]

'rules' [T: 4.0141, 5.476; B: 143, 178, 216, 311, *et. seq.*; R: 21, 26, 32, 47, 77, 81, 115ff., 127, 159, 163, 196]

(Notably 'rules of inference' [B: 134; R: 178ff., 185])

'convention' [R: 6, 159]

'decision' [R: 77]

'moves' and 'positions in games' [R: 94f.]

'pointers', 'paths', 'channels', 'handrails' [R: 82, 116, 122, 193]

'pictures', 'patterns', 'models' and descriptions thereof [R: 11f., 29, 75, 117]

(*N.B.*: In R, unlike in T, *pictures* and *models* are not themselves propositions, but rather instruments of conceptual control used to regulate what is to count as a proposition and to demonstrate connexions among propositions.)

'methods of experiment' and 'of prediction' and formulations thereof [R: 13, 65, 187]

'frameworks of description' [R: 160; also T: 6.341]

'impress a procedure' [R: 14]

'paradigms' [R: 45f., 82, 193]

'measures', 'standards', 'norms', 'controls' [B: 212; R: 47, 76, 99, 199, 194]; and the general idea of a criterion of identity [R: 96, 196], among others.

Proof, by bringing us into position to see things in a certain way [R: 13, 18], *makes visible and enables us better to comprehend what previously may have been only implicit and latent in the civil practice, e.g., which thing or what kind of thing we are talking about* [T: 6.232; R: 27], *or the 'possibilities' (which are the 'actualities' of mathematics) admitted by thought and language* [T: 2.0121, 6.361; B: 138, 157, 161, 164, 217, 253; R: 39, 116] *and to control those civil operations,* [B: 212; R: 117], *e.g. by guiding inferences* [T: 6.211], *or by supplying a criterion for mistakes in counting* [R: 27, 76]. *Coming into this position is no more a matter of discovery than is coming to know of the existence of the north pole* [T: 6.1251, 6.1261; B: 182, 189f.; R: 127].

Or, rather, the making of an expedition to the pole, which is something to be *done*, is like proof, in that *facts* are not in dispute in either case. What is important is not so much where one gets as getting there.

The illusion of discovery is due to an inadmissible switching back and forth between empirical and conceptual questions [R: 26, 126f.].

It is to be likened rather to 'nonobservational' reflective knowledge of one's own actions.

> (Could one argue that all 'transcendental knowledge' is of this kind?)

I think here of Wittgenstein's use of 'reflection' [T: 6.13] and of his later stress on 'doing', 'knowing how to go on', foreshadowed in the T idea of an 'operation' [T from 5.51; B: 191, 199; R: 3, 7, 117f., 123, 176, 179]. I find his example of untying knots particularly trenchant [B: 182, 184f.].

Wittgenstein sometimes put this in an exaggerated way by speaking of 'invention' [B: 186; R: 47, 59, 140]. When Wittgenstein gave up his 'static' conception of language as a unified system governed by the 'postulate of the determinateness of sense' with a single general form of proposition whose whole logic could be comprehended all at once [T: 2.0124, 3.23, 4.5, 4.53, 5.47, 5.476, 5.55, 5.557; B: 177f., 187f.], when the unity of language gave way to the variety of language games, a monolithic logic to the 'motley of mathematics' [R: 84, 194],

> (The seeds already were sown in the T discussion of mechanics [esp. 6.34–6.35]. He tried to hush up the incoherence at 6.3431. His use of 'Forderung' in the sense of 'demand' at 3.23 and 6.1223 also anticipated the future. Also in B [170], where Wittgenstein worries how proof is possible if proof depends only on sense which must be comprehended before proof can be attempted—this naturally leads to the thought that proof also alters or creates sense.)

and mathematical demonstration became in its applications comparatively unstable, like a four-legged table [R: 115, 180], he was faced with the problem of saying to what extent the demonstration of conceptual connexions also changes and creates concepts.

Wittgenstein was uneasy with this way of talking about concept alteration and innovation to which some of his commentators have attached so much importance [R: 126, 154]. The old concept, at all events, always is in the background [R: 121]. The fact is he had a number of different more or less acceptable things in mind. The most important was that of establishing new connexions between [old] concepts, and creating thereby the concept of a connexion [R: 79, 154, 188, 195].

> (But, he asks, is the conceptual apparatus a concept, is a 'conceptual path a concept' [R: 154, 188]? In this regard, it is worth noting that the *mathematical* concepts in question, e.g., *prime number*, typically have no civil use.)

But also: Turning things around so that they look different [R: 18, 122, 192];

extending old paradigms and rules to cover new cases [R: 47, 193];

changing rules and introducing new ones [R: 124];

introducing new paradigms [R: 78, 82];

introducing new paradigms for *internal* application within mathematics itself, e.g., recasting arithmetic in an algebraic mould [B: 202f.];

> (Wittgenstein's way of talking about creating concepts is, for obvious reasons, more appropriate for these 'internal' applications which Wittgenstein's general philosophy is calculated to play down and overlook. One could rewrite the mufti theme to say that mathematics is 'ultimately' created for increasing our reflective comprehension of unconscripted civil concepts which must be 'there' in advance of mathematizing.)

fixing criteria of identity, e.g., making it explicit that a cardinal number is unaffected by the direction from which an assemblage is counted.

Our description of the motley of mathematics should, at any rate, capture the natural conceptual order of the different techniques, an order which duplicates the relations of dependence within language [B: 244f; R: 7]. *This is an important instrument in Wittgenstein's criticism of attempts to reduce one part of mathematics to another, e.g., the theory of numbers to logic.* [For development, see theme 7 below.]

Theme 4. MATHEMATICAL RESULTS, WHATEVER ELSE THEY ARE, ARE ABOVE ALL CONTINGENCY AND MUST BE NECESSARY AND RIGID [T: throughout, but see esp. 2.012, 5.55 *et. seq.*, 6.111, 6.1222, 6.1233].

(In B and R, Wittgenstein repeatedly contrasts calculations, pictures, paradigms and other assorted mathematical instruments with causality, experiment, prediction [B: 125, 133, 152, 187, 209f., 213, 235, 238, 240, 313; R: 19, 28f., 32, 69, 81f., 91, 94 *et. seq.*, 113f., 119, 124f., 171, 186f., 189ff.; also T: 6.2331].

Axioms and consequences alike [R: 79, 114].

For this reason he approved of Frege's and Russell's campaign against 'psychologism' and 'empiricism' [T: 4.1121]. In T, the Axiom of Reducibility and the whole of set theory were held to be mathematically spurious because empirical [T: 6.031, 6.1232, 6.1233], and the classification of propositions according to form forbidden for the same reason [T: 5.553–5.5542]. The rule of necessity abetted Wittgenstein's suspicions about the deductive theories of mathematics which appealed to such empirical paradigms as the coordination of objects, and commonly treated possibilities as realities [B: 140, 164f., 212], and in which demonstration was assimilated to a pattern of deducing empirical statements from other empirical statements leading back finally to axioms which simply are self-evident or obvious [T: 5.4731, 6.1232, 6.127]. *A necessity, according to the early Wittgenstein, is something whose contrary cannot coherently be conceived and which, therefore, cannot meaningfully be doubted* [T: 3.03–3.0321, 5.4731]. *Transcendental arguments must establish necessities which are, so to speak, the other side of paradox. The truth of such propositions is determined with their sense* [T: 3.04, 3.05; B: 144], *and they have no justification except comprehension itself. He later would say that these propositions are not so much true as proven by use* [R: 4]. *They are a priori and known before the fact, from language alone* [T: 3.04; B: 143]. *The requirement of necessity for mathematical results is companion to Wittgenstein's early idea that the actualities of mathematics are the possibilities of daily life, coordinate with what we can say* [T: 2.0121; B: 135, 140, 153, 161, 164, 253; R: 116], *whose existence cannot be meaningfully questioned, because proven by their essence* [B: 124] *and guaranteed by language* [T: 5.525, 3.04]. *While Wittgenstein later sloughed off this way of talking he never forsook the thought that necessity is a kind of dependence on the use of language* [B: 135; R: 4, 20, 153], *though the sharpness of the dictum was dulled by his emendation that we sometimes put forward necessities in order to fix a sense previously underdetermined* [R: 113 et.

seq., 121]. *In* T, *Wittgenstein staunchly maintained that what is necessarily so is utterly without contingent consequences and in no way can depend upon the facts* [T: 2.0211, 5.551, 5.552, 5.5542, 5.634, 6.1222]. *This thesis, though still rather fashionable, probably is incoherent, and Wittgenstein himself gave it up in his later writings,*

(For an important anticipation, see T [6.342, 6.343]. The old view lingers on in B [212]. In this connexion, it is notable that Wittgenstein began his Tractarian journey by drawing our attention to the actual world of actual facts, suggesting thereby that logic presupposes *a* world. A similar interpretation may be put on the extremely obscure T: 5.5521, though he *appeared* to withdraw the thought in B [164 n].)

where he allowed that the sense of what we say, hence what our language requires and permits, does indeed presuppose and is grounded upon unquestioned facts about the human situation—upon our actual ways of living and acting [R: 20f., 36, 43, 98, 124, 159, 173] *and upon fundamental agreements among men* [R: 13, 34, 94, 97, 164]. *He did not think this in any way endangered the distinction between the contingent and the necessary.*

(Though he now allowed for synthetic *a priori* truths [B: 129, 178; R: 125f.].)

Necessities are, in any case, not 'about' their contingent presuppositions [R: 159ff., 170 et. seq., 187]. *And, however multi-form* [R: 125], *still function as controlling paradigms, rules, etc., and hence are not empirical statements of fact* [R: 32, 46f., 81, 159, 174]. *Though we indeed might have thought otherwise than we do, thinking as we do limits what is thinkable and determines what must be. What are recognized as necessary propositions would simply be unsayable in another world. If the world were very different from what it is, our actual concepts could not be made available, and some of what we now can comprehend wouldn't be intelligible; obversely, we cannot now intelligently conceive all of what would then make sense. Wittgenstein exclaims 'How can we describe the foundations of our language with empirical propositions?'* [R: 120; see also 4f., 14, 96 et. seq., 120, and Stroud's development of the theme, op. cit.] *These fundamental presuppositions are the contingent 'limits of empiricism'* [R: 96, 171, 176] *implied by what we cannot meaningfully question.*

Theme 5. MATHEMATICAL RESULTS ARE NOT GENERAL CONCLUSIONS
BUT PERSPICUOUS PROOFS.

(From the beginning, Wittgenstein worried about the
apparent generality of the propositions of logic. In letters to
Russell and in the 'Notes on Logic', he proposed that the
propositions of logic were complete closures. [See *Wittgenstein's Notebooks* 1914–16, pp. 119, 103, 126.] He
turned away from this already in 'Moore's Notebooks'
[*ibid.*, p. 107], and, in T, his dictum, 'The mark of logical
propositions is not their general validity' [6.1231, 6.1232],
became one of the foci of his criticism of Frege and Russell.
His sense of the importance of the thought that mathematical truth is not universal validity is evident throughout B [138, 144, 148, 150] and continues into R
[156].)

*The apparent generality of mathematical results is not that of a
universal proposition about mathematical objects but consists in the
open applicability of a particular rule, paradigm or control* [B: 150,
195, 312; R: 156].

It is a 'direction' (a *vector?*) [B: 163]; it is knowing how to go
on in a certain specific way, an 'induction' [B: 150, 250, 328],
which does not establish a proposition about 'all numbers'
but validates the use of a particular rule, e.g., that of binomial
expansion, to arbitrary special cases.

(It is significant that many theorems which nowadays
commonly are formalized according to recursive rubrics
could just as convincingly have been established by
consideration of an arbitrary special case, and indeed the
latter kind of proof usually has greater explanatory power
than the routine application of mathematical induction to
a given formula. Wittgenstein also observed that in
geometry we often begin with, e.g., 'Take a triangle' [B:
152]. He once put this by saying that in mathematics the
general and the special cases must be mutually intersub-
stitutable [B: 207; see also 214 where he discusses in-
compatibility between the general and the special in
mathematics]. This recalls Kant's view that in mathematics
we come to know synthetic necessities by 'intuition'. Both
Wittgenstein and Kant thought that mathematics deals
with general concepts. Kant put this by saying that mathe-

mathics uses 'Anschauungen', Wittgenstein by saying that particular and general coincide in mathematics. [For a non-technical explanation of the Kantian theory see J. Hintikka's 'Kant's "New Method of Thought" and his Theory of Mathematics', *Ajatus*, 1965, pp. 37–47].)

The apparent infinite extension can be grasped in one step [B: 146f., 149], and the indefinitely applicable rule finitely formulated [B: 149, 314, 329]. Mathematics demonstrates the particular essentials of our conceptions—singular necessities, if you wish [B: 152, 182, 200].

(At B 182, he observed that the contradictory of 'It is necessary for all' is not 'It is necessary for some not', but rather, 'It is not necessary for all'. Working on the assumption that all mathematical results are implicitly to the effect that something is necessary, the upshot would seem to be that the apparent universal statements of mathematics are not what they seem [also B: 249 f.].)

An example would be that a particular form of proof is valid [B: 198f.]. On this view, mathematical demonstrations do not establish that all the members of a certain totality have a certain property. [See theme 6 below.]

Wittgenstein's alternative to 'logical proofs in mathematics' [R: 84] *was perspicuous, memorable, reproducible* [these three words occur throughout R; see the index of that book], *geometrically cogent* [R: 83] *demonstrations, which reflect* [T: 6.13] *the essentials of civil language.*

(This is part of what is meant in calling Wittgenstein an 'intuitionist'. It goes well with his earlier concentration on verification and recursive procedures.)

Initially, recursive rules or operations for 'going on' were his favourite examples.

In T, the general form of proposition was given by exhibiting a putatively recursive rule [5.21–5.32, 5.5–5.503, 6.0–6.031] and everything in the domain of formal logic and mathematics was reduced to formal series and operations [4.1252, 4.1273, 5.1–5.150, 5.252, 5.2523, 6.0, 6.031] and calculation [6.126, 6.2331]. This trend of thought carried into B, where Wittgenstein continually returns to mathematical induction and formal sequence [throughout, but see 150, 182, 187, 202f., 250, 313 for some notable passages], holding, among other things, that the essence of a real number is an induction [234; for development see theme 10 below]. Induction still appears on the pages of R [e.g., 90], and, of course, Wittgenstein in this period was fascinated with 'knowing how to go on' [see early pages of R and parts of *Philosophical Investigations*].

(Kreisel traces Wittgenstein's impatience with Goedelian results to an alleged dissatisfaction with the appeal to some general but still indefinite idea of recursiveness [[2] pp. 245f.] I doubt this because of his own uncritical fascination with 'Knowing how to go on'.)

But in R, 'perspicuity' seems to cover almost any kind of 'knowing how to' [R: 3] and anything 'plain to view' [R: 83].

(There is little variety among Wittgenstein's examples— arithmetical and stick representations of reckoning operations, simple geometric constructions, topological problems, kinematical diagrams, conversions of units— and almost no detail.)

Perspicuous proof apparently may make use of most anything which is not brought into question at all [R: 45] because illustrative of what is essential [65], hence above all contingency [124] and about which the understanding cannot be deceived [75, 81, 90f.].

The demand for perspicuity was employed powerfully by Wittgenstein in his criticism of 'reductionism' in mathematics: alleged alternative proofs (e.g., logistical proof of arithmetical identities) lack the necessary perspicuity—what is proven rather, and proven perspicuously, is a general correspondence between two systems [R: 5 *et. seq.*; for development, see theme 7 below].

Wittgenstein has been styled a 'finitist' [Kreisel, [1], p. 148, and Bernays, op. cit., p. 11; but note Wittgenstein's own implicit denials at R: 63, 150]. I think part of what is meant has something to do with his demand for perspicuity. A proof must exhibit or demonstrate essential connexions. That can be done by making a 'construction' [e.g., B: 132], or by exhibiting an apparently concrete representation, or by allowing the machine to symbolize its own possible movement [e.g., R: 37f.]. Such representations are taken as self-applicable and hence have incontrovertible geometric cogency [see B: 132f.].

Consider the following demonstration of a negative answer to the question whether one can with seven 2 × 1 tiles finish tiling a bathroom floor already having 1 × 1 tiles in two opposite corners:

1	2	3	4
8	7	6	5
9	10	11	12
16	15	14	13

or the following 'shortest' proof of the Pythagorean Theorem

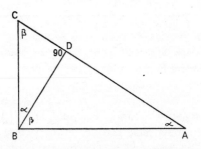

Observe that the area of ABC is the sum of the areas of ADB and BDC, all of which are similar.

Of course, one must recognize what is essential in the representation to be able to see them as proofs, and much preparation and prompting may be needed for that.

(Though I am perfectly certain that the 'shortest proof' above must be a proof, I'm not so sure of the proof.)

Theme 6. MATHEMATICS IS NOT THE ABSTRACT STUDY OF THE IN-FINITE.

Wittgenstein keenly appreciated that the use of a concept of infinity was both peculiar to and the hallmark of mathematics.

(In his 'middle' period especially, Wittgenstein was preoccupied with gaining a correct understanding of this concept of the infinite. See especially Part XII and first *Anhang*, both of which contain reminders of his use in T of the idea of an operation for going on.)

That is because mathematics is concerned with the unlimited possibility of applying rules which are implicit in the use of language. The mathematical concept of the infinite clearly is not an idea which belongs to civil language, but it can be comprehended only as part of the use of mathematical demonstration to control our understanding of civil language. Infinitude is not a feature of anything we talk about or conceptualize in civil language, but, so to speak, a feature of our forms of conceptualization themselves [a highly Kantian theme; see esp. B: 155–61].

Not something known by 'experience' [B: 154f., 157f., 304 *et. seq.*]. The appearance of 'infinite' in this usage shows that we are dealing with 'possibilities' [B: 153, 155, 159, 164, 313], with 'syntax', 'grammar', and 'rule' [B: 160f., 309, 313f.], and different kinds of mathematical infinity are features of different conceptions and not of different realities [R: 57].

In imputing infinitude in this sense one registers confidence that one has perspicuously apprehended the unlimited full range of application of a (single) concept (rule, form, etc.) [T: 2.0131; B: 153, 157, 313f.].

The assertion that a sure event will occur sometime in the infinitude of time is like a tautology [B: 153, 311].

But one is apt to misconceive a finitely formulated rule to be an unverifiable universal statement about a large aggregate of things—to take each possible application of a single rule as an actual mathematical object [B: 314; for 'unverifiability', see 149].

One regards the singular possibilities latent in our forms of thought as plural actualities. But an infinite possibility is not the possibility of an actual infinity [B: 164f., 159, 219, 312f.].

(In supposing, for example, that the possibilities of pairing things off—the natural numbers—can themselves be paired off like apples and pears [B: 140, 162].)

The mistake is in part a result of mixing up the material, temporal 'can' of capability and opportunity with the 'adverbial' timeless 'can' of logical possibility [B: 161f., 219, 311ff.; also R: 38f.]. It is a confusion of 'den Elementen der Erkenntnis' with physical questions [B: 168].

(This is an instance of the familiar theme of grammatical misassimilations.)

The possibilities are singular, and their alleged extensions cannot have independent existence.

(The existence of an infinite extension is proved by essence [B: 124, 221f.], e.g., the language has an unlimited number of names [T: 5.535].)

Supposed infinite sets always presuppose (logical) concepts and must be 'constructed' [B: 155, 221, 244].

The spuriously resulting world of 'sets' may present itself as the proper and autonomous subject-matter of mathematics to claim the titles of the discredited philosophies of empiricism and psychologism.

(There are precedents for this kind of 'Platonism' in the ancient idea that knowable, necessary, propositions must have their own special subject-matter—perhaps universals. Russell had advanced this kind of proposal in *Problems of Philosophy*.)

That has happened, in fact, with *Mengenlehre* towards which Wittgenstein's early criticism of Frege's 'logical objects' was redirected [B: 206f., 211].

(We already have seen that earlier he had held the subject was straightforwardly empirical [T: 6.031].)

Though this investigation can be pursued with exactness and precision, the claim that it provides a subject-matter and a foundation for mathematics is at best a pretence, based only on false pictures, which obscures essentials and unfailingly leads to mystery and paradox.

The set theorist seems to know what he is talking about because he uses borrowed pictures [B: 162, 218, 221; R: 62, 144ff., 149ff.] and imposes apparently unexceptionable principles like Excluded Middle [B: 176; R: 140, 149], but mostly because his concepts are introduced in application to familiar and compelling examples which unquestionably do make sense [B: 208f.: R: 60, 137, 148 *et. seq.*].

(I believe that Cantor's point of departure was the theory of Fourier Expansions.)

But he leaps beyond these to fanciful and underdetermined illustrations [B: 224, 232; R: 9f., 55, 148, 180].

(Where there is no way of perspicuously surveying the supposed infinite extensions or making 'selections' [B: 167, 224].)

And his operations become rootless [B: 211; R: 149f.]. The

result is mystery, glitter and darkness which widens the eyes and makes us gasp and reel [R: 142, 148].

(A kind of legerdemain, ceremony and incantation [B: 229; R: 60, 136f., and 53 for a different but similar instance], full of meaningless problems [B: 175f.], which Wittgenstein sometimes called 'alchemy' [R: 142]. He was an occasional and unimpressive practitioner in his own early days, e.g., in a letter to Russell in which he purported to prove that the Axiom of Reducibility was empirical and contingent.)

And the mathematician appears like nothing so much as a guardian of a cult, like the ancient priests and astrologers.

Set theory, whose general employment would result only in covering the distinctive features of different parts of mathematics with a uniform formal structure, least of all could be a foundation for mathematics [B: 206; R: 150: for development, see theme 7 below]. *Set theory (whose credentials, as one part of the motley, are not in question) can be redeemed philosophically only by deflating the theology of 'pure mathematics', with its pantheon of free floating objects* [R: 142] *and its fanciful images* [R: 60f., 180f.] *and scholastic questions* [B: 149; R: 59], *by returning the subject to its concrete illustrations and applications* [R: 62f., 133ff., 146, 152f.], *steering away from gratuitous abstractions* [see Kreisel [2]]. *Mathematicians in general, and set theorists in particular, are not giving general descriptions of amorphous aggregations but providing general schemes for dealing with particular cases. These applications to cases are of the essence, and we must always attend to the civil and mathematical rôles of mathematical concepts in their order of dependence.*

Regarding dependence, the real numbers presuppose the natural numbers and must be comparable with the rationals [B: 231f., 236ff.; see theme 7 and theme 10 below]. Our understanding of continuity and other such notions is built upon our familiarity with numbers [B: 207f.] and has important connexions with geometry [R: 148, 151]. Set theory should not try to reverse the dependencies or suppose it can make them disappear [B: 211], nor try to hide the distinctiveness of the various parts of mathematics with an amorphous, uniform elucidation [B: 206, 209; R: 146; for further development, see theme 7 below]. Civil rôles should dominate mathematics, Wittgenstein thought, but it is significant that set theoretical concepts are applied almost exclusively within mathematics itself [R: 186]. Writing about the compactness of the rationals, he says:

' "Fractions cannot be arranged in an order of magnitude." First and foremost, this sounds extremely interesting and remarkable.

'It sounds interesting in a quite different way from, say, a proposition of the differential calculus. The difference, I think, resides in the fact that *such* a proposition is easily associated with an application to physics, whereas *this* proposition belongs simply and solely to mathematics, seems to concern the natural history of mathematical objects themselves.

'One would like to say of it, e.g., it introduces us to the mysteries of the mathematical world. This is the aspect against which I want to give a warning.' [R: 60.]

It remains that the concepts of pure mathematics are in danger of losing their feet [R: 186]. Much of the so-called 'foundations of mathematics' seems to be dedicated to this possibility. Kreisel reproves Wittgenstein for not taking sufficiently well into account that logic '. . . provided concepts necessary for the description of mathematics, just as, according to Wittgenstein, mathematics provides the concepts necessary in the description of nature' [[1] p. 143]. Wittgenstein could have accepted that [see R: 145f.] and thrown in set theory too, and then have argued that for just that reason these subjects are ill-suited to serve as foundations.

Theme 7. NO ONE PART OF MATHEMATICS IS A FOUNDATION FOR ALL THE OTHERS.
The desire for foundations is in part due to a mistaken hankering for justification [R: 8f., 76, 82],

But, mathematics is the measure not the measured [R: 99]. Every part must fend for itself [T: 5.473; B: 131; R: 67], and must show in itself and in its application that it is true [B: 143f.]. We cannot explain the application with remarks in the margin [T: 5.452], nor can it be secured by any other part of mathematics [R: 67]. This is a kind of generalization of Brouwer's reliance upon 'basal intuition'. Ultimately, we just calculate as we do [R: 98], and the only justification for that is what we do outside of mathematics and in how we talk [T: 5.47, 5.472, 6.233; R: 9, 72, 82].

and to a methodology which demands a uniform presentation.

We feel that this insures comprehensibility and controls derivations, but logical notation is no better than prose [R: 155], and logical and set theoretic formulations hide important differences and defects in conception under an amorphous presentation [B: 206, 221; R: 76f., 89, 145f.].

From the beginning Wittgenstein objected to unified logistical formulations and doubted the claims of formal logic to be a foundation [R: 72f., 83, 145f.].

In T mathematics was described as a logical method of calculation, of making substitutions into equations [6.2, 6.233, 6.234, 6.2341, 6.24], and contrasted with the method of tautologies and contradictions used in formal logic for purposes of revealing relations of logical consequence [6.22]. Mathematics, so regarded, is neither part of logic (in the narrow sense of 'logic'), nor can it be deductively derived from logic.

(Russell's proposed definition of '$=$' in purely logical terms was banned on the grounds that objects are only contingently indiscernible [T: 2.0233, 2.02331, 3.221, 5.5302]. The essential, necessary 'pure numerical difference' needed in mathematics cannot be captured in this way [4.1272, 5.5303].)

But it is like logic in being a method of calculation which is derived from nothing at all, but reflected in the use of language. Logic and mathematics are true together in so far as, 'If a word [*sic.*, "God"?] creates a world so that in it the principles of logic are true, it thereby creates a world in which the whole of mathematics holds' ['Notes on Logic'], viz. by being together implied by the fact that we use language as we do, and by the consideration that totalities of elementary propositions with which logic operates and of objects whose mutual distinctness is presupposed by mathematics impose the same limits on thought and reality [T: 5.5561].

(There is in T, from 5.11 on, a strong tendency operating to reduce the concepts of logic and mathematics together to the idea of a putative recursive rule for going on. [See also 4.1252, 4.1273.])

Wittgenstein's whole unsatisfying doctrine about identity

and mathematics persisted into B, where he found new arguments to support his view that equations could not be reduced to tautologies [B: 141ff., also 126, which anticipates R].

(This appears to be a response to Ramsey's interpretation of T: 5.535 [see *Foundations of Mathematics*, pp. 60f.].)

He goes so far as to suggest that arithmetic, in its independence from logic and reliance upon its own form of autonomous insight, is an example of Kant's synthetic *a priori* [B: 129].

These objections and doubts later were directed against reductions of every kind.

First, because reduction would destroy the essential perspicuity of proof [B: 125f.; R: 62f., 68, 70, 81, 83, 91]. Second, it would not get us what we had and wish to retain, e.g., a logistical reduction would not teach us how to calculate or to solve differential equations [B: 127; R: 66, 71, 89]. Third, the result justifies the attempted reduction, and not vice versa—the shorter, original proof tells us how the longer ought to come out [B: 127; R: 73f., 81, 83, 91, 171]. And, finally, reductionism systematically confuses a representation of one theory by another with identification [R: 66, 72, 84, 89f., 91].

Wittgenstein places an exaggerated but interesting stress on difference and autonomy.

For instance, on the differences in mathematics among apparent existential statements and between existential statements and truth functions [B: 149; R: 141, 144], small and large numbers [R: 67, 74], equations and inequations [B: 249; R: 1].

His criteria for mutual independence of theories and for mathematical autonomy seemed to be these:

(1) *Could one theory (technique, etc.) have been learned independently of the other? [R: 86.]*

(2) *Does the subject have its own characteristic techniques [R: 85ff., 145];*

(3) *its own characteristic application, e.g., in surveying? [R: 88, 190.]*

(4) *Does purported reduction utilize or otherwise presuppose the analysed concepts? [B: 125ff.; R: 66f., 71f., 83, 85.]*

(5) *Finally, are the concepts in question immediately self-applicable, e.g., as when we count the numbers or use a geometric construction to illustrate a proof? [B: 132f.]*

Self-application guarantees perspicuity and independence of contingency. If the proof is an illustration of how it is, one cannot deny that that is how it is, anymore than one who is honestly screaming can fail to know that this is pain [B: 130, 132].

Wittgenstein's alternative to reductionism of any kind—whether to numbers, geometry, logic or sets—was attention to the varieties of language eligible for mathematical elucidation and to the consequent motley of mathematics.

(Though the 'motley' is not a theme in T, where Wittgenstein seemed to demand a single unified language, the idea is foreshadowed in his interesting but unsatisfying remarks about mechanics and the principles of physics [T: 6.3211, 6.33, 6.34 *et seq.*], which are made to appear to have a certain autonomy, even though they 'speak of the objects of the world' [6.3431]. On the other hand, [6.3751] *intimates* the idea that logical distinctions of every kind can be presented within the formalism of mathematical analysis.)

Theme 8. MATHEMATICS IS NOT SO MUCH DOCTRINE AS METHOD.

A 'method of logic' [T: 6.2, 6.234].

For exhibiting essential features of the civil use of language [T: 6.12, 6.1201, 6.121, 6.1221, 6.124, 6.22; R: 79]. In T, Wittgenstein was particularly exercised to combat the idea that logic and mathematics could be regarded as a corpus of propositions, ideally to be deductively presented as a unified theory à la Frege and Russell.

Apparent logical derivations can be replaced by calculations in which the distinction between proof and conclusion cannot easily be drawn [see below; T: 6.126, 6.2331]. Wittgenstein's method of truth tables abolished the artificially imposed distinction in rank as between alleged primitive propositions and their consequences [T: 6.126, 6.127]. He argued that there are no fundamental concepts in logic and mathematics [T: 5.45–5.4541], and that the classification of ideas which is so much a part of any kind of theorizing is here a symptom of error [5.554–5.555]. The logistical presentation falsely mis-assimilates the necessities of logic to contingent truths [6.113, 6.1263], and the formal concepts of mathematics to material concepts [4.1272, 4.1274, 6.1231–6.1233]. Construction of *theories* of logic and mathematics of this kind must presuppose anyway the mathematical *methods* Wittgenstein thought were fundamental [T: 6.123, 6.1263].

> (This position is strongly fortified by the argument Lewis Carroll advanced in his famous paper, 'What the Tortoise Said to Achilles' [*Mind*, 1895, pp. 278–80; T: 5.132].)

Wittgenstein was not concerned with special forms that might be defined in this or that alleged theory of logic, but rather with 'what makes it possible to invent such things' at all [T: 5.555].

The supposed conclusions of mathematical arguments are not really propositions which could be true or false, but integral parts of the whole logical demonstration which itself cannot be asserted or denied, only exhibited [B: 192, 198f.].

In T, Wittgenstein's ban was codified in the exaggerated dictum that what could thus be shown could not be said. He stuck to this in B, where he continued to look upon language as an untranscendable unity all of whose propositions have a perfectly determinate sense [B: 123, 139, 143f., 152, 168, 178, 198, 203, 208, 234].

> (At [208] he turns the principle that certain sets can only be described and not presented squarely on its head.)

The thesis that the results of at least some parts of mathematics cannot be formulated propositionally was additionally and incoherently supported by use of the verification principle [B: 172, 174f., 190, 336, 338]. A faint echo of 'showing' is still distantly heard in R [79], though by then Wittgenstein had broken out of this indefensibly tight position.

Wittgenstein always was chary about the conception of a mathematical proposition because, he argued,

(1) *they have no proper subject-matter* [T: 6.111, 6.211; see theme 6],

(2) *they convey no information* [T: 2.225, 5.142, 6.11, 6.122, 6.2321–6.2323; R: 31, 53f.];

(3) *they do not admit of meaningful alternatives* [T: 4.463, 6.1222];

(4) *they presuppose their own correctness* [T: 6.123, 6.1261, 6.1264, 6.1265, 6.23, 6.232–6.2322].

> Their sense presupposes their truth [B: 144], and they are no more assertable than their counterparts among the self-referential paradoxes.

Wittgenstein expectedly had hard words for the so-called conjectures and hypotheses in mathematics, e.g., the Riemann Hypothesis [B: 190f., 338]. An interesting and not entirely implausible consequence of his view is that the apparent propositions of mathematics do not have negations; rather, apparent negations (e.g., inequations) are independent determinations [B: 247–251]. In B and R, Wittgenstein was apt to classify these nonpropositions as commands [R: 49, 142ff.], rules and schematic applications of rules [B: 143, 194, 322f.; R: 47, 77, 118, 120], definitions [B: 198] or simply as techniques [R. 43]. He pointed out the possibility of imparting mathematical techniques without benefit of formulated propositions or apparent propositions, e.g., we teach a person to count or to integrate without bothering to impart such 'facts' as the fundamental theorems of arithmetic and the calculus [R: 49, 118]. Wittgenstein's thesis that mathematical results are not propositions holds especially well for his favourite examples of calculating [B: 172; R: 32, 76, 115]

where the distinction between proof and conclusion cannot be drawn easily [for development, see theme 9],

and knot-unravelling [B: 184f.], and for the kind of demonstration one witnesses in the physics lecture hall. But it is not entirely evident that these are what mathematicians are wont to call 'proofs'; certainly $13 \times 14 = 182$ *is not a 'theorem'.*

Theme 9. IN MATHEMATICS IT IS ALWAYS THE PROOF THAT MATTERS.
(Here there is a curious partial agreement with Frege who defined analytic necessity in terms of derivability from the axioms of logic.)

Mathematical results are proof constructions [B: 183; R: 92], for the proof is what shows the conceptual connexions [R: 25f., 75f., 80].
The 'real' mathematical proposition is the proof itself [B: 184].

(But that is no proposition.)

So-called mathematical propositions essentially are proof conclusions [B: 192; also Dummett, op. cit., p. 327].
If one may believe mathematical propositions at all, then that is to believe that one has a proof [B: 204; R: 32].

(I think the thought would be true if read, '. . . that there is a proof'.)

To know a mathematical proposition is to know how it can be proved, and to know that is to have proved it [B: 199].

They cannot be understood when cut off from the proof [B: 183; R: 26f., 52, 77].

(Like the surface of a body [B: 192].)

With reference to Wittgenstein's favourite example of calculation, there is here no clear distinction between proof and conclusion [T: 6.126–6.1265; B: 130; R: 26, 32f.; and see Kreisel [1], p. 140].

(Discussing Goedel's Incompleteness Theorem and the common way of speaking of it in terms of asserting something of itself, he says, 'In this sense the proposition "625 = 25 × 25" also asserts something about itself: namely that the left-hand number is got by the multiplication of the numbers on the right' [R: 176].)

Wittgenstein plausibly claims that the alleged conclusion is itself a form or an indication of a form of proof in the 'application', e.g., it is a form of Modus Ponens [T: 6.1264] or a rule telling how many objects there should be if we have arithmetically melded two groups of things [B: 145; R: 77].

The conclusion so regarded is given its sense by the mathematical demonstration [B: 180f.; R: 52 (an example where the application is within mathematics), 77] by schematically showing how the alleged conclusion is applied as a rule of inference in civil life: the proof of the 'conclusion' shows how the conclusion may be used as a rule of proof. The conclusion in its turn tells us how to read the demonstration. Its sense is to tell us how to use the proof of which it is the 'conclusion' [R: 76]. The sense of the alleged conclusion is that *this* has been proved [B: 181, 192].

(He also says—if I understand the passage—that in inductive proof—the kind he liked best—the conclusion is to proof as a sign is to signified [B: 328f.].)

From this Wittgenstein concludes that the sense of the conclusion is its proof [T: 6.1265; B: 192].

(And that is why it *must* be so, on Wittgenstein's theory of necessity. See theme 4 above.)

Apparently Wittgenstein believed that this way of thinking about proof and conclusion is supported by the fact that the alleged conclusion is often self-applying [B: 130, 132]. He summed it all up in the maxim that in mathematics process and result are the same [T: 6.1261; R: 26].

(But this maxim bears other interpretations too, e.g., that there are no processes in mathematics.)

An obvious and strong objection is that Wittgenstein's thesis, if true, makes it meaningless to speak of establishing the same conclusion in two different ways [R: 92f.].

Sometimes he appears to accept the conclusion that there cannot be two independent proofs of the same mathematical proposition [B: 184, also 193].

(But note the word 'independent'.)

Sometimes he incoherently allows that we can be brought to accept the same rule in different ways [R: 92f.], through new connexions, but one way dominates, e.g., that defined by multiplication [R: 93]; again, he allows that we might get to the same place by two routes [R: 92, 165], or that we are working in distinct systems [R: 165], always with the suggestion that the application furnishes the connecting fabric. Wittgenstein also says that alternate proofs supply equally suitable instruments for the same purpose [R: 165] and persuade us to 'stake the same thing' on the truth of the proposition [R: 186].

These replies do not meet the objection and reveal what I feel may be the weakest place in Wittgenstein's whole philosophy of mathematics, his failure to say how the different proofs for all sorts of different things, throughout the many parts of mathematics, can be related.

Theme 10. IN HIS MIDDLE AND LATE PERIODS WITTGENSTEIN SHOWED A WAKENING INTEREST IN THE APPLICATION OF MATHEMATICAL CONCEPTS WITHIN MATHEMATICS ITSELF, ESPECIALLY IN CONNEXION WITH THE CONSISTENCY PROBLEM (WHICH WE SHALL CONSIDER NEXT BELOW) AND IN SET-THEORETIC INTERPRETATIONS OF THE CLASSICAL REPRESENTATION OF REAL NUMBERS BY NON-TERMINATING DECIMALS. [For the latter, see B throughout, but especially parts XII, XV–XVII and first *Anhang*; R: Appendix II.]

Wittgenstein was gravely suspicious of the idea that real numbers could be regarded as arbitrary infinite sets of nested intervals of rationals or as arbitrary Dedekind 'Cuts', conceived of as existing outside our conceptions without need of rule or specification. This is the worst form of 'extensionalism', where we only seem to know what we are talking about,

*based on fanciful images and full of all sorts of spurious problems and
misapplications* [see themes 2 and 6 above].

We think of a real number as a definite but infinitely long
string of things which we could systematically tick off and,
after an infinite time, look back upon as a job done, a state
we might now already be in had we lived from the beginning
of time [B: 149, 164 *et. seq.*, 236f.]. We are apt to think in
this way about infinite strings and infinite processes because
we mistake and project accidental features of the representation as essentials of the conception [B: 231f.; R: 251].

(The powerful dialectic Wittgenstein directed against the
easy assumption that the representation of a real number
simply either does or does not contain a certain pattern of
digits carries the germ of a genuine mathematical point,
viz., the distinction between generally recursive and merely
recursively enumerable sequences. See esp. R [139ff.]
where he makes the supporting observation that the
denial of 'There exists a law that p' is not 'There exists
a law that $\sim$p' [R: 141; also B: 228f.].)

He objected particularly to the idea of arbitrary 'free choice
sequences' speciously thought of as generated by some
mechanical temporal process, such as flipping a coin [B:
165ff., 218ff., 233].

Wittgenstein also had doubts about Cantor's 'Diagonal Argument',
In apparently presupposing familiarity with a real number
still not defined, the proof seems to require us to act in
ignorance and without concrete comprehension [B: 226]. The
proof assimilates the introduction of a new concept to a deep
and mysterious discovery. But the depth is an illusion and the
mystery due to the fact that, even after the argument has been
understood, it remains unclear where and how the concept
applies, and we try to fix its sense in terms elsewhere appropriate, e.g., in terms of comparisons of magnitude [R:
54 *et. seq.*].

*and about Dedekind's theorem that the real numbers are closed over
additional cuts* [B: 224f.; R: 148ff.].

He objected particularly to the image of 'fitting in' reals
among the rationals [B: 223, 339; R: 151].

*Apparently Wittgenstein did not object to the classical conception of a real
number as the limit of a sequence of partial sums, represented perhaps*

by assigning an argument to a well-defined power series expansion. Here we still can discern the relation of real numbers to the civil institution of measurement [B: 230, 235; my perhaps incorrect interpretation of 'messen'], *and are less apt than with the more abstract conception to obliterate clear lines of dependence of the reals upon other mathematical theories and especially upon the system of rational numbers* [B: 228; R: 148].

A particularly insistent theme in B was Wittgenstein's demand that particular real numbers should effectively and uniformly be comparable with the rationals upon which they depend [B: 227, 236 *et. seq.*].

(The rule of development of a real is the method of comparison with rationals [B: 236–44].)

The introduction or definition of a real number should make clear from the outset what those relations are and not leave it as something to be discovered later on [B: 238f.].

Wittgenstein sometimes appeared even to allow that the general idea of an infinite decimal had a useful, non-mysterious sense, capable of covering a variety of different systems [R: 58],

(perhaps still other forms of numbers different from [e.g.] 1/3, $\sqrt{2}$ and π, themselves first introduced in quite different connexions)

all of which he once was inclined to bring under the umbrella conception of a rule for going on—an 'induction' (a 'recursive rule') [B: 223f., 234ff.]. *Positively, Wittgenstein identified particular real numbers with particular such rules* [B: 227–34, 308f.; R: 144].

Theme 11. THE NUB OF WITTGENSTEIN'S OBJECTIONS TO THE CONSISTENCY PROBLEM SEEMS TO HAVE BEEN THAT THIS IS JUST ONE KIND OF MATHEMATICAL QUESTION WHICH HAS BEEN GIVEN AN EXAGGERATED IMPORTANCE BY THE FASHIONS OF CONTEMPORARY THEORIES OF THE FOUNDATIONS OF MATHEMATICS [R: 52, 107].

The earliest extensive examination of the matter by Wittgenstein of which we have a printed record is the transcription of conversations with Schlick and Waismann incorporated as the second *Anhang* in B, although there is a clear anticipation at B: 189ff. He returned to the topic of consistency and consistency proofs frequently in R, esp. in parts II and V. It is clear, however, that Wittgenstein's thinking about the question was conditioned largely by the turn of the century concern with the logical paradoxes, which he regarded merely as confusions to be resolved by analysis and not by proofs [B: 320].

(But note his suggestion that mathematical demonstration is never anything else but 'analysis' [B: 192]. Usually Wittgenstein illustrated his observations with Heterological and kindred paradoxes [R: 51, 102, 104f., 150f., 166, 170, 175, 182]. This may explain why he so thoroughly misunderstood the aims and results of metamathematics.)

Wittgenstein's polemic squared at all points with his negative attitude towards 'foundations' and with mathematical theories about mathematics [B: 320, 327, 330, 336; R: 109].

He had just as little patience with the related metamathematical concern with the questions of independence and completeness [B: 189f., 319, 324, 335ff.].

He held that the fear of an hitherto undisclosed contradiction was either a pretence or neurotic [B: 318f., 323, 325, 332, 338, 345f.; R: 181], *first, because the appearance of a contradiction isn't the only thing that can go wrong in mathematics* [B: 325; R: 105, 130, 196]; *second, because the demonstration of a contradiction itself would be just another mathematical result, although in a system other than the one in which the supposed inconsistency would be found* [B: 189, 320, 328, 330, 335, 341; R: 167f.];

He argued that only formalized, derivational mathematics could pretend to view a contradiction as a disaster. But in fact a formal contradiction would be interesting only if it were also an inconsistency, thus presupposing that the system had truth, meaning and application [B: 321ff., 333, 337, 339; R: 104, 166].

(A contradiction is just another piece in the imagined *game* of formal mathematics [B: 318f., 326, 331f.].)

Wittgenstein believed that his own views about the meaning and application of mathematics left no place for significant philosophical questions about provability and consistency [B: 189, 322, 329ff., 339; R: 104, 109, 166ff., 178, 181].

(This claim was sometimes unsatisfyingly supported by use of *Tractarian* principles about what can only be shown and not said, and about the impossibility of meaningfully crossing the limits of language [B: 326, 330, 336].)

third, contradictions can always be taken in stride [R: 51, 101, 141, 150f., 166, 168, 170, 181f.], *and even be used* [R: 150f., 166, 171, 183]. *Systems with contradictions can at the very worst always be patched up with more or less* ad hoc *repairs* [B: 319, 333, 345; R: 102, 181]. *At all events, a consistency proof would not give us the controls we would want and the confidence we would lack if we really were sceptical about mathematics* [B: 330, 345; R: 104, 106f., 109f., 181].

CONCLUSION

I hope to have created a convincing sense of constancy and continuity in Wittgenstein's thinking about mathematics, a constancy in basics which swells under a continuity of surface changes in emphasis, and interests and occasionally in doctrine. Certainly the hard lines of T were softened in later days, but a recognizable doctrine survived to be given a broader and looser application.

Constructively, the two dominant continuing themes in Wittgenstein's thinking are that mathematics is an assorted kit of instruments for the conceptual control of civil language and life at large, and the conception of mathematical proof as the perspicuous demonstration of essentials, viz. necessities. The doctrine was illustrated for the most part by examples of simple arithmetical calculations and the calculation of tautologies with some occasional attention to other parts of 'intuitive mathematics'. Critically, we find a persisting scepticism about the deductive paradigm of mathematical demonstration, a stiff resistance to the conception of mathematics as an autonomous subject-matter which is best codified in a growing corpus of propositions about mathematical objects; Wittgenstein never really became reconciled to mathematical *propositions* and never accepted the historically recurrent thesis that mathematics can be unified into a single theory. His distrust of the claims of 'pure mathematics' was sustained by a serious inattention to the actual contemporary conduct of mathematical theory, only partially compensated for by his waxing and then waning concerns with the idea of a real number and the conception of the mathematical infinite and his still later critical reaction to metamathematics (Wittgenstein apparently was pretty ignorant about recent work in algebra, analysis and geometry, from which he might have received some moral support). This late and grudging and lazy interest in pure mathematics did not have entirely happy consequences, for it seems to have abetted his occasional indifference to the distinction between civil and mathematical applications of mathematical concepts, which throws a darkening shadow of suspicion over his whole philosophy of mathematics. Something at once more interesting and more compelling might have emerged from an investigation of how internal applications (e.g., of probability concepts to the theory of numbers) finally reach down into 'life'. Wittgenstein would have done well to take seriously the thesis that nondenumerability is an inescapable implication of the physical and technological applications of mathematical analysis. [See Bernays, *op. cit.*, p. 14.]

The most obvious surface change was that the unified language of T was fragmented into a welter of language games regarded as forms of behaviour, and mathematics in train became dependent upon conventions and upon agreements among men, on the ways we act and forms of life. He became ever more apt to formulate his thoughts in the vocabulary of 'rules', 'pathways', 'paradigms' and 'norms' and to pay perhaps exaggerated attention to the conceptual transformations effected by mathematical demonstrations. The original thesis that formal logic and mathematics are distinct logical methods was softened into the 'motley'; the apparently crystalline conception of 'and so on' was diffused into the general notion of perspicuity. Wittgenstein expressed uneasiness about sharp lines [see R: 155, 163, 186] and imputed an over-rigid theory about language to his own earlier self [R: 182].

This naturally was attended by a generally more relaxed attitude towards language at large. Most notably, Wittgenstein, after putting up a staunch resistance, finally abandoned the idea that even propositional language was a unified system analytically resolvable into a 'totality' of elementary judgements, themselves anchored to the 'totality' of objects to which reference ultimately is made—a view which issues in what I have elsewhere called the 'Absolute Spielraum Principle' [*Inquiry*, 1964, pp. 411f.] The rigid distinction between *saying* and *showing* is broken and therewith is destroyed the 'transcendental metaphysics' of the other 'world' on the other side of the limits, the world of 'possibilities' which must have the perfect structure of an 'ideal' to hold language inflexible inside.[1] It seems to me that the most important change of all, deeper and less visible and more consequential than the others, was in his view of *necessity*. What was proposed rhetorically in the T question, 'What must *be* the case in order that something can be the case?' [5.5542], finally gave way in the concession that 'There correspond to our laws of logic very general facts of daily experience' [R: 36]. Otherwise, the ideal world of logic of which he speaks so eloquently in the *Philosophical Investigations* would have remained starkly separated from the contingency of fact. But now the benchmarks of contingency, the 'limits of empiricism' are themselves posted in other contingent facts.

I think Wittgenstein was right but not right enough. Mathematics is built on the presuppositions of everyday life and therefore has contingent implications. But I doubt that Wittgenstein saw this with sufficient clarity or perspicuity in R, nor did he follow up with enough detail. Surely the facts that we walk on two legs and speak a babel of tongues—important in the human situation—are not among the bourning stones of empiricism. But why not? We need many cases of at least as much detail as Wittgenstein devoted to his lumber merchants [R: 43f.]. Then perhaps we could begin to understand what is so important, that every part of the motley of mathematics has a motley of applications [see e.g., R: 152].

Assessment. We have already observed a number of defects in Wittgenstein's presentation and unresolved problems for his theory of mathematics.

Wittgenstein simply didn't know what to do about pure mathematics, where the 'civil application' is already mathematics. It is important here to see what Wittgenstein himself sometimes failed to notice, that mathematical concepts are not themselves civil concepts. The natural numbers are not the numbers of 'how many?' or 'which one?', but simply the numbers which we can calculate with and prove theorems about, doubtless often for civil purposes of regularizing our ideas of 'how many?' etc. The number 6 is just as much a mathematical notion as *perfect number* or $\aleph_0$. Perhaps Wittgenstein already was bumping unwittingly

---

[1] The first break came with his abandonment of the requirement that the elementary judgements be mutually independent. This is documented in the 1929 paper on logical form and in B, parts VIII and XXI and on p. 317, where he rewrites T: 2.1512 to say that not single sentences (as he thought before) but the whole, still rigid system of language is applied to reality.

against the difficulty in B with his frequent application of the verification principle to the supposed propositions of number theory. The application is, I believe, entirely reasonable regarded by itself, but hardly coherent with Wittgenstein's ban on mathematical propositions. The problem stayed to haunt him in R, e.g., where he found himself unable to find a civil technique for $2^{\aleph_0}$ to be a property of [R: 186]. He seems to have felt deceived by the two-facedness of mathematics, which looks outwards to its civil application and inwards to its own theory. [See R: 117ff. That is one way of taking the 'twofold character of the mathematical proposition as *law* and as *rule*'; R: 120.] Since he didn't want to deny anything, Wittgenstein had to find some adjustment to the fact that mathematicians work within their own walls and establish all sorts of interesting things like the irrationality of $\sqrt{2}$ and the transcendence of π. That dulls the sting of Wittgsenstein's criticism of metamathematics which is, in its operations, not all that different from Galois theory or any other part of pure mathematics in which men have reasoned successfully about mathematical objects. Wittgenstein allowed that the demonstration of a contradiction would show that we don't know our way about [R: 104]. Agreed, and that is an important result, which may resemble the discovery of the irrationality of $\sqrt{2}$; but it is also a problem, which may have a similar though doubtfully as grand a significance for mathematics as the discovery of irrationality; we don't see immediately what is wrong with our intuitive idea of class abstraction in the way most of us are able to see why division by 0 is forbidden. I don't think Wittgenstein was wrong in stressing civil applications—on the contrary; but I doubt whether he could have resolved the difficulty without going into unwonted detail with the aim of explaining how internal applications of mathematical concepts also, in a perhaps refracted and diffused way, reflect the essentials of civil, nonmathematical language.

This first difficulty is tied up with the unsatisfactorily indefinite state of Wittgenstein's ideas about conceptual change. The most obvious alterations occur in connexion with internal applications, e.g., the closing up of the projective plane by the introduction of a point at infinity, the extension of the real number field, the algebraic reworking of arithmetic and geometry, and the systematic use of set theory as a formulary.

We have also noticed that Wittgenstein was never really able to say how different proofs could have the same conclusions. Otherwise put, he had no place in his framework of thought for the idea of a *theorem*. The availability of alternative proofs goes together with the common assumption that one can understand a theorem one has never seen proved, which Wittgenstein apparently also wanted to deny, not without conceding the ring of paradox [see B: 183; R: 92]. Here again I think Wittgenstein could have dispelled the difficulty only if, contrary to his every inclination, he would have looked at many different particular cases in considerable detail. I don't know how to do this; but I believe that what we must come to understand better is the obvious, open, multivalent applicability of interesting mathematics to cases of every kind, both inside and outside; this perhaps would better reveal how one thing can be looked upon as a model for another kind of thing and (to speak figuratively) how the same case can be rotated in different directions into the same position.

Another major problem which Wittgenstein himself recognized is to explain how mistakes in calculation specifically and in demonstration generally are possible. Either you do or you do not know how to calculate; but if you do, then your calculation gives the right result. So far the problem sounds a bit like accounting for mispelling. But it is given special consequence by Wittgenstein's maxim that process and result are the same in mathematics and poignancy by the consideration that if proof were (as Wittgenstein held) the revelation of sense, then it would be hard to explain how we could, with understanding, set about to prove something if we didn't know the result in advance [see B: 170]. We can agree up to a point with Wittgenstein's confessional declaration, 'I have not yet made the rôle of miscalculating clear. The rôle of the proposition: "I must have miscalculated." It is really the key to an understanding of the "foundations of mathematics".' [R: 111; see also 33, 95, 120.]

There are a number of other, smaller unresolved problems. Wittgenstein was ill-prepared to cope with the obvious, if only occasionally relevant, distinction between axioms and theorems [see R: 79]. Why, for instance, were the ancients so chary about the parallel axiom—it generally was thought to be true? (And see Wittgenstein's own remarks at R: 113f.) Again, how does Wittgenstein account for the fact that mathematicians do 'discover' proofs if not theorems? Where do trial and error methods fit into his scheme? Though I can believe that something I don't see led Euler to his calculated disproof of the Fermatian conjecture, that all numbers of the form $2^{2^n}+1$ are prime, most of us see $2^{2^5}+1$ as a concrete counterexample [for partial recognition, see B: 134 and R: 188]. All these are obvious, still unresolved difficulties for Wittgenstein's philosophy of mathematics.

Switching onto another critical track, I think most commentators would agree that Wittgenstein's style and manner were inappropriate to the subject. The flickering images of his variable terminology are regrettable; and he uses it in a careless analogical way, with little discrimination. Just think how many different things have been and could be called 'rules'; think how very different are the rules of English from the rules of calculating. In no other part of philosophy is detail more in demand. Wittgenstein draws our attention to the 'motley'; but where is it in his book? He works with a few jejune examples, notable chiefly for their vague similarity to more important ones. (Wouldn't the Koenigsberg Bridge Problem have done better as an illustration than the joints in the wall [R: 174]?) Wittgenstein was inexcusably lax about technicalities, and sometimes they matter. Everyone has felt, with Wittgenstein, that there must be an important formal difference between the sequence of primes and (say) the sequence of even numbers [see B: 251]. I believe that mathematicians, some of whom are of a like mind with Wittgenstein about the real numbers, have tried unsuccessfully to say what that difference is.

The otherwise finely wrought T is unbelievably bad on important technical questions. The main such defect is that Wittgenstein's operation for generating propositions was not, as he later could have put it, generally recursive, as it had to be. I have racked my brains trying to figure out how a theory of descriptions could be fitted into the T theory of language, as Wittgenstein intimated it could be at T: 3.24. But, more to our point, the T theory of mathematics *per se* is simply a mess. First, the equations in question are not even degenerate sentences, so it is not clear how they can be *sinnlos* but not *unsinnig* singular points of logical revelation. Second, these equations are described as containing *names* and not (e.g.) numbers, though Wittgenstein's examples are framed for number. I suspect Wittgenstein had something like trigonometry in mind; but for the reason just given, his theory is inadequate even to simple calculations. He briefly sketches out a theory of number, which *may* be congruent with the Peano scheme; but then one wonders how *this* can be applied to apples and oranges. It would take more than two applications of joint denial to get 'apple$_1$ is in the bowl and apple$_2$ is in the bowl'. There are ways out of this, but they lead into still deeper difficulties.

Yet, after all this has been noted down, I think that Wittgenstein was substantially right in his proposed if fragmented alternative to the other 'philosophies' of mathematics. In the course of tracking through these texts, I found myself becoming more and more agreeably disposed to the thought that the formal derivational method of presenting mathematical proof against which Wittgenstein polemicizes is *only* a method of presentation, and a rather artificial one at that, a kind of uniform which I had been taught to respect from training by the professors of logic. I am completely convinced by what he intimates regarding the 'meaning' of mathematics. I should now like to try to convey this conviction.

Many share Wittgenstein's distaste for the theology of pure mathematics and his wish to dispel the arcane mysteries of the cult. But perhaps the mysteries are preferable to saying that mathematics is something it patently is not (who would exchange the mathematics we know for psychology?), and to the naturalism of the 'meaningless game'. Wittgenstein's view of mathematics as a kit of instruments for conceptual control is at once a refuge from empiricism and an alternative to Platonism. We must try to see how mathematical objects are creatures of human conception in a way in which coconuts and thoughts are not. Wittgenstein's guiding thought is that they are features of our originally nonmathematical ways of thinking about the world, and they owe their apparent superpalpability to the fact that they may be presented 'nonobservationally', in this most immediate manner. We explain the meaning of mathematics by attending to those applications, to the dominating illustrations, and not by appeal to borrowed images. Wittgenstein also fortifies us against those obviously false but still dangerously inviting ways of thinking of mathematical sequences as like actual physical processes which go on perhaps for a terribly long time. The infinitudes of mathematics are not processional, but features of the open if regular application of single rules. I believe that many practising mathematicians share Wittgenstein's idea that real numbers must answer to 'rules'.

Evidence for the correctness of Wittgenstein's way of thinking about mathematics appears in many places. Consider that until quite recently only in geometry among the many mathematical disciplines were proofs supposed to proceed from stipulated axioms and postulates. Why? Because elsewhere demonstration began with the mathematician drawing our attention to what everyone could see had to be the case, e.g., one could see that the numbers were unlimited just because one had learned a rule of civil language, to count thus, permitting one always to count higher than 'this'. Even in geometry, axioms were formulated as reminders that geometric proportions and not (e.g.) sensation intensities were the subject-matter, and postulates were stipulated where a kind of generality was needed for which civil practice did not provide immediately validating construction. Geometric demonstration remained for the most part a matter of getting one to 'look and see', where what one looked at was the 'application'. Outside of geometry, with the growth of pure mathematics, this application was commonly already something mathematical (e.g., the order and the number of the exponents of polynomial functions).

There is something right in Wittgenstein's ideas about proof 'creating' concepts. One first thinks of the important if hackneyed examples from the history of the extension of the concept of number, which I shall not dwell on except to observe the differences. We get to $\aleph_0$ by generalizing upon one application of the numbers and ω by generalizing upon another; the complex numbers, by way of contrast, arose out of a demand for algebraic roundness. The final resolution of the classical geometry problems affords a different kind of illustration. Wittgenstein once saw these as establishing connexions between previously separate 'language systems' [B: 177]. Suppose, what is historically inconceivable, that Archimedes knew what he did about geometric magnitudes and was also somehow master of the complete algebraic theory of equations, the concept of a derivative function, and the analytic theory of power series expansion. He, like Lindemann, might have been able to prove that *e* was the root of no polynomial equation; and hence not πi; and hence not π; but not even Archimedes could have seen immediately that therefore the circle could not be squared. Lindemann's proof would have been incomprehensible to the ancients and would not have answered *their* question. The sense of 'π' has since undergone a continuous but marked change, mostly as a result of applying a growing body of analytical technique to problems that originally arose elsewhere. The original concept of a geometric ratio was, however, always there, as Wittgenstein might have said, in the background. One may tendentiously interpret Lindemann's demonstration as an explanation of why the geometric problem could not have been (hence never was) solved.

This case description, which I hope is acceptable, is meant to illustrate how application makes meaning; here the main 'application' was mathematical, but the mathematical application itself got its meaning from the nonmathematical superimpositional procedures of comparing areas. Now we really don't want to deny anything, and the question arises whether this way of thinking would make any useful sense if directed to more recondite and abstract parts of mathematics which begin with long enlisted, highly regimented applications. I hazard the suggestion that it might, though here my ignorance may betray me. I have been bemused to observe the excitement generated by Cohen's recent proof of the independence of the Axiom of Choice. The great question is what will the mathematicians do now. The consensus seems to be that they will go on as before with a sense that their previous confidence in using the Axiom has been vindicated.[1] I feel that one could 'philosophically' explain that 'decision' along the following, Wittgensteinian lines. Start with Wittgenstein's thought that mathematical conceptions of the infinite are introduced for purposes of fixing in a nonarbitrary manner the limits of already available concepts. A proof of denumerability exhibits a rule by which that can be effected. A proof of nondenumerability shows that there is no such procedure. Still, in order that anything should be limited, a concept with an

---

[1] There may be some holdouts, chiefly because the Axiom of Choice has some counterintuitive consequences—observe the immediate appeal to the non-mathematical application!—notably the Tarski-Banach theorem. But that kind of intuition is always on the defensive anyway. Recall Wittgenstein's own favourite example of the distance a band around the earth would stand off the surface if its length was increased half a foot.

allegedly nondenumerable extension must be pinned down to something we can comprehend. Proofs employed in the stratosphere of set theory get their sense from their connexions with closer, gravitating, 'constructive' things. The limits are drawn to enable us to survey *those* cases in a nonarbitrary way. Now, if we are sure that a principle holds for any such finite or otherwise 'constructive' case, it behooves us to adopt it, if it is also known to be consistent with all other such principles. I believe that that is now the situation with the Axiom of Choice. I'm not entirely confident that what I say makes sense; but it is, at all events, an example of Wittgensteinian thinking.[1]

It must be evident already that I am sympathetic with Wittgenstein's thesis that mathematical proof is perspicuous demonstration and not logical derivation; or, better, that logical derivation is only one kind of demonstration. I believe that this in fact would have been the traditional sentiment, and Wittgenstein's philosophy represents a significant return from recent fashion. I am inclined to think that Hilbert was wrong and Euclid right, that postulates are not to be laid down as assumed truths, but are rather to be posted here and there to tell you what you can *do*. Anyway, I agree with Wittgenstein that it is the proof that matters most and not the conclusion. Mathematicians discover proofs, not theorems. Mathematical propositions are indeed essentially last lines of demonstrations. One could not properly claim to know a *theorem* if one thought it had not been demonstrated, and for one to *believe* a mathematical proposition would imply one believed it could be demonstrated.

Wittgenstein's maxim that process and result are the same is an extreme formulation of the position. Even that has a certain initial plausibility for examples of nonsystematic demonstrations, such as Cauchy's proof that the sum of the numbers of the faces and the vertices less the number of the edges of a polyhedron is always 2, and the solution of the Koenigsberg Bridge problem. One could argue for the thesis by concentrating (as Wittgenstein

---

[1] Similar reasoning might lead us to adopt the Axiom of Reducibility were it shown to be independent of the other axioms of the Ramified Theory of Types. The Axiom obviously holds for finite models, for there we can easily form predicative functions which define the extensions of impredicative functions, e.g., *x has all the properties of a great general* has the same extension as some function or other rather like x = Epaminondas . . . v x = Alexander . . . v x = Hannibal . . . v x = Caesar . . . v x = Sabutai . . . v x = Marlborough . . . v x = Napoleon . . . v x = Rommel.

does) on calculations, where the calculation seems to be a proof that the calculation can be done. I don't like this defence, since I doubt whether calculation is itself ever demonstration, notwithstanding the fact that Goedelian exercises seem finally to culminate in an elaborate but still elementary computation. I should prefer saying that the theorem is that there is a calculation that can be so regarded. Generalizing upon this, one can preserve *something* of Wittgenstein's doctrine. A demonstration shows that a certain construction exists, and that cannot be better effected than by exhibiting such a construction. One thinks here of the classical precedent of Euclidean geometry, where constructions were exhibited with proofs appended. But the doctrine applies best to nonsystematic examples. I recall the experience of a mathematician friend (the same one who showed me the 'shortest' proof of the Pythagorean Theorem) who was engaged to present TV lessons in elementary geometry to classes of second graders. Axiomatics was out. One week he taught them to bisect a line. The next week he showed them how to draw a circle, and then he asked how one might find the centre of a circle. Two children were reported to have seen the solution immediately. What I find interesting about this and also about our two examples given on pp. 87f. is the near impossibility of seeing the demonstrations that attend the conclusions as deductions from axioms. Where indeed *are* the axioms? Well, perhaps they are 'implicit'. Perhaps, but how do they figure as premisses? I do not deny that we could find derivational proofs from axioms for the claimed conclusions. But the proofs I have mentioned are not of that kind. I say that the proof gets us to see the construction in a certain way which may flick off and on and, indeed, we may actually have something rather more like a duck-rabbit situation than a derivation.[1]

I have read somewhere that compound interest was invented by the Genoese bankers of the fifteenth century. I can imagine that they could have supported their introduction of this new form of merchandising with the following demonstration: if liquidity has its price, then, in an ideal frictionless economy, interest should be compounded continuously, for a perfectly

---

[1] I once was set and solved the problem of showing that a triangle with two equal bisectors is isosceles. I have not been able to recapture the proof though I do recall that the conclusion came when I saw a relationship which, like the faces in the trees, has now disappeared into a jumble of lines.

rational investor could continuously withdraw and reinvest his principal with accrued interest. This kind of 'proof' must, I think, resemble the early and consequential discovery by the Babylonians of an explanation of why fields with equal perimeters do not produce equal yields, and the explanation of why Del Cano's log-book was off a day when he put in at a Portuguese port in Africa towards the end of the first circumnavigation of the world. I think these are the kinds of demonstrations Wittgenstein had most in mind. They do not proceed deductively from axioms; they take on their meaning from their direct connexions with an application which is immediate and palpable. At the same time, it also is evident that nature doesn't always behave as the demonstration seems to demand. The economy is not frictionless; it is too much trouble to be 'perfectly rational'; 'fertility' as well as area may affect the crop. But again the proof puts us into position to spot these other factors, and thus may be used as an instrument of conceptual control.

In everyday usage words like 'demonstration', 'proof', and 'inference', in company with 'explanation', 'elucidation' etc. cover activities which while essentially linguistic also go beyond the use of language to what can be gained in the way of creating conviction and organizing knowledge. The modern formal conception of proof as logical derivation, like the currently popular 'covering law' conception of explanation, would lop off the non-linguistic factors as something extraneously psychological and reduce the notions of demonstration and explanation to their purely linguistic components. Indeed, one of Goedel's achievements was to show how *formal* proofs could be regarded as purely linguistic structures. Still, subsumption is not enough to explain, and formal proof is demonstration only under important if implicit caveats.

Now, subsumption under general laws is a form of logical derivation: in reversal of that, I'm also inclined to think that mathematical demonstration is at its best a kind of explanation.

That thought taken together with the examples considered just above brings me back to 'concept formation'. The nonsystematic demonstrations we have been considering are successful only if they get us to see something in a new way, or if they reveal distinctions previously overlooked. They do that the more effectively, the more they also 'explain'; they are 'perspicuous' if not immediately convincing. I am, after reading Wittgenstein, frankly puzzled by the fact that there can be different proofs of the same theorems. But now, with an eye to examples selected from the little mathematics I learned at school, I am impressed by the fact that some proofs do explain better than others. Go back to the 'shortest' proof of the Pythagorean Theorem cited earlier which makes use of this construction.

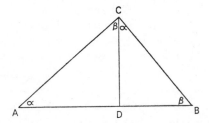

Compare this with another very convincing, 'short' proof using the construction

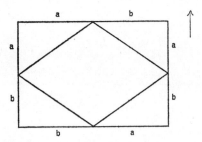

$(a+b)^2 = a^2+b^2+2ab$, where, of course, the four corner triangles have a combined area of *2ab*. I confess that I am still not sure that I see why the first shortest proof is a proof; I am perfectly convinced by the other. Nonetheless, I believe that the first proof is probably the 'better' one because it intimates an explanatory connexion with the fundamental principle that corresponding parts of similar figures have proportional magnitudes.[1]

One last example. All of us have seen the classical proof for the irrationality of $\sqrt{2}$ ascribed to Pythagoras. We begin by assuming

[1] Perhaps the other proof also intimates a deep explanation connected with consideration of symmetry. What I don't see at all are the connexions between these proofs, and with the others which idle minds have produced over more than two millennia.

that $2 = m^2/n^2$, where m and n are relatively prime. I once complained to a mathematician friend that, although I found this perfectly convincing, I felt that I didn't really understand what was happening. He sympathized and told me to look at the demonstration as a special case of the Unique Factorization Theorem. Now I understand (as I had 'implicitly' in school when I 'saw' that $\sqrt{5}$, $\sqrt[3]{10}$ and $\sqrt[3]{49}$ are all of them irrational). The Unique Factorization Theorem itself seems or once seemed to me perfectly obvious, though I confess that the standard proof, ascribed to Euclid, strikes me as 'unperspicuous'. I understand or would understand things better from some proofs of a given theorem than from others because the 'better' proof relates the conclusion more closely to the civil applications with which my thinking began—to the operations of adding and multiplying which support the theory of numbers or to the construction and use of Euclidean triangles for measuring areas.

IV

HUMAN BEINGS

John W. Cook

> Only of a living human being and what resembles (behaves
> like) a living human being can one say: it has sensations; it
> sees; is blind; hears; is deaf; is conscious or unconscious.
>
> WITTGENSTEIN

IT seems fair to say that there is no very general agreement on what
exactly Wittgenstein has contributed to our understanding of the
problem of other minds. Some will attribute this to the perplexing
nature of Wittgenstein's style, and perhaps there is some justice
in this. On the other hand, it may be that the difficulties that we
find in his style are partly the result of preconceptions that we bring
to our reading of him. When it comes to the problem of other
minds there is surely a readiness on our part to find the main
lines of his position running along certain well-known paths. We
expect to find some element of Cartesianism or some element of
behaviourism in his position, for these seem to divide up the field
without remainder. True, he may have disavowed certain consequences, such as the idea of a private language, that others
thought they saw in these alternatives, but he cannot have rejected
both in their entirety. Perhaps he struck a compromise by
adopting elements of each. Against this way of reading Wittgenstein I will try to show that he did indeed reject both Cartesianism
and behaviourism in their entirety. He rejects an element that
these alternatives fundamentally share, namely, a certain way of
saying what a human being is. In order to bring this element into
the open, I will begin by reviewing those features of philosophical
scepticism that give rise to the problems of other minds.

117

I

In his First Meditation Descartes makes clear the following features of philosophical scepticism: the sceptic is to set aside doubts about particular cases ('Has the cat been put out?', 'Is the gun loaded?') and instead is to search out grounds for calling in question an entire class of judgements. This is to be accomplished by undercutting in some way the ordinary sort of justifications we give for judgements of the class in question. Now scepticism thus understood has given rise to a set of demands that philosophers have usually tried to honour in the answers they have given to the sceptic. First, in answering the sceptic we are debarred from merely appealing to justifications of the ordinary sort ('I looked'), for it is precisely these that he purports to have undercut. (This is what Moore seemed so often to disregard.) Secondly, if the sceptic is to be answered on his own terms and we are to progress from merely moral certainty to metaphysical certainty, as Descartes would have put it, we must begin from premises that do not themselves have questionable presuppositions of any sort. We must find some way of grounding our ordinary judgements in what have been called 'protocol statements'. (For simplicity of exposition I will retain this phrase, drawing on the etymological significance of 'proto'.) Thirdly, this grounding of our ordinary judgements is to be accomplished by either (i) a justification of some extraordinary sort for making inferences from protocol statements, e.g., Descartes' appeal to the veracity of God, or (ii) a construction (in letter if not in spirit) of our ordinary judgements out of protocol sentences by purely formal means. (I will call these the demands of scepticism.) Philosophers, as I said, have usually honoured these demands. There have been exceptions, such as Moore and Thomas Reid, but their responses to the sceptic have proved to be more puzzling than helpful. Accordingly, modern philosophy has been chiefly a contest for finding suitable ways of meeting the sceptic's third demand. Thus, we have witnessed a succession of reductionists, on the one hand, and those they call metaphysicians, on the other. These are the lines, then, between which the skirmishes are carried on. Every so often a philosopher has tried to find middle ground, but the others call 'Foul' and the contest goes on with added subtleties.

This, in outline, is the background against which we read Wittgenstein. It will be well to review, then, the content of the sceptic's demands as regards the problem of other minds. The first demand requires that we set aside our ordinary justifications for the statements we make about other people's mental states, events, and processes, such as 'I know she is worried; I've been talking to her', 'I could see he was in pain; he was grimacing and holding his elbow', etc. (These must be excluded, if for no other reason, because 'She told me' and 'He was grimacing' seem to be, at least implicitly, statements of the sort the sceptic means to be calling in question.) The second demand is now the requirement that the protocol statements on which we ground any statements about other people's mental (or 'mental') states, events, and processes are to be statements about human bodies. (Behaviourists sometimes talk about descriptions of 'colourless movements'.) We might put this demand most graphically by saying that the protocol statements are to be free of any suggestion that the subjects to which they apply are essentially different from automata. The third demand is most commonly met either (i) by the argument from analogy, which is allowed to be less than what the sceptic will settle for but the best we can do if we are Cartesians, or (ii) by some form of behaviourism. Now let us ask where Wittgenstein is supposed to stand in response to the sceptic. There seem to be three interpretations: either Wittgenstein is trying to meet the third demand with his notion of criteria and is thus, despite his disclaimers, a subtle behaviourist; or he is carrying on, in a sophisticated way, Moore's tradition of refusing to accede to the first demand and is thus what might be called an 'ordinary language Cartesian'; or he is attempting to combine somehow these seemingly antithetical approaches and is thus perhaps the first crypto-Cartaviourist. What no one seems to have considered in all of this is what Wittgenstein has to say about the second demand and in particular the idea of 'body' or 'bodily movements' from which the whole problem begins. If in fact he advanced substantial considerations against this very root of the problem, he will have done something very different from anything suggested by current interpretations. It will be my claim in this essay that Wittgenstein struck at the root.

In order to make clear what such an approach to the problem would involve, it will be well to review the status of the second demand in the problem about the external world. There the demand is that we begin from protocol statements about sense-data or, more leniently, about appearances. I think it would now be widely conceded that the notion of sense-data is hopelessly confused and also that although we do understand and commonly make remarks about the appearances of things, these could not serve as the logical-epistemological foundation for our statements about such things as chocolate bars ('It's melted') and footballs ('It has a leak'). Some of the reasons for this can be stated briefly. First of all, it is obvious that children do not first master the language of appearances and then move on to construct or derive physical object statements. Moreover, there are good grounds for holding that there is a great deal in our physical object statements, e.g. words like 'melted' and 'leak', that could not occur in descriptions of appearances, and in any case learning the language of appearances logically presupposes a mastery of the language used in talking about physical objects. Indeed, the language of appearances is a highly sophisticated use of words. Who, after all, can easily describe hues and highlights and shadows and apparent convergence of lines and the like? And when do we take notice of such things? Children's drawings do not suggest that they take much notice of appearances. For these and other reasons the idea that the language of appearances constitutes an epistemologically basic language has now been pretty well abandoned. One of the additional reasons for this is that we no longer find plausible those sceptical arguments, such as the argument from illusion, that seemed to create the need for—and to give us the very idea of—a protocol language. (No one thought there were sense-data before they found such arguments appealing.) I make particular mention of this point because it illustrates the essential connexion between sceptical arguments and the idea of a basic description or protocol language of the sort the sceptic demands. Thus, philosophers who would answer the sceptic on his own terms by meeting the third demand in some way share an assumption that is far more fundamental than the differences there may be between their opposing ways of meeting the third demand. In the problem of other minds this means that behaviourism and the argument from analogy are brothers under the skin: both rest upon the assumption that we are forced to recognize descriptions (or observations) of bodily movements as being epistemologically basic in our knowledge of other persons. Now it is just this assumption that Wittgenstein rejects. I refer especially to sections 281-7 of *Philosophical Investigations*, where he first introduces questions about bodies, souls, and human beings, and also to the way in which he follows this up in sections 288-316 with an attack on the idea of an inward or private identification of pain or thinking.[1] What I want to bring out is the connexion between these two groups of passages. In order to do this, however, it will be necessary to begin by working back through the problem itself, for much of the published discussion of Wittgenstein's views is simply the result of having got the problem of other minds badly out of focus. I will begin, then, by asking what this problem is.

II

Consider how we are to state the problem of other minds. We might ask: 'Do other people have a mental life, as I do?' But this clearly won't do, for they are not people, surely, if they do not have thoughts, emotions, sensations, desires, and so on. After all, we do not mean to be asking in the ordinary way whether this or that person is in a coma or something of the sort. So we had better retreat to this formulation: 'Are the things that I take to be people really people, that is, do they have thoughts and emotions and so on?' But this, too, is unsatisfactory, for it is left unspecified what distinction we are being asked to make. If the question is whether they are people or not, we must ask: 'People as opposed to *what*?' And here the answer is not at all clear. If I look at my son playing near by and ask, 'What else might he be?', no answer readily suggests itself. He is clearly not a statue, nor is he an animated doll of the sort we sometimes see looking very lifelike. He is my own child, my own flesh and blood.[2]

The problem of other minds seems to be in danger of foundering

---

[1] At section 316 the discussion does not end but is given a new turn; the investigation of the concept *thinking* and others in sections 316-76 should be seen as containing a further account of the way in which Wittgenstein means to oppose the idea of an inward or private identification of a mental state or process. He makes this connexion explicit in the next group of passages, 377-97, and then in section 398 the discussion returns to the question raised in 281-7 about the nature of the *subject* of pain or thought. Here he first discusses (398-413) puzzles about the first person pronoun and the idea that the 'self' is discerned by an inward gaze, and he then concludes the discussion of the whole topic by taking up questions about human beings, souls, and automata (414-27). He comes back to the topic in Part II, p. 178.

[2] See *Philosophical Investigations*, p. 178.

at the outset. It is clear, at least, that we cannot get the problem stated so long as we allow the concept *human being* (or *person* or *child*) to have its usual place. Somehow we must shunt it aside by setting some other concept over against it. Descartes sought to raise a doubt about the furniture of the world by supposing that he dreamed, and in this way he could talk not only of ships and shoes and beeswax but also of dreams of these. It is just such a move that is required if we are to launch the problem of other minds. But this move, too, ought to be found in the *Meditations*, for wasn't it Descartes himself who launched the problem? *Sum res cogitans.* How did Descartes manage this?

He began with the following reminder about himself: 'As though I were not a man who habitually sleeps at night and has the same impressions (or even wilder ones) in sleep as these [mad]men do when awake!' The reminder is that he goes to sleep and dreams. But then he continues: 'When I reflect more carefully on this, I am bewildered; and my very bewilderment confirms the idea of my being asleep.' This provides Descartes with that challenge to his former opinions that he was looking for: he may be only dreaming that he sees and hears. It is the next sentence, however, that approaches our present problem: 'Well, suppose I am dreaming, and these particulars, that I open my eyes, shake my head, put out my hand, are incorrect; suppose even that I have no such hand, no such body. . . .'[1] Here we have the beginning of an answer to our question: with the supposition that he is dreaming Descartes sees a place to enter a wedge between himself and his body, a wedge that is driven further in the remaining Meditations. But there is a difficulty here. Descartes begins by reminding himself that he is 'a man who habitually sleeps at night' and dreams, and he adds that these dreams occur while 'I am undressed and lying in bed'. This is Descartes' beginning and the point at which we must grasp what he says. There is no difficulty, of course, in understanding at least a part of this. People go to bed, usually undressed; they sleep, calmly or restlessly, and they dream. Dreams, of course, are what people tell when they wake up or perhaps write in a diary or keep to themselves. So a dreamer here (and this includes Descartes) is a human being: he gets dressed and undressed, sleeps on a bed or

---

[1] *Descartes: Philosophical Writings* (Edinburgh, 1954), eds. G. E. M. Anscombe and P. T. Geach.

pallet, tells dreams while eating breakfast, and so on. If this is
what we are to understand by Descartes' opening remark, we need
not put up resistance yet. But then comes the wedge: 'suppose
even that I have no such hand, no such body'. Here we must call
a halt. We were to think of Descartes as a man who, undressed
and in bed, often dreams. It was only with that understanding that
we were able to take his first step with him. Does this still stand?
If so, what is this 'body' that he now supposes himself not to have?
Can he, without this 'body', sleep, either calmly or restlessly, and
dream? Or has Descartes unwittingly contradicted himself here?
Has he appealed to the possibility of dreaming only to take back
something that the very possibility of dreaming itself requires? This
does appear to be the case. But if that is so, then we can go no
further with him. Either we are to think of him—and he is to
think of himself—as a man who, undressed and in bed, often
dreams, and then we understand him, or he takes this back and
wipes out all he has said. And this holds for the remaining
Meditations, for everything that Descartes goes on to say in the
Meditations is said under the supposition that he may be dreaming.
Whatever sort of philosophical doubts this may raise, there is
at least one thing certain; if he should ask himself 'What am I?',
he can answer that he is a man who sleeps, undressed and in bed,
and often dreams. To take back this beginning is to take back
everything.

So the wedge that Descartes would drive between himself and
his body is never really driven. Or rather, no place is found for
the wedge to enter. For it is not that we understand about
Descartes *and his body*. We understand only about Descartes, that
philosopher who habitually undressed and went to bed at night
and whose dreams, by his own testimony, were sometimes wilder
than the fantasies of madmen. But this is not to say that we understand only about his body. No, to say that we understand only
about Descartes is to say neither more nor less than we mean, for
no place has been found yet for the word 'body'—at least not in
the special sense (if it is a sense) that Descartes requires. This is a
point we tend to forget. Descartes introduced a highly extraordinary use of the word 'body'. He has to be understood to be
using it always in the context of his distinction between *himself*
and his body. So his use of the word is not at all like these: 'His
body was covered with mosquito bites', 'His body was found at

the bottom of the cliff', 'He has a strong body but no brains', and so on. In saying such things as these we do not use 'body' as the one side of a Cartesian distinction. We are not saying, for instance, 'His body, but not his mind, was covered with mosquito bites'. That would be utter nonsense. If I say that someone's body was covered with mosquito bites, I could also say 'He was covered, etc.' The word 'body' comes in here as part of the emphasis: not just his ankles and wrists, but his back and stomach, too. Again, in speaking of a corpse we can say either 'His body was found, etc.' or 'He was found dead, etc.' The word 'body' in the first of these is used to make the contrast between dead and alive. No special ontology need come in here. As for the third sentence in the above list, it might be found in a requested letter of recommendation, and from it we should take the warning that the man can do heavy work but should not be expected to go at his work with much intelligence. In these and in other ordinary cases our understanding of the word 'body' is tied to particular contexts to a variety of particular distinctions of the kind just illustrated, and none of these provides a place to drive a conceptual wedge between Descartes and his body. But once again, this should not lead us to conclude: Then Descartes was *only* a body. For what distinction would that be making? It was not, after all, a corpse that wrote the *Meditations*.

There is a bit of a clue, in what Descartes says, to how he may have failed to realize that he was introducing an extraordinary use of the word 'body'. He says: 'suppose even that I have no hand, no such body', and thus it looks as though he supposed that 'hand' and 'body' are words of the same sort or that 'hand' and 'body' are related as 'shirt' and 'clothing' are, so that one could work up from supposing that you had no hand, no foot, etc. to supposing that you had no body, as you might work up from supposing you had no shirt, no coat, etc. to supposing that you had no clothing. This would perhaps be encouraged by the fact that we do use both the expressions 'my whole body' and 'my whole suit of clothing', and we also say 'He lost a hand' as well as 'He lost a shirt'. But the parallel fails just where it is crucial for Descartes. I could understand, given a certain context, a man's believing that he had no right hand, that he was a one-armed man, but I can make no sense of a man's believing that he has no body, that he has never had a body. I might have occasion to worry about a child being born with no hands, but there is no occasion to worry about a child being born with no body. And this is not merely because bodies are required for birth. Bodies are not born; they are stillborn. What are born are babies, human beings.

We may summarize our results as follows: Descartes' use of the word 'body' presupposes that he has driven his wedge, that he has provided the right sort of contrast between 'I' and 'my body', but on the other hand there seems to be no place for his wedge to be driven unless his use of the word 'body' is itself presupposed, and these requirements are incompatible. (If anyone should wonder about the locution 'my body' and ask what the body belongs to if not the mind, he need only remind himself of the locution 'my mind'.)[1]

We began by trying to formulate the problem of other minds and encountered a difficulty in discovering what could be contrasted with a human being in such a way as to allow the problem to arise. In turning to Descartes we hoped to find the required contrast in his use of the word 'body', but it now appears that this has only further exposed the difficulty. Is the case hopeless, then? To answer this it is necessary to take notice of a reply that might be made to the foregoing arguments. The reply is this. Names of mental states, events, and processes, including the word 'dreaming', get their meaning from private ostensive definitions. For this reason it does not follow that if Descartes begins from the reminder that he dreams, he must allow ever after that he is a man who goes to bed and sleeps. To speak of dreaming carries no such implication, for the state we call 'dreaming' is something known to us by means of introspection or inner sense, and introspection discloses nothing of a bodily nature.[2]

It is to this account of words like 'dream' and 'pain' and 'thinking' that we must ultimately trace the problem of other minds. Putting the matter in unabashed metaphor, it is the idea that since

---

[1] Frank Ebersole once remarked in another context that philosophers often talk of people as if they were speaking of zombies, which the dictionary describes as corpses that, by sorcery, are made to move and act as if alive. At the time I did not fully appreciate the significance of this remark, but very likely it did something to help focus my thoughts for the present essay. (See also the excellent chapter on human actions in Ebersole's book, *Things We Know* (Eugene, Oregon, 1967), pp. 282–304.)

[2] See Descartes' *Principles*, I, xlvi, lxviii, where he maintains that what is clearly and distinctly perceived as a sensation is something that 'takes place within ourselves' and involves nothing of a corporeal nature.

the inner sense that reveals our mental states does not discover anything bodily, it must be possible to conceptually skim off a mental side of our nature leaving a physical remainder called 'the body'.[1] It is this idea of a physical remainder, the 'senseless body' which some mind may 'have', that gives us our problem, for it is a consequence of this idea that when we look at another person all that we really see is something that, in itself, is no more an appropriate subject of pain or thought than a stone is. Philosophers have puzzled over the question 'Why shouldn't we regard a complicated automaton as we do a person', but what ought to puzzle us is the question 'If all that we see of other "people" are "senseless bodies", how could we have got as far as connecting the concepts of thought and sensation with them at all?' The argument from analogy should not impress us here unless, as Wittgenstein saw (283), we are willing to go a step further and allow that perhaps stones have pains and machines think. For if I identify pain and thinking inwardly, if I do not learn these concepts in learning a common language, then my concepts *pain* and *thinking* are not essentially related to living human beings (in the ordinary sense), and so my body might turn to stone or into a pillar of salt while my pain continues. But in that case I should allow that the pebbles I walk on may be in pain, too. It would be gratuitous to restrict the concept to human beings and to what more or less resemble (behave like) them.[2] But the real difficulty here is not to account for our restricting our concept of pain to human beings but to account for how we extend it beyond our own case. For on the supposition we are here considering (that I learn what 'pain' means from my own pains) it will not do to say

[1] This idea is seldom made as explicit as it was by C. J. Ducasse, who wrote: 'What thought, desire, sensation, and other mental states are like, each of us can observe directly by introspection; and what introspection reveals is that they do not in the least resemble muscular contraction, or glandular secretion, or any other known bodily events. No tampering with language can alter the observable fact that thinking is one thing and muttering quite another; that the feeling called anger has no resemblance to the bodily behaviour which usually goes with it; or that an act of will is not in the least like anything we find when we open the skull and examine the brain. Certain mental events are doubtless connected in some way with bodily events, but they are not those bodily events themselves.' *Is Life After Death Possible?* (Berkeley, 1948), p. 7.

[2] Locke was bold enough to draw this conclusion. Having said (*Essay* II, I, 4) that we get the ideas of the operations of our own minds from 'internal sense', he can later see 'no contradiction' in the supposition that God might give to some 'systems of matter' the powers to think, feel, and enjoy. (*Essay* IV, III, 6.)

that I extend the concept to others by simply supposing that they sometimes have the same thing that I have so often had, since this explanation presupposes the very use of words, namely, 'same sensation', that we ought to be explaining (350-2). But this means that I could never get as far as using the argument from analogy or anything like it. I could not even understand the question whether there are other beings that feel what I call 'pain'. The only recourse here is to admit that I cannot extend the use of 'pain' from myself to others and to hold to a strict logical behaviourism: when I say that other people are in pain, I am merely speaking of the movements of those senseless bodies that I see. What this would fail to account for, of course, is my pity or concern for them. Since I can no more think of my children as *suffering*, in the sense that applies to me, than I could think this of a stone, my pity for them should strike me as a logical incongruity. It's as if I were to fall passionately in love with a fleck of dust.

It should now be possible to get an understanding of Wittgenstein's discussion of the problem of other minds. In particular, we can see the connexion between those passages (281-7) in which he first introduces questions about bodies, souls, and human beings and the next group of passages (288-316) in which he attacks the idea of an inward or private identification of mental states, events, and processes. The essential point is that if there is confusion in the idea of an inward, private, identification, then there is also confusion in the idea of conceptually skimming off a mental side of our nature, leaving a physical remainder called 'the body'. The philosophical idea of a 'senseless body' must be dropped. But in that case we must also reject the idea that when we look at another person we see only a 'body', i.e., something which is no more a possible subject of pain or thinking than a stone would be. And finally, in rejecting *that* idea, we eliminate the only grounds of scepticism with regard to other 'minds' and in this way eliminate, too, the only source of the plausibility of behaviourism. In short, by rejecting the idea of a private identification, we get back our ordinary concept of a living human being. In place of 'colourless bodily movements' we now have human actions and reactions; we are back in the world of people running from danger, telling us their woes, nursing painful bruises, grimacing, frowning in disapproval, and so on. Thus,

Wittgenstein's primary contribution to the problem of other minds was his attack on the idea of a private language, of a private identification of mental states and processes. Although he has a number of other important things to say about such words as 'pain' and 'thinking', these cannot be understood apart from a grasp of his primary contribution. His reminders about such words will be of no use until we have eliminated the philosophical notion of 'body' and have brought human beings back into our discussions. I will return later on to consider some of these reminders and in particular to consider the objection that may now have occurred to the reader, that it must be a question-begging move to make the concept *human beings* primary in any account of mental predicates.

At the beginning of this essay I remarked that our difficulty in understanding Wittgenstein's contribution to the problem of other minds might be the result of preconceptions that we bring to our reading of him. These preconceptions should now be clear. The philosophical ideas of 'body' and 'bodily movement' have simply become unquestioned notions; they set for us what we take to be the problem of other minds. The problem, as we understand it, is that of grounding or justifying our ascriptions of mental states and processes on observations of bodily movements. Thus, when Wittgenstein speaks of 'behaviour', we inevitably read into this our own concession to the sceptic; we think of Wittgenstein as trying to solve the same problem that others have tried to solve with behaviourism or the argument from analogy, only it is not clear what his own solution comes to. In struggling with this people have seen that he allows no place for the argument from analogy or at least that he makes no appeal to such an argument, and this has given rise to suggestions that, despite all he says to the contrary, Wittgenstein settled for some form of behaviourism. In defence of this suggestion interpreters have fastened on his concept of criteria and have argued that he puts forth a 'criteriological' theory of meaning that could not amount to anything but a subtle form of behaviourism. I believe that I have already given sufficient reasons for dismissing this interpretation, but because the misunderstandings about the rôle of criteria have run so deep, I will digress from my main topic to say something about this.

III

The view that I want to discuss is that Wittgenstein came to talk about criteria as a means of solving the problem of other minds, where that problem is understood in the usual way as a problem of our *knowledge* of other minds. This interpretation has been set forth in detail in a recent article by C. S. Chihara and J. A. Fodor,[1] and it will be useful to look carefully at what they say. They first give us their account of Wittgenstein's aims in the following passage:

> Among the philosophical problems Wittgenstein attempted to dissolve is the 'problem of other minds'. One aspect of this hoary problem is the question: What justification, if any, can be given for the claim that one can tell, on the basis of someone's behavior, that he is in a certain mental state? To this question, the sceptic answers: No good justification at all.

Just what this claim is that needs justification is not explained to us at this point, but apparently it is to be thought of as a claim made in answer to the sceptic. Of course, whether it is a claim that one should make will depend upon what it is that the sceptic denies and why he denies it. Is he thinking (quite correctly) that the movements of a 'senseless body' would provide no logical foothold for words like 'pain' and 'thinking' and then supposing (quite incorrectly) that all we see of other 'persons' are such 'bodily movements'? Apparently Chihara and Fodor are so oblivious to there being any difficulty about this philosophical idea of body that they do not even see it as the challengeable point in the sceptic's position, which on their view seems to arise out of nothing. They characterize scepticism as follows:

> It is assumed as a premiss that there are no logical or conceptual relations between propositions about mental states and propositions about behavior in virtue of which propositions asserting that a person behaves in a certain way provide support, grounds, or justification for ascribing the mental states to that person. From this the sceptic deduces that he has no compelling reason for supposing that any person other than himself is ever truly said to feel pains, draw inferences, have motives, etc.[2]

[1] 'Operationalism and Ordinary Language: A Critique of Wittgenstein', *American Philosophical Quarterly*, Vol. II, pp. 281–95.
[2] *Ibid.*, p. 281.

Now because these authors do not see that scepticism arises out of a challengeable notion of 'body', they can only understand Wittgenstein to be meeting the sceptic head on. 'Wittgenstein's way of dealing with the sceptic,' they tell us, 'is to attack his premiss by trying to show that there do exist conceptual relations between statements about behavior and statements about mental events, processes, and states.'[1] We are also told that on Wittgenstein's view there is a 'logical connexion . . . between pain behaviour and pain' and that 'Wittgenstein used the term "criterion" to mark this special connexion'.[2] The position thus described is then further characterized in the following way: 'To hold that the sceptical premiss is false is *ipso facto* to commit oneself to some version of *logical behaviourism* where by "logical behaviourism" we mean the doctrine that there are logical or conceptual relations of the sort denied by the sceptical premiss.'[3] In a footnote to this sentence Chihara and Fodor offer the following, highly significant, justification for using the word 'behaviourism' in the classification of Wittgenstein's philosophical position:

> . . . insofar as C. L. Hull can be classified as a behaviorist, there does seem to be grounds for our classification. Hull's view, as we understand it, is that mental predicates are in no sense 'eliminable' in favor of behavioral predicates, but that it is a condition upon their coherent employment that they be severally related to behavioral predicates and that some of these relations be logical rather than empirical—a view that is strikingly similar to the one we attribute to Wittgenstein. Cf. C. L. Hull, *Principles of Behavior* (New York, 1943).

This comparison of Wittgenstein with Hull is significant for the reason that it shows most clearly what Chihara and Fodor understand by the word 'behaviour', which they use in describing the positions of both men. The authors are surely aware that in *Principles of Behavior* what is thought of as 'behaviour' is what Hull calls (in contradistinction to purposive action) 'colourless

---

[1] *Ibid.*, p. 282.

[2] *Ibid.*, p. 283. Chihara and Fodor cannot, I think, be putting this in just the way they want, for it would seem to be merely redundant to say that there is a logical connexion between *pain*-behaviour and pain. What they mean, I suppose, is that Wittgenstein thought that there is a logical connexion between such and such 'bodily movements' and pain.

[3] *Ibid.*, p. 282.

movements'.[1] Hull, in other words, is engaged in an attempt to respond to the sceptic's demands on the sceptic's own terms. So one point that becomes clear in this comparison of Wittgenstein with Hull is that these authors think of Wittgenstein as using his notion of criteria to connect mental states with 'bodies'. A second point that begins to emerge here will be seen if one recalls that it is Hull's stated aim to begin from 'colourless movements and mere receptor impulses as such' and build up (or 'deduce') such concepts as *purposive action, intelligence, intention* and other mental verbs and predicates. Now Chihara and Fodor see clearly enough that Wittgenstein did not think that there was a *deductive* relation to be found here, but it is also clear that they believe that he was engaged in the same programme as Hull and differing from him, perhaps, only in settling for a looser logical relation. So the second point that emerges from the comparison is that they think of Wittgenstein as having held an empiricist theory of 'concept formation', which they describe as the view that in learning mental predicates we are learning 'criterial connexions which map these terms severally onto characteristic patterns of behaviour'.[2] In section II of their essay they assert that Wittgenstein held 'an operationalistic view of the meaning of certain sorts of predicates', including such words as 'pain', 'motive', and 'dream'. Since this is a highly implausible interpretation of Wittgenstein, given his general remarks about language, it is important to see that their sole reason for thinking that Wittgenstein held such a theory of language is their belief that he meant to be replying to scepticism on the sceptic's own terms ('bodily movements') and that he introduced his concept of criteria in order to accomplish this. Wittgenstein's criteria, on their view, are quite particular patterns of behaviour that are related, in some way, to the meaning of a word such as 'pain', where 'behaviour', once again, is thought of as being 'bodily movements'.

I want now to show that this interpretation is wrong on both counts. That Wittgenstein did not introduce his concept of criteria in order to answer the sceptic will have to be shown by making clear the quite different problem for which he did introduce it. I will come to this presently. As for the other part of the interpretation, we have already seen reason to reject the idea that

---

[1] *Principles of Behavior* (New York, 1943), p. 25.
[2] *Ibid.*, p. 292.

Wittgenstein meant to answer the sceptic on his own terms and so thought of behaviour as 'bodily movements'. Indeed, it is by rejecting this very notion of 'body' and 'bodily movement' that Wittgenstein undercuts the whole problem. It is true that he sometimes speaks of certain behaviour as being a criterion for something, but we must see whether what he counts as behaviour is anything that the sceptic would be prepared to allow. In his discussion of 'saying something to oneself in the imagination' Wittgenstein speaks of criteria in the following passage: 'Our criterion for someone's saying something to himself is what he tells us and the rest of his behaviour; and we only say that someone speaks to himself if, in the ordinary sense of the words, he *can speak* And we do not say it of a parrot; nor of a gramophone' (344). Here what Wittgenstein calls 'our criterion' includes someone telling us something, and it is clear from the contrast made with parrots and gramophones that he is thinking of this as a human action and not merely certain sounds emanating from some 'senseless body' (whether the shape be human or otherwise). Also what the person tells us might be: 'When I saw him enter the room, I said to myself . . . ,' and surely the sceptic does not want to concede at the outset that 'persons' (or 'bodies') *see*. Moreover, Wittgenstein's specification here includes that the person in question speaks a language, and this means that he does such things as answering questions, giving orders, telling jokes, giving directions, asking advice, stating his business, giving lectures, confessing his ignorance, complaining of aches and pains, and so on. In short, before something can be understood as a criterion for a man's saying something to himself, there must already be known about him all of the sorts of things that the sceptic means to be calling in question. So by 'behaviour' Wittgenstein cannot have meant anything like what the sceptic must mean. But in that case reference to criteria cannot be relevant to scepticism. This point will be even clearer if we notice that in some cases Wittgenstein even counts sensations and thoughts as criteria. In one passage (160) he presents two cases of which he asks: 'Should we here allow his sensations to count as a criterion for his reading or not reading?' In the first of these cases it is clear that the man's sensations would be irrelevant, but in the second case this is not so. Elsewhere Wittgenstein gives an example in which a man's having 'thought of the formula' is both his and our justification (criterion) for saying that he knew how to continue the expansion of a series. Then this explanation is added: 'The words "Now I know how to go on" were correctly used when he thought of the formula; that is, given such circumstances as that he had learnt algebra, had used such formulae before' (179). Now if thoughts and sensations are among the things that Wittgenstein will count as criteria, then not only are criteria not at all the sort of thing that it would be relevant to mention in replying to the sceptic but also criteria are not in every case behaviour, even in the ordinary sense of the word. There seem to be no grounds here for thinking of Wittgenstein as a behaviourist.

It should by now be clear that it must have been some quite different problem from the problem of other minds that led Wittgenstein to introduce his concept of criteria. And in fact it is not difficult to discover what that problem is. Since much of the misunderstanding has arisen from that passage in *The Blue Book* (pp. 24–5) in which Wittgenstein first introduced the pair of terms 'symptom' and 'criterion', it will be well to begin by looking there. He tells us that he is introducing these terms 'in order to avoid certain elementary confusions', and from the context of the few pages immediately preceding and following this remark it is clear that these are confusions that arise out of asking 'What is expecting?' or 'What is knowledge?' or 'What is time?' and so on while hoping to 'find some common element' in all of the applications of the general term. Here is Wittgenstein's account of the difficulty:

> We said that it was a way of examining the grammar (the use) of the word 'to know' to ask ourselves what, in the particular case we are examining, we should call 'getting to know'. There is a temptation to think that this question is only vaguely relevant, if relevant at all, to the question: 'what is the meaning of the word "to know"?' We seem to be on a side-track when we ask the question 'What is it like in this case "to get to know"?' But this question really is a question concerning the grammar of 'to know'. . . .

When, several paragraphs later, Wittgenstein explains the words 'criterion' and 'symptom' it is clear that he has two purposes in mind. The first is to use this pair of terms to characterize the idea that there must be a common element in all cases of the application of a general term; the second is to characterize his own objection to that idea. The first of these comes to this: we have the idea that there is a 'law in the way a word is used' (p. 27), some single test for deciding the applicability of the general term to particular cases. We can call this 'the defining criterion'. Now if there were such a defining criterion, then whatever else might be true of the various particular cases will be only indirectly relevant to deciding whether the general term is applicable. Such a piece of evidence can be called 'a symptom'. Now the philosophical idea that there must always be a common element in virtue of which a general term applies can be described as the idea that for such words as 'expecting' and 'knowledge' there should be a defining criterion. It is because we have this idea that we are tempted to say, when particular cases are brought up for consideration, that the varying details of those cases are irrelevant to the question 'What is expecting?' We think the details, since they are not common to all cases, are only symptoms and so have no bearing on the grammar of 'to expect'.—And now I think we can see the rationale for introducing this pair of terms. First of all, the claim that in the various particular cases of expecting we can discover only symptoms is self-contradictory, for how could we set out to search through these cases for that common element which we complain of not finding if we did not know that they were cases of expecting. If there must be a defining criterion, and we admit to not having discovered it (but only 'symptoms'), then we should also allow that we do not even know whether we have been considering cases of expecting. But this is absurd. Accordingly, since we did know that these were cases of expecting, it must be that the idea of a defining criterion is a piece of confusion.[1] Our demand that we find the 'common element' is

> a very one-sided way of looking at language. In practice we very rarely use language as such a calculus . . . We [in philosophizing] are unable clearly to circumscribe the concepts we use; not because

[1] The foregoing argument is not made explicit in *The Blue Book*, although the conclusion is stated in several different ways on page 25. That the argument is not made explicit here is perhaps to be explained by the fact that these notes were 'meant only for the people who heard the lectures' (p. v), where Wittgenstein may have made explicit use of the argument. In *Philosophical Investigations* he makes use of the argument in section 153, which concludes: 'And if I say it is hidden—then how do I know what I have to look for? I am in a muddle.'

we don't know their real definition, but because there is no real 'definition' to them. To suppose there *must* be would be like supposing that whenever children play with a ball they play a game according to strict rules' (p. 25).

Not only do we not 'use language according to strict rules—it hasn't been taught us by means of strict rules, either'. But if the idea of a 'defining criterion' is a bogus notion, then in considering the details of particular cases we are not considering merely 'symptoms'. These details, which vary from one case of expecting or knowing to another, *can* show us something about the grammar of the words. That is, it is useful in philosophy to ask ourselves what in this case and in that case would enable us to recognize (would justify us in saying) that someone was expecting a visitor. In one case it might be that the man is pacing up and down the room, occasionally looking at his watch, and at the same time talking about how good it will be to see his old friend again. In another case it might be that, although he is not thinking about the expected visitor at all, he has the man's name on his appointment calendar and has laid out certain items in preparation for the man's visit. That is, if we were asked how we knew that this person expected a visitor, *these* are the sorts of things we would mention. The relevant point, then, is that there is not some one thing, the same in all cases, that justifies our use of the word 'expecting', and if anything has a right to be called a 'criterion' it is (Wittgenstein seems to imply) such details of particular cases that we would find it relevant to take notice of in our everyday life.

It is worth remarking, perhaps, since the opposite has been so often supposed, that Wittgenstein nowhere suggests that a philosopher, by using this concept of criteria, can bring out everything that is of philosophical interest in the use of a word. It is only the misguided inclination to see Wittgenstein as a behaviourist that would lead one to think that he intended to offer an 'operational analysis' of the meaning of a word like 'expecting'. The words 'symptom' and 'criterion' were introduced as a means of dealing with a certain philosophical problem, as a way of breaking the hold of a certain picture of the workings of language, namely, the idea that words are learned and used according to strict rules and that accordingly we can reject as irrelevant the varying details of particular cases when asking, for example, 'What is expecting?' In *Philosophical Investigations* he expresses this idea by saying that we think there is 'nothing at all but symptoms' (354). This is explained in an earlier passage as follows:

> In case (162) the meaning of the word 'to derive' stood out clearly. But we told ourselves that this was only a quite special case of deriving; deriving in a quite special garb, which had to be stripped from it if we wanted to see the essence of deriving. So we stripped those particular coverings off; but then deriving itself disappeared. —In order to find the real artichoke, we divested it of its leaves. For certainly (162) was a special case of deriving; what is essential to deriving, however, was not hidden beneath the surface of this case, but this 'surface' was one case out of a family of cases of deriving.
>
> And in the same way we also use the word 'to read' for a family of cases. And in different circumstances we apply different criteria for a person's reading. (164)

One point to gather from this passage is that in so far as Wittgenstein uses the concept of criteria to oppose the notion of 'the hidden', this is *not* the notion that arises in the problem of other minds, the problem that grows out of Descartes' metaphysical use of 'body' but rather that notion of the hidden that arises out of looking for a common element and finding none. I take it that Wittgenstein's opposition to this notion of 'the hidden' does not make him a behaviourist.

Several misunderstandings can be cleared up by noticing how the word 'criterion' comes into Wittgenstein's treatment of two related confusions that can grow out of the search for a common element in all cases of expecting or understanding or thinking. The first of these can be roughly indicated by considering the word 'calculate'. We use this word to say what someone is doing when he is using paper and pencil to calculate how much material will be needed for a building job, but there are also cases in which we say that someone has calculated although nothing is written down or said aloud. The latter we sometimes speak of as 'calculating in the head'. Now if we expect to find in cases of the two sorts a common element which will be what calculating really is, we will immediately want to say that the use of paper and pencil is no part of the essence, since this is not common to the two sorts of cases. We will want to say that the essence of calculating is some quite particular mental process to which the learning of arithmetic in the usual way, i.e., with written and spoken calculations, is inessential. (See 385 and 344.) Now it is cases of this sort that Wittgenstein has in mind when he says that 'the fluctuation in grammar between criteria and symptoms makes it look as if there were nothing at all but symptoms' (354). That is, because we learn the word 'multiply', for example, in cases in which someone, teaching us, works out problems on paper (in which case it is indifferent to us whether he uses his results for anything further on these occasions), and because later on, when we speak of a man's calculating in his head, it is *not* indifferent whether he uses the result (here a criterion would be his setting his saw in a certain place or drawing a line or gathering up the right amount of material after taking some measurements and pausing to think), we have a 'fluctuation' of symptoms and criteria. We keep the same word, 'calculate', even though what was a criterion in the first sort of case drops out in the second. Noticing this, we may think that, because it is sometimes possible to calculate without writing or speaking, it would have been possible to calculate had we *never* had a written or spoken language (arithmetic). Moreover, this same idea will occur to us with respect to concepts other than calculating, for we have similar shifts in the following pairs of cases: 'speaking(aloud)' and 'speaking to oneself in the imagination' (344-8); the use of 'expecting' both for cases in which the expectant person is thinking and talking about what he expects and for cases in which he is not (572-83); and the use of 'thinking' both for cases in which the thinker is writing or talking and for cases in which he is neither writing nor talking (318-42). In each of these cases we may be tempted to suppose that the essence of speaking, expecting, or thinking is something that could be identified apart from the mastery of language, and as a result we get such questions as 'Could a deaf mute who had learned no language still speak to himself in the imagination?' (348), 'Can a machine think?' (359-360), and so on. Now it is important to notice exactly the way in which Wittgenstein treats this kind of idea. He does not do so simply by saying that there are certain criteria for thinking, etc. He does not, that is, argue in the manner one would expect him to if he thought of criteria in the way described by Chihara and Fodor. Instead, there are a number of quite different considerations brought to bear on the problem. One is simply the use of analogies (316, 365). Another is to call into question the premise

'What sometimes happens might always happen' by giving some clear counter examples (345: see also p. 227). Still another is to remind us that a misleading metaphor can lead us to think that something that is logically primary in a use of words is really inessential (354–6).

The second and related confusion in connexion with which Wittgenstein uses the concept of criteria can be seen by comparing the following passages:

> When we do philosophy, we should like to hypostatize feelings where there are none. They serve to explain our thoughts to us. (598)

> ... We are tempted to say: the one real criterion for anybody's *reading* is the conscious act of reading, of reading the sounds off from the letter. (159)

> In order to get clear about the meaning of the word 'think' we watch ourselves while we think; what we observe will be what the word means!—But this concept is not used like that. (316)

> 'But you surely cannot deny that, for example, in remembering, an inner process takes place.'— ... When one says 'Still, an inner process does take place here'—one wants to go on: 'After all, you *see* it'. And it is this inner process that one means by the word 'remembering'. (305)

> How should we counter someone who told us that with *him* understanding was an inner process?—How would we counter him if he said that with him knowing how to play chess was an inner process? —We should say that when we want to know if he can play chess we aren't interested in anything that goes on inside him.—And if he replies that this is in fact just what we are interested in, that is, we are interested in whether he can play chess—then we shall have to draw his attention to the criteria which would demonstrate his capacity, and on the other hand to the criteria for the 'inner states'. (p. 181)

What Wittgenstein is suggesting in these passages is that we tend to assimilate concepts of one sort to concepts of a quite different sort, and this comes about in the following way. Since a person can read or think or remember or understand something without, on the particular occasion, *saying* anything, we are tempted to exclude the mastery of language from consideration when asking what thinking is, what understanding is, etc. Accordingly, in our search for the essence of each of these we gravitate towards a kind of concept, namely, *sensation*, that can be applied to a subject that has no mastery of language. (Brutes and infants can have sensations.) Putting the matter in another way, we concentrate on the 'silent' cases of thinking or understanding or remembering and 'look into ourselves' for the essential element, i.e., take notice of feelings, images, words going through our head, and so on. In this way we come to assimilate concepts like *thinking, understanding, remembering,* and so on to sensation words. (See p. 231.) Now one of Wittgenstein's ways of opposing this is to ask us to compare, for example, the criteria for understanding or knowing how to play chess and the criteria for mental states (pp. 59 and 181). What will come out of such an investigation are such things as the following. We might say to someone, 'Raise your finger the moment the pain stops', but not, 'Raise your finger the moment you no longer know how to play chess'. At the very least there will be this difference: to be able to say whether the pain has stopped I need not try to do anything, whereas I might need to try reciting some rules of chess or try making a few moves in order to learn whether I could still play chess. (Contrast 'in pain' with 'sore to the touch'.) Again I could confidently plan to deceive someone into thinking that I am in pain, i.e. plan to act the part without being in pain, but I could not, by acting the part of a chess player, deceive someone who knew the game into thinking that I could play chess—or at least I could not do so without the aid of a confederate giving me signals. Or again, I might be shown by someone that I only imagined that I understood a certain word, that the explanation I would have given of it or the use I would have made of it is actually confused, whereas I could not be shown by someone that my arthritic fingers do not really hurt, that I haven't been in pain at all. Now a misunderstanding can arise about Wittgenstein's use of such considerations as these. For it might look as though he meant to deny that thoughts and images are ever essential to playing chess, understanding, remembering, and so on. But this is not at all what he means to deny. He is saying rather that it requires certain surroundings in order for there to be such a thing as the thoughts of a chess player or for an image that I have to be the image of the expression on a certain man's face. His point is succinctly illustrated in the following passage: 'The words "Now I know how to go on" were correctly used when he thought of the formula: that is, given such circumstances as that he had learnt algebra, had used such formulae before' (179). In such a case if the man had not thought of the formula, he might not have known how to go on with the series of numbers. But Wittgenstein's point is that it is not from an inventory of the man's present mental contents that either he or someone else can see that he knows some algebra or that he even knows how to count. Or rather, since his present mental contents include his thought of the *formula*, i.e., something algebraic, we had better say that what is 'present' in this sense is essentially connected with what has gone before. (See p. 174.) A thought, then, is nothing like a sensation.

IV

Let us return now to the problem of other minds. At the end of section II I suggested that Wittgenstein's rejection of the Cartesian notion of 'body' and his insistence on making the concept *human being* primary might strike someone as being a question-begging move. One may want to know how we get that concept in the first place and what right Wittgenstein has to inject it into the discussion of the problem without providing a justification. This is the point I want now to speak to, and I will approach it through a brief discussion of the argument from analogy.

Mill, in his classic statement of this argument, says: 'I must either believe them [other human beings] to be alive, or to be automatons',[1] and he explains how, by means of an analogical inference, he 'concludes' that they are alive and are like him in their sensations and emotions. Now what is odd about Mill's argument is that it is difficult to see at what point the supposed analogical inference would have any work to do. At what point in my life is it supposed to have been an open question for me whether my friends and family are people or something else? Disregarding the puzzle about what else they *might* be, let us ask: When was I in need of the argument from analogy? When did I suffer from ignorance or doubt of the sort that that argument is supposed to remove? Is the analogical inference thought to assist us out of some state that we are in only in earliest childhood or

[1] J. S. Mill, *Examination of Sir William Hamilton's Philosophy*, London, 1872, p. 244.

out of some state of doubt that may beset a person in his adult years? The latter alternative surely cannot be the right one. There is not an undercurrent of uneasiness that runs through all my various encounters with other people tempting me to recoil from them in horror or suspicion. I do not, for instance, suffer queer feelings that my children may be altogether unlike me in some essential respect. When one of them comes crying to me with a bumped head or a bleeding foot, I do not gaze wonderingly at the child, thinking: What can be happening here in this thrashing, noisy thing? And when I speak with people I do not feel foolish in the thought that my remarks may be only activating circuits in them or something of the sort. Although there may be some such form of insanity, some kind of dissociation, in which the victim simply cannot find his feet with any other human being, this is not a condition from which very many of us suffer. And yet if it is thought that we all stand in need of the benefits supposedly conferred by the argument from analogy, then it seems that we are all being represented as suffering from this form of insanity. But even the proponents of the argument from analogy do not believe this, and I conclude, therefore, that the argument could have no relevance for us in our adult years. Perhaps, then, the analogical inference is to be thought of as having its place in our childhood and as being our means of coming to understand others as human beings in the first place. This, if I understand them, is something like the view set forth by Chihara and Fodor. They maintain that as children we encounter in others complicated syndromes of behaviour (bodily movements?), for which we want some explanation. For instance, we repeatedly encounter the 'pain syndrome' and are 'in need of an explanation of the reliability and fruitfulness of this syndrome, an explanation which reference to the occurrence of pain supplies'.[1] And this being so, they reason, the 'application of ordinary language psychological terms on the basis of behaviour' is to be thought of 'as theoretical inferences to underlying mental occurrences'.[2] This is offered as an account of how we come to use psychological terms in speaking of other people, and the authors dismiss the objection that their account saddles the child with too great an intellectual burden by appealing to the fact that we all learn a language with a complicated grammatical structure and do so, apparently by natural capacities the

---

[1] *Op. cit.*, p. 293.   [2] *Ibid.*, p. 294.

exercise of which involves 'the use of an intricate system of linguistic rules of very considerable generality and complexity', which system of rules is not explicitly taught to us.[1] This is the account that they offer as an answer to the sceptic and as an alternative to behaviourism. What they are offering, then, is an account of how the child passes from an earlier stage when he sees his parents and others as mere 'bodies' moving about to seeing them as human beings.

Before commenting on this I should like to contrast it with the quite different account that Wittgenstein gives of the way in which we come to use a word such as 'pain' in speaking of other human beings. First of all, throughout *Philosophical Investigations* Wittgenstein opposes the idea that in learning language there is somehow imparted to us an understanding that logically compels us to use a given word in a certain way. In place of this Wittgenstein puts the suggestion that learning language depends on certain 'normal learners' reactions' (143–5), that is, certain primitive responses that get encouraged and developed as one learns words. In one place (p. 224) he speaks of language-games arising as 'something spontaneous', and there is one passage (310) that suggests that our using words like 'pain' and 'hurt' in speaking of others begins with something 'instinctive'. (See also his use of the word 'attitude' in 284 and on p. 178.) In *Zettel* these suggestions are made more explicit.

> It is a help here to remember that it is a primitive reaction to tend, to treat, the part that hurts when someone else is in pain; and not merely when oneself is—and so to pay attention to other people's pain-behaviour . . . (540)

> But what is the word 'primitive' meant to say here? Presumably that this sort of behaviour is *pre-linguistic*: that a language-game is based *on it*, that it is the prototype of a way of thinking and not the result of thought. (541)

> . . . Being sure that someone else is in pain, doubting whether he is, and so on, are so many natural, instinctive, kinds of behaviour towards other human beings, and our language is merely an auxiliary to, and further extension of, this relation. Our language-game is an extension of primitive behaviour. (For our *language-game* is behaviour.) (Instinct.) (545)

[1] *Ibid.*

What makes it possible for Wittgenstein to give this account, it seems to me, is that he, unlike the behaviourist or Chihara and Fodor, rejects the idea that what the child is initially confronted with are 'bodies' that he somehow comes to see as human beings.

Behind the account offered by Chihara and Fodor lies an unspoken assumption that it is somehow natural for us in our infancy to see human beings as 'bodies', mere things, and this sends these authors in search of an account of the way in which we pass from seeing them in that way to seeing them as living human beings. But why should we think that the child is initially 'set' for seeing people as things? Indeed, what does it mean to speak of seeing a person as a thing? Where would we say that this has happened? This is something that we would describe in this way that might happen to an adult. I might have an uncanny experience in which I see a number of people as automata when they all begin to perform some task at the sound of a bell. Or perhaps this experience could occur as I stand observing the rush hour crowds pushing their way, stony-faced, along sidewalks and into subway entrances. (The subway tunnel is a great maw devouring spent machinery.) What this would involve, however, is something that is not yet there in the child. In these uncanny experiences I imagine a particular surrounding for what I see; I expect in these people what I have learned to expect of machines. For instance, if another bell rings, they will all cease work simultaneously and remain motionless until some other signal is given. Or in the rush hour crowd I perhaps look at the people's legs to discover the mechanical nature of their movements or stare into their faces, thinking 'Unseeing eyes'. And then the spell is broken when someone speaks to me.—Now if *this* is seeing a person as a thing, then, as Wittgenstein says, 'the substratum of this experience is the mastery of a technique' (p. 208). That is, I must have learned considerable language in order to see human beings as machines. Therefore, this cannot be the account we should give of the human infant's way of seeing his parents. But of course it would also be wrong to say that infants see their parents and others as human beings, that they come 'set' in this way. For what does it mean to speak of seeing something as a human being? We might say this of an adult who is watching an ingeniously made human-like automaton and has an urge to go up to it and ask a question or something of the sort. But we speak of 'seeing as' here just because if the machine were to give a few clicks and stop, the spell would be broken; the person would not try to wake it up nor would he treat it as he would a corpse. So this is an account to give of someone who knows what a machine is, and we do not want to give that account of the child learning language.

Now Wittgenstein's account escapes these difficulties, I believe, just because it does not saddle the child at the outset with that philosophical notion of 'body' which has called into existence both behaviourism and the argument from analogy. Behaviourism is left with the logical incongruity of the child's laughing with and pitying those 'bodies' that it sees around it, while Chihara and Fodor trade this logical incongruity for the logical anachronism of getting the child over a philosophical hurdle before he is out of the cradle. Wittgenstein, by both rejecting the philosophical idea of 'body' and by tracing language back to primitive responses, can allow the child's laughing with others and pitying them and so on without either the incongruity or the anachronism. And now I think we can see how Wittgenstein would reply to the charge that he has introduced the concept *human beings* without justification and so has begged the sceptic's question. He speaks to this point in another connexion when he writes: 'What we have rather to do is *accept* the everyday language-game, and note *false* accounts of the matter *as* false. The primitive language-game which children are taught needs no justification; attempts at justification need to be rejected' (p. 200). What I have been trying to show in this essay is the way in which the problem of other minds arises from a false account of the matter, of our language-game. It is this false account that leads to the idea that we all hold some unsupported belief, and this idea, in turn, gives rise to the demand for a justification. Wittgenstein's alternative to this is summed up in his remark: 'My attitude towards him is an attitude towards a soul. I am not of the *opinion* that he has a soul' (p. 178).

V

If a human being is thought of as consisting of a 'senseless body' plus mental entities (or plus a mind with mental states), the logical category of mental states will be seriously misrepresented. They cannot, on this view, be states of a living organism and must be thought of in an altogether different way. What this difference is must be made clear if we are to understand Wittgenstein's rejection of the idea that sensations are private objects. The important point here is that if sensations are not thought of as being states of a living organism, then it will be impossible to think of them as having a natural expression in the behaviour of living organisms. Instead, we will think of sensations, as most philosophers since Descartes have, as being objects perceived by means of 'inner sense'. Accordingly, words such as 'pain' and 'dizziness' will not be thought of as tied up with the natural expressions of sensation; they will be thought of as being names for objects that the speaker alone can perceive. Now this shift from 'state of a living organism' to 'object of inner perception' is the subject of Wittgenstein's well-known beetle-in-the-box passage (293), which concludes with the remark that 'if we construe the grammar of the expression of sensation on the model of "object and name" the object drops out of consideration as irrelevant'. This passage has been misunderstood by people who have failed to appreciate Wittgenstein's insistence that sensations are states of living organisms; they have taken him to be saying that sensations do drop out of the language-game as irrelevant.[1] Yet Wittgenstein explains his meaning when he says that a sensation 'is not a *something* but not a nothing either' and explains that in saying this he has 'only rejected the grammar which tries to force itself on us here' (304). These passages are often taken to mean that a word like 'pain' can have a public use despite the privacy of sensations. But such an interpretation is wrong; Wittgenstein is rejecting a metaphysical account of what sensations are. When he remarks that he is rejecting 'the grammar which tries to force itself on us here', we ought to connect this with his remark further on that 'grammar tells us what kind of object anything is' (373). When he says that a sensation is not a *something*, he is saying that a sensation is not an object of 'inner sense', is not something having its essential characteristics apart from a living organism.

What is at issue here can be seen more clearly by recalling Hume's account of mental states and events, where the grammatical transformation that Wittgenstein is rejecting is made explicit. Hume remarked that if 'any one shou'd [say] . . . that the definition of a substance is *something that may exist by itself*; . . . I

---

[1] See, for example, Alan Donagan's interpretation in 'Wittgenstein on Sensations', in *Wittgenstein: The Philosophical Investigations*, ed. George Pitcher, p. 347.

shou'd observe that this definition agrees to everything that can possibly be conceiv'd'.[1] That Hume thought of mental states and events (which he called 'perceptions') as being substances in this sense is shown by his remark that 'as every perception is distinguishable from another, and may be consider'd as separately existent; it evidently follows that there is no absurdity in separating any particular perception from the mind; that is, in breaking off all its relations with that connected mass of perceptions, which constitute a thinking being'.[2] Thoughts, images, desires, sensations, and so on 'have no need of anything else to support their existence'.[3] This leads Hume to suggest the following thought-experiment as a means of discovering what a 'thinking being' or 'self' is:

> We can conceive of a thinking being to have either many or few perceptions. . . . Suppose it to have only one perception, as of thirst or hunger. Consider it in that situation. Do you conceive of anything but merely that perception? Have you any notion of *self* or *substance*? . . . For my part, I have a notion of neither. . . .[4]

If this passage were read apart from the context of Hume's remarks about 'perceptions' being substances, one would suppose that he was here asking us merely to consider what it would be like for someone to have nothing on his mind but his hunger or thirst. In that case it would be natural to suppose that we are to consider a human being who has not eaten or drunk for a good many hours and whose hunger or thirst distracts him from all other matters. In any case, what we should think of here is a living human being, a creature that can want food and drink and can try to get them. It would then be clear what this 'self' or 'thinking being' is. But if we were to understand Hume's passage in this way, we would not have understood his proposed thought-experiment. The experiment is to begin by our considering an impression: the *impression* known as *hunger* or the *impression* known as *thirst*, and we are then to consider whether we can discover any 'real connexion' of that impression with anything else. Now the crucial difference between these ways of reading the passage lies in Hume's notion that hunger and thirst are substances and so can be considered without considering a creature that can eat or drink. Hunger and thirst are to be thought of as 'distinct exis-

---

[1] *A Treatise of Human Nature* (Oxford, 1951) ed. L. A. Selby-Bigge, p. 233.
[2] *Ibid.*, p. 207.   [3] *Ibid.*, p. 233.   [4] *Ibid.*, pp. 634–5.

tences' rather than as states of living organisms. They are to be thought of, in other words, in the grammatical category of 'object and name'. Now it is just this way of thinking of mental states, including sensations, that entails that idea of a private language that Wittgenstein argues against. On the Humean view, the meanings of words like 'hunger', 'dizziness', and 'pain' must be specified without mention of human beings and what more or less resemble (behave like) them. That is, learning these words will not involve learning to use them in such sentences as these: 'I thought he was hungry, but he didn't eat the food I brought him', 'If I get dizzy, please catch me', 'I can't walk on this foot; it hurts too much', 'I dropped the pan because it was too hot to hold'. On the Humean view, if someone never said such things and did not understand others saying such things, this would not count against his knowing what words like 'hunger' and 'dizziness' mean. The question, then, is: What *would* count against his understanding such words? Or count for it? If we answer that he understands 'dizziness' if and only if he always uses it as the name of the same sensation, we will have begged the question, for we cannot suppose that 'same sensation' could, given Hume's view, have a use when what is in question is whether, on that view, 'dizziness' and 'pain' could have a use. And for the same reason it will not do to say that he could remember having called *this* sensation 'pain' before: the expression 'this sensation' could not have a use if words like 'pain' and 'dizziness' could not. But all of this is, in a sense, beside the point, for we are already under a misconception if our account of what sensations are entails the consequence that sensations could only have names with 'private meanings'. If we reject the idea that sensations are, as Hume thinks, individual substances, i.e., objects of 'inner sense', and acknowledge that sensations are states of living organisms, then we can allow that words for sensations are tied up with the natural expression of sensations.

There is, then, an essential connexion of sensations with living organisms. But to admit this is not to accept some form of behaviourism. We can avoid behaviourism while acknowledging the essential connexion if we also acknowledge a certain complexity in the creatures to which sensation words and other psychological concepts apply. We can see this clearly by taking Hume's example of hunger. It seems perfectly clear that the concept *hunger* (employed primarily in the adjectival form 'hungry') applies only to a being that eats. Yet there is no need to *identify* hunger with eating or even with trying to get food, for human beings are also the sort of creatures that can diet and go on fasts and so can properly be said to be hungry even when refusing good food. Now surely there is no paradox here. There can be both the essential connexion and the exceptional circumstances, and this is just because human beings are the complex creatures they are. One can turn down food for a great and indefinite variety of reasons, for example, because one cannot pay for the food, because one suspects the food is tainted, because one is trying to lose weight, because accepting the food would deprive someone else more in need of it, because it is food that is forbidden by divine commandment, because remaining to eat would mean missing a train, and so on. In cases such as these one can be hungry without eating the food that is available. Yet such cases do not destroy the essential connexion of hunger with eating, for in such cases one would be prepared to say (or might think to one-self) that one would eat were it not for such and such or that one would have eaten had such and such a reason not occurred to one. Moreover, if someone does not eat the food available to him, we will judge that he is not hungry, unless we suspect that there is some overriding reason he might have for passing up the food on this occasion. The essential connexion, then, allows of certain exceptions and most certainly does not amount to an identification of hunger with eating or with trying to get food. Now the same considerations hold for a sensation word. There are natural expressions of pain, such as drawing back from the cause of pain, crying, favouring the injured part (e.g., limping), seeking relief from the pain, and so on, but also there are many reasons people can have for restraining the natural expression of pain. A child may hold back his tears in order to show that he is brave; a man may try not to limp or wince in order that the person who stepped on his foot will not have to apologize; a cook may not draw back from a painfully hot pan for fear of spilling its contents; someone may stifle a groan so as not to wake another person or may hold back an exclamation so as not to disrupt a meeting, and so on. Also we learn not to be startled or frightened by pain and so gain some control over our reactions. Now the use of the word 'pain' is certainly tied up with the natural expression of pain, but this is not to say that there is pain only in case there is pain behaviour. So there is no reason for thinking that to admit an essential connexion here is to invite behaviourism. There is no plausibility of behaviourism here in any case, for the grammar of the word 'pain' is completely different from the grammar of 'the expression of pain'. For example, a pain can throb but there is no way of behaving throbbingly, and whereas a person in pain can wail loudly or whimper softly, a pain can be neither loud nor soft.

What I have tried to make clear here is that Wittgenstein has rejected the Cartesian-Humean metaphysical account of sensations. This needs emphasizing because it is widely supposed that Wittgenstein accepted that metaphysics and merely argued that that metaphysics does not entail the privacy of the language of sensations. This interpretation gets its plausibility from the assumption that the only alternatives here are the Cartesian-Humean account or behaviourism. But it is just this assumption that Wittgenstein rejects: a sensation is not a something but not a nothing either.

VI

I should now like to return to Descartes once again to ferret out one further source of the whole problem. In the following passage in the Second Meditation he gives us what we can now see to be a metaphysical redescription of a human being. He writes:

> First came the thought that I had a face, hands, arms,—in fact the whole structure of limbs that is observable also in a corpse, and that I called 'the body'. Further, that I am nourished, that I move, that I have sensations, that I am conscious: these acts I assigned to the soul. . . . As regards 'body' I had no doubt, and I thought I distinctly understood its nature; if I had tried to describe my conception, I might have given this explanation: 'By *body* I mean whatever is capable of being bounded by some shape, and comprehended by some place, and of occupying space in such a way that all other bodies are excluded; moreover of being perceived by touch, sight, hearing, taste or smell; and further, of being moved in various ways not of itself but by some other body that touches it.' For the power of self-movement, and the further powers of sensation and consciousness, I judged not to belong in any way to the essence of body . . .; indeed, I marvelled even that there were some bodies in which such faculties were found.[1]

---

[1] Descartes, *op. cit.*, pp. 67–8.

Now in one respect Descartes is quite right about this last part: a corpse is not the sort of thing of which we can say that it has sensations, sees, is blind, is conscious or unconscious. And if a soul is that of which we *can* say these things, then of course a living human being is a soul.

The difficulty in Descartes' remarks lies in the move that looks quite innocent, namely, in 'I have a body'. And I think we can now see a further source of this move. Descartes' redescription is a kind of rehearsal of two quite different kinds of language-games. On the one hand, there are those in which human beings are central (complaining of aches and pains, telling dreams, guessing at a man's motives, etc.), and on the other hand, there are those in which human beings have roughly the same status as sticks and stones (weighing and measuring, etc.). This is a difference that stands out in sharpest relief; it is manifested in hundreds of ways. (Compare: 'I am as tall as this tree' and 'The rock hit a tree, so no one got hurt'.) Now when we come to reflect on this difference it is surely inevitable that we will treat this difference in the use of words, that is, the special status of human beings in the one case and their non-special status in the other, as marking out two different sorts of things composing a human being. This, of course, is the Cartesian account. Behaviourism, then, starting from this account, rejects the language-games in which human beings have a special status. Unlike either of these, Wittgenstein rejects the first step, which escaped unnoticed: the redescription of a human being. We can now express this result as follows: these two kinds of language-games *taken together* mark off human beings from sticks and stones. If someone now should want to re-open the question, asking: 'But how can something that lies undressed in bed at night, something of a certain height and weight, have thoughts and sensations?' we shall have to say, as Wittgenstein suggests (284, 412, 421): Look at someone engaged in a conversation or think of a child just stung by a bee and ask yourself what better subject there could be for thoughts and sensations. In this way we are brought back to earth, turned aside from misleading pictures, and we will find nothing odd in saying that these creatures are thinking or in pain.

Getting these two language-games back together—and in the right way—is not, of course, a simple matter. The problem is rather like that of getting substance and quality to lie down together again: the separation has been so prolonged as now to seem virtually in the nature of things. In each case the difficulty seems to be that we have saddled ourselves with a pair of spurious entities. In the latter case it is the 'bare particular' and qualities designed to 'clothe' it; in the former case it is the 'body' and 'private objects'. It is only if we let go of these that we can find those 'real connexions' that Hume was looking for.—Yet other matters are bound to intrude here. One of these Wittgenstein mentions when he remarks that 'religion teaches that the soul can exist when the body has disintegrated' (p. 178). Seen in the context of the philosophical problem we have been considering, it is natural to think of this teaching as requiring an interpretation along lines that now seem impossible. It is natural, that is, to think of this teaching as requiring a Cartesian ontology. Yet it would be obtuse to insist on this, for, as Wittgenstein goes on to remark, the teaching has, after all, a point. It is one way of announcing the promise of a life everlasting. And that promise does not itself specify a Cartesian ontology. If we do not at once see how a non-Cartesian account of the matter is possible, then we can only confess ignorance.[1] In any case, it would seem presumptuous of a believer to insist that the promise shall be fulfilled in the way that he has been accustomed to thinking of it. At the same time, it would be equally presumptuous of a non-believer to boggle at this talk of soul and body. After all, we all still speak of the sun rising and setting, and no one is the worse off for that. Indeed, it seems unlikely that we shall ever speak otherwise.

[1] Wittgenstein says that he 'can imagine plenty of things in connexion with' the teaching, and here we should bear in mind that the promise has been filled out with an account of 'resurrection bodies'. On this point I have been greatly benefited by conversations with my colleague Robert Herbert. See his essay 'Puzzle Cases and Earthquakes', *Analysis*, January, 1968.

V

WITTGENSTEIN AND
STRAWSON ON OTHER MINDS

L. R. Reinhardt

WHEN, in the *Philosophical Investigations*, Wittgenstein writes of 'criteria' and when, in *Individuals*, P. F. Strawson writes of 'logically adequate criteria', they do not mean the same thing. But in both cases a relation is involved which is neither a matter of evidence contingently being evidence for something else nor a matter of entailment holding between propositions. It is important to the understanding of Wittgenstein's work that the issue is not obviously one of a relation between propositions. I shall later argue that certain points follow from Wittgenstein's views which are about logical relations between propositions, but that the core of his view cannot be put this way. Given this caution, there is a measure of agreement between the two philosophers which may be put as follows: that some human being is behaving in a certain way or has certain things happening to him entitles us to assert that he is in some mental state. And, to repeat, the entitlement does not arise out of empirically ascertained regularities nor is it a matter of entailment. (I am here using 'mental state' loosely to include pains, intentions, beliefs, and even dispositions; the looseness should not matter for present purposes.)

Another area of agreement between Wittgenstein and Strawson is the thesis, in Strawson's terms, that the concept of a person is logically primitive, that a person (or human being) is neither an animated body nor an embodied anima. Both philosophers reject the idea that it is not the very same thing to which I refer when I say 'Jones is fat' and 'Jones is thinking of home'. With human beings it is not as it seems plausible to say it is with, e.g., the name 'Iceland' in the pair of sentences 'Iceland is an island' and 'Iceland is bankrupt'. It can seem quite appropriate in this case to hold that the apparent unitary referent of 'Iceland' is only apparent. Bodies of land cannot be bankrupt and states cannot be bodies of land, have geographical properties. Thus, it seems plausible to say, a sentence such as 'Iceland is a bankrupt island' is a zeugma, as is 'The cape is stormy and loose about her shoulders'. (I expect the right answer here is that 'Iceland' refers to a *country*, and that countries, rather like Strawsonian persons, just do take predicates from two different categories. This is why I say it 'seems plausible'.)

Further, and to make a brief historical digression which will remind us of the origins of our problem about other minds, the duality of reference which we might find plausible with 'Iceland' is, Descartes would insist, also the case with human proper names. Moreover, just as the state of Iceland might continue to exist if relocated in a portion of Canada, the Cartesian real person is only contingently related to its body. (It is harder to find a parallel for existence without any body at all; perhaps a government in exile after a revolution might do.) I mention Descartes because, while we all admire him for appreciating that the relation between person and body is not like that of a captain to his vessel, we do not perhaps appreciate sufficiently just how he arrived at the view that the relation was 'mysterious'. I shall argue shortly that representing a human body as a moving and changing thing in space-time, as Descartes would have done, is a device which focuses us sharply on the problem of other minds.

To return to Strawson. For him the fact that certain behaviour takes place is logically adequate for saying that certain thoughts, feelings and intentions are present. But, as is notorious, there is some difficulty in seeing just what this thesis comes to. In fact, it is not clear whether criteria should be called instances of behaviour. It is not clear whether the criteria for a P-predicate being true consist in a number of M-predicates being true or whether the criteria are something quite other than either P-properties or M-properties. Nor are we justified in equating Strawson's symbol 'P' with 'psychic' or 'mental'; though we are justified in equating his symbol 'M' with 'physical' or 'bodily'. The sort of case which comes to mind most readily with Strawson's view is one where a man is writhing and groaning and where that settles for us the question whether he is pain. But the question arises whether 'writhing' and 'groaning' are M or P predicates. Strawson would classify them as P predicates. But then *they* apparently need criteria; and one cannot see what these criteria are to be.

The temptation is to suppose that we must eventually get to M-predicates being true as the criteria for P-predicates being true. I wish to explore this temptation. But a word of apology to Strawson is in order first. The temptation is, I believe, itself a symptom of the reluctance to accept P-predicates as just as well-grounded and basic as M-predicates. Being part of a certain tradition in philosophy, we are subject to this temptation. It is very likely a deep-rooted prejudice connected with idolizing the physical sciences. Since I believe that Strawson has contributed greatly to withering this prejudice, it would be unjust of me to claim that the picture I am about to present is an accurate representation of his views. But Strawson does not do enough to show us what is wrong with the picture; and Wittgenstein's strength, relative to this problem, lies in the fact that he can free us from the grip of the picture. I believe also that it is a widespread interpretation of Strawson to read him as saying that the truth of M-predicates is the ground for the truth of P-predicates.

Suppose then that we take seriously the suggestion implicit in the temptation, the temptation to hold that M-properties constitute the criteria for P-properties. To do this, let us imagine a mode of description for a phase in the life of a human being which consists solely of chemical, spatio-temporal, topological and physiological predicates. We need topology to deal with the alterations in configuration of what we ordinarily call a human face, alterations we ordinarily call grimaces, frowns, smiles, sneers, etc. For convenience, let us call this mode of description the Cartesian mode, the allusion being to Cartesian coordinate geometry. Immediately we can see that we are precluded from using any terms such as 'writhing', 'groaning' or any of the terms mentioned just above. Moreover, since our predicates in the Cartesian mode are all Strawsonian M-predicates, we cannot specify actions, but only bodily movements. Hence, we cannot justify a claim that the object being described is 'raising an arm';

we can only say that a certain appendage is changing its spatial position relative to the rest of a certain body.

The Cartesian mode is available to us if, for certain purposes, we choose to adopt it. As I have already suggested, it was something along these lines that Descartes had in mind when he said the relation between body and mind was 'mysterious'. And we can see why he thought so. For once we have done things this way, it will be impossible to build a bridge to our ordinary ways of talking about human beings. There are several things which it might be thought I am suggesting here which I am not suggesting, or which, at least, do not follow from what I am saying; and they are worth a brief mention. First of all, I am not claiming, *a priori*, that it would be impossible to establish correlations between actions, writhings, groans, smiles, etc., and the elements described in the Cartesian mode. I think there are bound to be enormous difficulties about such a project. But, even if further conceptual inquiry shows that the project is incoherent and not merely unlikely to occur, what I have said does not establish this, nor does my point make determinism impossible. Nothing I have said rules out the possibility of finding the sorts of correlations which would enable us to exhibit the counterpart in the Cartesian mode of any act or mental state as occurring when and only when (or only when) some antecedent set of states—in the Cartesian mode—occur. So long as we accept that some bodily movement or change occurs in connexion with actions and mental states, we cannot rule out, without a lot more argument, the possibility that these movements and states are determined by antecedent conditions. If the envisaged programme is possible, it seems reasonable to hold that any determinist should be happy. Hence, the identity theory of sensations and mental states with brain or bodily states, while perhaps of some interest in its own right, is not a requirement for determinism.[1]

---

[1] I must confess that I write here with my tongue veering towards, if not completely in, my cheek. I do think the envisioned project is incoherent. Suppose a determinist said that, on the basis of the bodily states of a group of people at a given time, he could predict their bodily movements in a year's time. He does this without any reference to psychological or mental concepts, leaving it to us to supply the action descriptions. Apart from the stock objections about informing the subjects about the issue, thus allowing them to change their minds, it should be noted how hard it is to stop from having to take into account a huge portion of the universe. For example, a falling meteorite in Australia might cause the death of a relative of

[*continued on p. 156*

Still, we can see that nothing in the Cartesian mode can give us grounds for our ordinary ways of talking about other human beings and ourselves. At most, we might get a theory off the ground about the *causes* of our responsive behaviour. Such a theory would have to be tied in with a theory about our perception of those bodily movements and changes. Now, where the prejudice I mentioned earlier asserts itself most perniciously is in the temptation to believe that, strictly speaking, all we observe in reality is what can be described in the Cartesian mode. This raises problems about the concept of observation, and I do not want to go into any detail about that. But if, as I think would be agreed, we would implausibly say that we were observing a gambit in chess if we knew nothing of the rules, we would then with equal implausibility say that we observed the Cartesian counterpart of a frown if the description of that frown involves topology and we knew nothing of that science. Similarly, in observing a man lifting his arm above his head, we are not observing an increase in the angle between an upper bicep and the left or right side of an upper torso. Further, concerning what we can observe and perceive, there is no barrier to saying that we see pain in a man's face or hear anger in his voice. We also observe the gracefulness of his walk or the firmness of his stance, attributes which are revealing of personality and character.[1] If it is replied to this point that we do not literally see his pain or hear the anger, an explanation is owing of what 'literal' is contrasted with here. It is not figurative

---

[1] Miss Cora Diamond has pointed out to me that while nothing does seem to be said by saying that we do not literally see pain in a person's face, it is plausible to talk here of a *different sense* of 'seeing'. And this does distinguish such cases from the case of seeing pieces on a chessboard and seeing a threatened gambit. In the latter case, there is no inclination to talk of different senses of 'seeing'. Similarly, if a man raises his hand at a meeting to attract the speaker's attention, we may say either that we see him raise his hand or that we see him trying to attract the speaker's attention. Again, it is not a different sense of 'see' here. J. L. Austin cautioned philosophers against multiplying senses beyond necessity, but, in the case of seeing pain, it certainly does seem a natural thing to say that the sense is different. Of course, a different sense is not thereby a non-literal use.

[*continued from p. 155*

one of the subjects, and lead to him or her having to be elsewhere than predicted. The same point obviously applies to predicting the movements of inanimate objects on earth. We just get the old Laplacean picture, requiring a God's-eye view, a mere assertion that the thing could be done. Still, the weaker point that, *after the fact*, what happened can be exhibited deterministically, seems to me all a determinist really has to insist on.

to talk this way as it would be to talk of floorboards groaning or of causing suffering to a flower by cutting its bloom. Such modes of speech are figurative precisely in contrast to the way we talk about human beings.

As I said above, this picture of our situation, one in which we find no way to bridge the gap between the Cartesian mode or M-predicates and the way we talk of human beings, is not a representation of Strawson's view or anything which follows from his view. I presented it to illustrate a difficulty in that view, namely that it is not easy to stop oneself from interpreting it along these lines. The picture of our situation represents the correct line of development if it is held that M-properties are the criteria for P-properties. But if they are not, and cannot be, it would appear that whatever these logically adequate criteria for P-predicates are, they cannot be stated with either M-predicates or with P-predicates. And this is a puzzling result. There is a passage in Strawson which hints at the right direction we must take to resolve the puzzle.

> If one is playing a game of cards, the distinctive markings of a certain card constitute a logically adequate criterion for calling it say, the Queen of Hearts; but, in calling it this, in the context of the game, one is ascribing to it properties over and above the possession of these markings. The predicate gets its meaning from the whole structure of the game. So with the language in which we ascribe P-predicates. To say that the criteria on the strength of which we ascribe P-predicates to others are of a logically adequate kind for this ascription, is not to say that all there is to the ascriptive meaning of these predicates is these criteria. To say this is to forget that they are P-predicates, to forget the rest of the language-structure to which they belong.[1]

The suggestion here is that it is the entire system of P-predicates of which we gain a mastery in understanding what persons are. And there is perhaps a further suggestion in Strawson that we just do learn to apply this system without the system having to have a foundation in something else. I should want to argue, and I think that this is Wittgenstein's view, that we grow into a mastery of this system. It is even misleading to say we are taught it, though we may be said to learn it. The system of P-predicates contrasts

[1] *Individuals*, P. F. Strawson; London, 1959; page 110.

sharply with the Cartesian mode in that the latter does involve teaching and learning in the most banal sense of those terms.

I suggested that we just do use the system of human predicates without having to find a foundation for it. I think this is the import of many remarks of Wittgenstein's, of which I will cite only a few. First, consider what he writes on page 223 of the *Philosophical Investigations*:

> If I see someone writhing in pain with evident cause I do not think: all the same his feelings are hidden from me.

And on the following page:

> 'But, if you are *certain*, isn't it that you are shutting your eyes in face of doubt?'—They are shut.

Now what is noteworthy here, relative to Strawson, is that, even if we do call writhing and groaning and the evident cause the criteria or the grounds for a man's having feelings, these grounds include both Strawsonian P-properties and M-properties. While Wittgenstein certainly has something like a theory about criteria —he contrasts criteria with symptoms for example—he is not obviously using the term 'criteria' as a central tool in his investigations of the problem of other minds. What I mean is that we cannot say that, for Wittgenstein, criteria are always something different from necessary and sufficient conditions, always something special which is related to the issue of other minds. Criteria may very well be necessary and sufficient conditions with respect to some matters. If they are not with respect to other minds, then it does not adequately illuminate Wittgenstein's views about other minds just to say that he resolves the problem with the idea of a criterion. The concept of a criterion is a formal concept. Knowing what it comes to in any area is knowing what counts as this or that in that area.

We should read what Wittgenstein says about criteria keeping in mind always what he says about grammar. In the *Blue Book*,[1] he writes: 'It is part of the grammar of the word "chair" that this [here we must, I think, imagine the speaker actually performing the action of sitting down in a chair] is what we call "to sit in a chair".' The comparable point with respect to an issue about other minds would involve a remark such as 'It is part of the grammar

---

[1] *The Blue and Brown Books*, L. Wittgenstein; Blackwell's; Oxford, 1959; page 24.

of the word "headache" that this [and we imagine someone condoling with someone and offering him an aspirin] is what we call "to sympathize with and help someone with a headache".' So long as criteria are construed as something we observe which justify us in saying something, we shall miss Wittgenstein's point. Suppose someone (in a philosophy class perhaps) argues that a table might be in pain. It will be part of the answer to such an argument to ask what could count as an expression of pain coming from a table; but it is also part of the answer to note that we have no idea what will count as sympathizing with a table or feeling relief from anxiety when the table is all right again. It would also be to the point to ask what would count as enjoying seeing the table suffer, what will count as sadism with respect to tables.

The tendency to persist in interpreting criteria as observable features which justify making statements is a persistence of the Humean tendency to see ourselves in the world as onlookers. As much as anything, Wittgenstein is trying to break us of this philosophical habit.

The passages I have already quoted indicate that Wittgenstein is not concerned to justify the way we do carry on. It is more a matter of reminding us of pervasive features of our lives. What he writes at paragraph 445 applies throughout the *Investigations*: 'What we are supplying are really remarks on the natural history of human beings; we are not contributing curiosities however, but observations which no one has doubted, but which have escaped remark only because they are always before our eyes.'[1] We are told some things about how it is not. It is not a matter of having opinions or beliefs that the bodies around us are human. Wittgenstein puts this point dramatically: 'My attitude towards him is as towards a soul; I am not of the opinion that he has a soul.' We do not have a situation where we can allay the doubts of the sceptic by producing further evidence or grounds. Recall the passage quoted earlier about the man writhing with the cause of his pain evident. Wittgenstein says our eyes are shut to doubt. To have opinions is, by definition we might say, to be open to doubt.

[1] Cf. the remarks of C. S. Peirce about metaphysics scattered thoughout his writings, that it is an empirical study but about such pervasive facts that they are hard to notice. For example: 'It is, on the contrary, extremely difficult to bring our attention to elements of experience which are continually present'. *Collected Papers*, Vol. I, page 55.

Wittgenstein's remarks about criteria have been interpreted in the following way: When a man is writhing with cause of pain evident, we are entitled to say that he is in pain *unless* specific reasons for doubting are offered. If all the putative doubter points out is that the proposition that a man is writhing and groaning does not entail that he is in pain, this point carries no weight and there is nothing odd about the fact that it does not. To think the lack of entailment does carry weight is to assume that the grounds in this region of our lives must conform to models taken from elsewhere. I do not think that Wittgenstein would disagree with what is said here. Consider page 224 of the *PI*: 'Am I less certain that this man is in pain than that twice two is four? Does this shew the former to be mathematical certainty? Mathematical certainty is not a psychological concept. The kind of certainty is the kind of language-game.' But this, as I said earlier, seems not so much to be the heart of Wittgenstein's view as a kind of consequence of it. The trouble is that the interpretation in terms of entitlement to assert unless specific reasons are offered against the assertion, does not get at the force of the sentence, 'They are shut', cited earlier. This is clearly not a resolution to be decent about the feelings of others. To be utterly beastly about others' feelings is consistent with our eyes being closed to doubt. Indeed, how could the sadist take his pleasure if he doubted?

Let us consider a case where a story about entitlement to assert unless specific reasons for doubting are offered is just the right story. The contrast between such a case and the case of the suffering of another human being should then be evident. Consider the legimate inference from 'He promised to F' to 'He will F'. When you ask me if Jones will be at the party and I say confidently that he will, I can support my claim by replying to your query 'How do you know?' just by saying 'Jones promised to come'. And here, in the absence of a specific reason for doubting, my claim is justified. It is no rebuttal to point out the obvious truth that promising does not entail performance. But suppose we try to fit into this story the idea that our eyes are closed to doubt. If I knew Jones very well and had acquired great respect for him as a man of his word, it might very well be that my eyes would be closed to doubt. I might even say 'My eyes are closed to doubt here; nothing you say will make me change my conviction that he will be here'. But this avowal of mine is now an avowal of faith in Jones. And this is surely not so in the kind of case Wittgenstein asks us to imagine. It is not due to some general faith in human nature that, in such cases, doubt simply does not get any purchase. If human nature enters the picture anywhere, it is that it shows itself in the fact that we do not doubt in situations like this.

If criteria have to be interpreted as a matter of logical relations between propositions, the interpretation suggested does seem to be the only one available. Sometimes this interpretation is expressed by talking of what is *normally* so, and this is contrasted with what is *usually* so. This has the merit of indicating that the relation is not a matter of empirically ascertained regularities. This is why I think that the thesis can be said to follow from what Wittgenstein says. But he is going further than to tell us what justifies us in saying something in the absence of specific reasons for doubting. It is more as though he is telling us of points in our lives with each other where we are helpless and cannot even think meaningfully about justification and grounds. It is tempting to say that Wittgenstein is indicating places where, so to speak, the gap between reasons and causes virtually closes up. Yet I am not sure this is the right general characterization of his view. Let me develop my reasons for saying this, however. I think the reasons are correct even if it is not a matter of reasons and causes after all.

What I have in mind is that there is a kind of scale running from, at one end, 'take to be' and 'believe to be' through 'respond to as', 'regard as', 'treat as', to, at the other end, 'describe as'.

One end of the scale is 'describe as'. I have already mentioned describing a stretch in the life of a man in purely mechanical, physiological and topological terms. This is a possible activity just as it would be possible to describe a chess game purely in terms of the physical properties and spatial relations of the pieces. The range of choice open to us for 'describing as' is enormous, as many choices are available as there are modes of description in our language; and the stuff of new ones is there too. I have suggested already that one reason the problem of other minds disturbs us is that we come to think that we have to *get from* one available mode of description to another. And we think that we have to find in the one mode the stuff out of which to build the bridge to the other. But if we consider when we might actually have to justify or give reasons for talking of someone in a certain way, the whole issue is surely the other way about. If we were engaging in describing a human being strictly in the Cartesian mode, the question 'Why are you talking that way?' would get an easy hold. Of course, the question might also have a ready answer. I may just have found to my surprise and delight that his movements can be described in the Cartesian mode, that a certain vocabulary works, that I have mastered it. But the same question directed at someone talking as we ordinarily do about a human being could get a grip only if the person questioned were supposed to be doing something else. Imagine a man trying to use rigorously the Cartesian mode. He slips up and begins to talk of what the human being there is doing and feeling. So he is asked 'Why are you talking that way?' The answer might be 'Oh, I slipped up; got interested in him'. We should note with respect to the problem (so-called) of bridge building, that we can no more *get from* one way of talking to the other than the other way around, if getting from consists in finding grounds in one mode of description for the other.

So we have available to us, on the level of 'describing as', a good deal of choice and we can imagine different interests and purposes to which these choices are appropriate. But, that we can describe in different ways, adopt different modes of description, does not show that we are regarding what we describe in a certain way or treating it in a certain way or seeing it in a certain way or responding to it in a certain way. Least of all, does it mean that we are taking it to be what we describe it as. We do not cease to believe a man is before us when we adopt the Cartesian mode; or, at least, that we are using the Cartesian mode does not itself show that we cease to treat him as a man or respond to him as one. This *might* happen to someone though.

Any mode of description is, at least, a collection of predicates and of any such collection the general point Strawson made about P-predicates will apply. That is, that all there is to the meaning will not be the criteria for the application of these predicates. Their rôle in the system, in the wider setting will be relevant as well. A similar point, I believe, is made by Wittgenstein when he discusses children in our society playing with toy trains; they will be children who also know about real trains. Some children in a primitive tribe might be taught merely how to run the toy trains. Wittgenstein says of such a possibility that the primitive children's activity will have a different sense. If we were, for example, to give definitions of words like 'pain' and 'groan' which would enable us to use them in the Cartesian mode, thus relocating these words in a strange setting, a similar change in sense would take place.

To each mode of description, there is a range of attitudes or responses to which the language, the vocabulary of the mode of description is internally related. We might say the vocabulary expresses the interrelationship between us and the things we are talking about, though it does not *describe* that relationship (describing it is what I am trying to do here). A mode of description, a vocabulary, presents a creative mind with an opportunity, and an attitude of, say, wonder, might be evoked by any vocabulary if it were deployed by the right man. Some attitude terms seem general enough that we may be loath to rule out their applicability relative to just about any mode of description. But this does not seem to be so with every case. An attitude of reverence or religious awe, for example, could hardly be expressed with *any* mode of description.

While we may adopt and follow the rules of various modes of description, it does not follow that the understanding I have of these rules enables me to feel just any way about what I am describing or to respond in just any way. When I attribute understanding of a vocabulary to a man, there is an implication that he is susceptible to certain kinds of responses. And while there may be choices as to how to go about describing a situation, there is not the same kind of choice as to how I shall feel or as to what feelings I can make intelligible to others. (We might say that a way of talking can grab you by the heart, virtually pull out of you certain responses.) In many cases, if a way of talking does not affect a man in certain ways, we shall be entitled to doubt whether he understands the words he is using. Hamlet cannot say 'How weary, stale, flat and unprofitable seem to me all the uses of this world' and then inform us that he is glad to be alive.

At one end of the scale are 'take to be' and 'believe to be'. Now we do not have a choice about that. And this is because if what is there is a human being, then it is one and you cannot, on pain of madness, mistake it for something else. Or if we do, as in bad light in a forest where we think it is a tree, we have ordinary error. But if I cannot grasp how to describe something as this or that, it does not follow that I have made an error about what it is. What I meant by 'on pain of madness' comes out if we consider briefly 'treating as' and 'responding to as'. A man might very well treat another man as merely a piece of stuff (say a slave trader loading a ship efficiently). But he does not necessarily take the slave to be a piece of stuff; or, if he does, this is not shown merely by the fact that he treats him that way. We should have to know more about our slave-trader first. We might want to know, for example, whether he is racked with unconscious guilt. To say the trader takes the man in the hold to be just a piece of stuff is actually exculpatory, allowing a clear plea of insanity. That the trader treats the slave in a certain way, an inhuman way even, does not show that he responds to him in a way got at by 'as a piece of stuff'. He may, sometimes, slip into pangs of compassion as he distributes water to his captives. We may not be able to say, in any general way about the trader—and especially not about ordinary deckhands—just how it is with him or them towards the cargo in the hold. It is vastly too easy to say they do not believe them to be human beings.

If a man takes an x to be an F in one situation, but to be a G in another (where F and G are incompatible and no change has occurred) he is mistaken in a straightforward way in one case or in both. If a man treats another as a hunk of stuff in one situation but as a human being in another, this is not contradiction or contrariety, but a different sort of human muddle. Even that is too strong; for often there will be nothing sinister in a situation where it is plausible to say one man is concerned about others only as matter (consider a pilot making calculations to assure a safe takeoff; still, this is motivated by concerns which are human).

It might be thought that when I am 'describing as', I must also be right in my description and thus be taking the things to be what I describe them as. But this is a mistake. When I 'describe as', all that needs to be so is that what I describe is *as I describe it*. Suppose we adopt the Cartesian mode in connexion with a cricket player going for a six. We shall leave out all reference to intention and action and make no mention of aims internal to playing cricket. If I describe his swing as a motion of a certain kind including flesh, bone and wood, the Cartesian mode predicates must be true of what is happening for me to get it right. But what I am describing is still *his swing*, an action of his. I do not forget this in adopting the Cartesian mode. With human beings, there is a primacy to our ordinary ways of identifying and describing them. We take what we see or believe what we see to be actions even if we can describe them as mere bodily movements. We do not *slip into* the Cartesian mode from our ordinary responses as we can easily slip in the other direction.

It is worth noting here that one factor contributing to the prejudice I mentioned earlier in this essay is that human beings can be much more easily brought under the Cartesian mode than inanimate objects in *rerum natura* can be brought under our human ways of talking. In these cases, we shall readily concede that we speak figuratively (as with groaning floorboards). This universality of applicability is a powerful inducement to believing that the Cartesian mode alone gets at how things ultimately are. It is easy to see how this universality leads to this belief; but it is a different matter to establish that it justifies it, and I cannot see why it should be thought to.

What I have said about the primacy of our human vocabulary of action and feeling suggests that this vocabulary is not one we can choose to use or not to use, but that it is constitutive of our human nature. Of course we can, in many circumstances, choose not actually to *say* anything in this language. But Wittgenstein's view, as I understand it, is that we have no choice in taking things this way, in the way got at by the vocabulary. The responses we have and the related attitudes can only be understood by considering the language in which they express themselves, along with the ways of acting which, with the vocabulary, constitute a form of life.

VI

PAIN AND PRIVATE
LANGUAGE

Anthony Manser

THOUGH this issue has been considerably discussed in recent years, it seems worthwhile to raise it again for two reasons. First, because of a certain dissatisfaction with contemporary examinations of Wittgenstein's treatment of the matter in *Philosophical Investigations*, which itself is intimately connected with puzzles that arise in the readers of that work. Second, because the problem of pain was one that occupied Wittgenstein a great deal from the time of his return to Cambridge. I have been told[1] that the group of students that surrounded him in 1929–30 were referred to as the 'Toothache Club' so often was this example the subject of their discussions. G. E. Moore says that in his lectures for the academic year 1932–3 Wittgenstein dealt at 'great length with the difference between the proposition which is expressed by the words "I have got toothache", and those which are expressed by the words "You have got toothache" or "He has got toothache", . . .'[2] The example of toothache is also used in a similar discussion in *Philosophische Bemerkungen*.[3] In trying to get clear about what Wittgenstein said on the subject of pain and private language, it will be necessary to investigate why pain was such an important issue to him; it presumably originally arose from consideration of the 'solipsism' and other matters in the *Tractatus*, though here I am more concerned with examining the later doctrines than

---

[1] By Professor A. M. MacIver, in a private communication.
[2] 'Wittgenstein's Lectures in 1930–33' in *Mind*, Vol. LXIII, 1954, p. 5.
[3] pp. 88–96.

tracing their history in Wittgenstein's thought. Also, care will have to be taken to avoid being so captivated with the examples that Wittgenstein uses that their function in the argument is forgotten. This is particularly the case with the notion of 'private language'.

Wittgenstein invokes the example of a 'private language' in the context of his discussions of pain and other sensations, and it is in this context which it has philosophical interest. Some writers have taken the notion in a wider sense, that of a complete language made up by an individual for himself alone, as distinct from a mere code into which he translated a pre-existing language. Such a code would be only 'accidentally' private, in that its translation could be discovered and the private diary of the individual made public. An example of this wide use of the notion occurs in Professor Ayer's paper in the symposium 'Can there be a private language?'[1] where he says: 'But if we allow that our Robinson Crusoe (an individual brought up in complete isolation) could invent words to describe the flora and fauna of the island, why not allow that he could also invent words to describe his sensations?' The trouble with this suggestion, as Rush Rhees pointed out in his reply to Ayer's paper,[2] is that even without the question of sensations arising it is hard to see what such a Robinson Crusoe would need words to describe the flora and fauna of the island *for*. This is the central problem with such a private language, and arises prior to that mentioned by Wittgenstein in connexion with the 'sensation E' but which also applies here: 'But in the present case I have no criterion of correctness. One would like to say: whatever is going to seem right to me is right. And that only means that here we can't talk about "right".'[3] Ayer thinks that Crusoe would discover, for example, that a certain bird was good to eat and hence give it a particular name, giving another name to one that was not good to eat to distinguish between them. Then the next time he sees a bird of the first kind, he utters the name and shoots it. But why utter the name here? It doesn't play any part in the process, for if he can re-identify the bird on the second occasion, the name doesn't serve any purpose. His uttering it is idle ceremony. And if he confuses the two kinds of birds, how does the prior naming help?

[1] *Supplementary Proceedings of the Aristotelian Society*, 1954, p. 70.
[2] *Ibid.*, pp. 77–94.
[3] *Philosophical Investigations* (in future referred to as *PI*), § 258.

What has happened here, as so often in such cases, is that a normal social situation has been smuggled in. Names would be given to the two kinds of birds in order to assist in teaching children which to catch, and there would consequently be some kinds of rules which could be appealed to. It would make sense to talk of someone making a mistake; if someone uttered the word and raised his bow to shoot at the bird named, a companion could say 'No, it isn't, so don't shoot it'. If Crusoe were to shoot a bird of the type not good to eat he would certainly have made a mistake, a misidentification. But this would not be affected by his utterance of a particular noise, which is all his so-called name could be. There are two points here; first, language must play a rôle in some way of life, second, it must involve public rules. On both these counts Ayer's suggestion fails; it appears that he is making an intelligible claim, but on examination it is meaningless. Whatever noises a linguistically isolated individual might make, they would not count as a 'language'. In this sense a 'private language' is a chimera, for language is always a social activity, involving the rules that only a social situation can provide. This general conclusion seems to be completely established by Wittgenstein, but it has nothing to do with the question of the meaning of sensation words in our normal vocabulary.

Confusion is liable to occur at this point from consideration of Wittgenstein's 'sensation E', which he introduces in *PI*, § 258: 'Let us imagine the following case. I want to keep a diary about the recurrence of a certain sensation. To this end I associate it with the sign "E" and write this sign in a calendar for every day on which I have the sensation.' He concludes the section by saying: 'But in the present case I have no criterion of correctness. One would like to say: whatever is going to seem right to me is right. And that only means that here we can't talk about "right".' It seems at first sight that it would be quite possible for me in some way to identify a new sensation; the normal way to do this would be to refer to the circumstances in which it occurred. For example, the first man to experience an electric shock from touching the terminals of his new electrical machine felt a new sensation. He could identify it either by mentioning or remembering the mechanism which gave it to him, 'What I get from that device when I do such-and-such' or by the kind of sensation he received, which he could describe in terms of his existing sensation vocabulary. And then there would seem no reason why he should not use the sign 'E' to refer to it in his diary if he wished to register recurrences. But in such a case 'E' would not be a *name* for the sensation, but a mere code-word, for the rest of language has come to the aid of the inventor of the sign; he could communicate his meaning to others; it just so happens that he hasn't bothered. For we do attempt to describe sensations to others, even though some are fairly indescribable.

It might be objected that I am talking about describing a sensation rather than about naming it. In a sense this charge is true, because, as the possessor of an adequate language, naming is not a necessary procedure for me to be able to refer to, talk about or remember a sensation—I already possess criteria to enable me to decide that this is the 'same thing again'. These criteria are the rules for all the words in my vocabulary which I use in referring to the sensation; they are the criteria for its identity. Naming, as Wittgenstein stresses, is a particular kind of ceremony: 'When one says "He gave a name to his sensation" one forgets that a great deal of stage-setting in the language is presupposed if the mere act of naming is to make sense.'[1]

There are well-known contexts in which naming takes place, e.g. the christening of children, the launching of ships, the discovery of a new species of plant. And these new names play a definite rôle in our social life, so that there is no question about the performing of an individual act of naming falling under one of these headings; its purpose is obvious. In each case there is something new to be named. But it is not immediately obvious what would qualify as a 'new sensation' and hence deserve a name in this sense. If it came to be recognized that a certain sort of sensation or set of sensations had diagnostic value then it might be given a name for the convenience of medical workers; 'The patient has Wittgenstein's sensation'. This can be compared with the definition of 'aura' in the *Oxford Dictionary*: '4.*Path*. A sensation, as of a current of cold air rising from some part of the body to the head, a premonitory symptom in epilepsy and hysterics'. The very fact that a definition can be formulated in such terms shows that it is not a genuinely 'new' sensation which is at issue here. In fact the idea of a new sensation is worrying in the way in which Ronald Knox's 'New Sin' is worrying; we can

[1] *PI*, § 257.

conceive a sin which is now more important because more widespread than it used to be, but not a sin which had only just been discovered, which had been overlooked by the Church Fathers.

However, the various instances considered in the last paragraph still don't really amount to 'naming' in the sense that Wittgenstein used the word in § 257: ' "What would it be like if human beings shewed no outward signs of pain (did not groan, grimace, etc.)? Then it would be impossible to teach a child the use of the word 'toothache'!"—Well, let's assume the child is a genius and itself invents a name for the sensation!' His problem is that of the original introduction of the sensation word into our vocabulary, not the building of further structures with an already existent one. In this sense my examples were of no help, were not of real *naming*. This is clear in the case of 'aura', where the so-called name was really only a shorthand method of referring to a description, another example of the code-word mentioned earlier. And proper names represent a somewhat different problem which need not be gone into here, though it is perhaps worth remarking that the child genius of § 257 might well be using only a proper name for his sensation. For in the case envisaged the name invented would not function like a word in everyday language: 'And when we speak of someone's having given a name to pain, what is presupposed is the existence of the grammar of the word "pain"; it shews the post where the new word is stationed.'[1] Without such a post there would be nothing to distinguish between it and a proper name.

For Wittgenstein the discussion is centred on pain because it is the commonest example of a sensation word to be used in philosophical arguments of the 'private language' type. And this is a natural way to proceed because we expect it to be one of the first such words to be learnt, and one which may well form a basis for future extensions of the sensation vocabulary. Hence no *definition* of it will be possible; there will be no 'elements' into which it can be resolved. If you have not experienced pain, there is no way in which I can explain it to you. Neither would an ostensive definition, such as sticking a pin into you, help here. For only if you already know what pain is will you know what to attend to in this apparent ostensive definition, the sensation

[1] *PI*, § 257.

rather than my action, etc. In the case of the original introduction of such a sensation word there is 'no post where the new word is stationed'; we cannot presuppose the background of the rest of our sensation language. Hence to those who wish to talk in terms which involve a private language, pain is rather like an 'object' in the *Tractatus*: 'Objects can only be *named*. Signs are their representatives. I can only speak *about* them: I cannot *put them into words*. Propositions can only say *how* things are, not *what* they are.'[1] Two further comments from the *Tractatus* may help to show the relevance of this: 'A name cannot be dissected further by means of a definition: it is a primitive sign.'[2] 'The meanings of primitive signs can be explained by means of elucidations. Elucidations are propositions that contain the primitive signs. So they can only be understood if the meanings of these are already known.'[3] It would therefore seem that if the word 'pain' is to be introduced into the language immediately, the sentence expressing pain would be very like an elementary proposition in the sense given to this term in the *Tractatus*. Part of the trouble here is that those who are trying to argue for the irreducible and primary nature of sensation language have not seen the full consequences of their arguments, the special status that must be given to assertions about pains (or about other sensations) if what they say is true.

For in an important sense the notion 'pain' is only being taken by Wittgenstein as a representative one; his discussion is ultimately about a whole class of philosophical views, roughly to be characterized as sense-datum empiricism, the idea that our language must have a foundation in a certain special class of experiences, namely sensations. And this is why there seems to be a link between this view and another which sought for a 'foundation' of language, that of Wittgenstein himself in the *Tractatus*. The idea that in the final resort there is only one way in which our everyday language can get its meaning is the doctrine which is variously attacked in the *Philosophical Investigations*. Pain is in many ways the most difficult of the sensations to deal with, and to account for our use of 'pain' the idea of a sensational foundation is most plausible. Hence it is natural for Wittgenstein to concentrate his attention on this area.

[1] *Tractatus Logico-Philosophicus*, 3.221.
[2] *Ibid.*, 3.26.   [3] *Ibid.*, 3.262.

It is often assumed in philosophy that though it is possible to communicate the fact that I have pain, I can't communicate my pain, in other words that sensations are irreducibly private. From this it would seem to follow that I can only learn the meaning of the word 'pain' from my own experience. Yet when I say 'He has a pain' I mean the same as when I say 'I have a pain'; I am asserting that he has the same as I have. The problem for Wittgenstein is how this can be. Normally we can discover that two attributions 'mean the same' by some process of validation. One way of doing this is by producing the referent, e.g. 'He has a watch and I have the same' is validated by our both producing watches for inspection. But in the case of pain there doesn't seem to be such a procedure, for pain seems to be a 'private object', not one that can be produced or indicated to validate the identity. And it would seem that unless there were some such validating procedure the claim that there is an identity does not make sense: 'It is as if I were to say: "You surely know what 'It is 5 o'clock here' means; so you also know what 'It's 5 o'clock on the sun' means. It means simply that it is just the same time there as it is here when it is 5 o'clock".—The explanation by means of *identity* does not work here. For I know well enough that one can call 5 o'clock here and 5 o'clock there "the same time", but what I do not know is in what cases one is to speak of its being the same time here and there.'[1] If I learn about my own pain directly and about that of other people only by inference from their behaviour, there would appear to be a gulf of just this kind. 'If one has to imagine someone else's pain on the model of one's own, this is none too easy a thing to do: for I have to imagine pain which I *do not feel* on the model of pain which I *do feel*. That is, what I have to do is not simply to make a transition in imagination from one place of pain to another. As, from pain in the hand to pain in the arm. For I am not to imagine that I feel pain in some region of his body. (Which would also be possible.)'[2] And, it would appear, there must be a difference in the meaning of the term 'pain' as applied to myself and to him. For, given that I feel my pain, then I can *know* I have it, whereas in the case of his I may be mistaken. In his case the word refers to behaviour, not, it would seem, to feeling.

I don't want to spend much time on the epistemological

---

[1] *PI*, § 350.   [2] *PI*, § 302.

question, for it seems clear that we can be *certain* that someone else is in pain. ' "But, if you are *certain*, isn't it that you are shutting your eyes in face of doubt?" They are shut.'[1] The question of whether I can say that I know that I am in pain seems not a very central one in this context. The difference between this problem and that which Wittgenstein's talk of introducing the name 'E' might suggest can now be seen. In the latter case it was the problem of introducing a new sensation word into the vocabulary; here it is a matter of how a word, already in the vocabulary, can ever have entered it. We all do use the word 'pain' of ourselves and others; the question is how this can have come about. The likeness with sensation 'E' can also be seen, for it appears that I have learnt the word from my own private experience. The fact that we have a set of sensation words coupled with the doctrine that sensations are private gives rise to a rather different notion of 'private language', one arising in the midst of our normal public language. Wittgenstein argues in the *Investigations* that the insistence on trying to explain all language on the model 'object and name' is the source of the trouble, though it is a quite natural way of proceeding. 'Now someone tells me that *he* knows what a pain is only from his own case!—Suppose everyone had a box with something in it: we call it a "beetle". No-one can look into anyone else's box, and everyone says that he knows what a beetle is only by looking at *his* beetle.—Here it would be quite possible for everyone to have something different in his box. One might even imagine such a thing constantly changing.—But suppose the word "beetle" had a use in these people's language?—If so it would not be used as the name of a thing. The thing in the box has no place in the language-game at all; not even as a *something*: for the box might even be empty.—No, one can "divide through" by the thing in the box; it cancels out, whatever it is. That is to say: if we construe the grammar of the expression of sensation on the model of "object and name" the object drops out of consideration as irrelevant.'[2] If it were the case that we learnt the use of the word 'pain' only from our own private experience there would be no guarantee that the word was being used in the same sense by different people. The object which is meant to be named being a purely private one there is no way of checking its identity in different cases. The tendency to say 'But I know that I am feeling

[1] *PI*, p. 224.   [2] *PI*, § 293.

this!' must be resisted, for the 'this' in question cannot, on the theory being attacked, be given any public meaning. It might be added that anyone who believed that there could be a private language in this sense would be unable to explain how it was possible for us to get from this situation to that of our normal use of pain-vocabulary.

But it is only on the assumption that is made by this theory that the problem arises; 'dividing through' can only take place where the 'object' can be named and not described, where a whole way of talking is being introduced into the language, not just an isolated word. 'Only I can see my after-image' is clearly a grammatical truth. But I can tell someone how to obtain an after-image and check that he has indeed succeeded by questioning him about details of his experience. Here the rest of language, in particular the language used to describe physical objects, comes to our aid. After-images can be described; they don't need to be named, so there is no problem about the place of the word in our language. 'Pain' is also a word of everyday language which we do use correctly, but on the account which Wittgenstein is attacking it is puzzling to see how it can have its everyday use. Therefore he has got to give a different account of the way in which the word comes into use, one which will escape from the difficulties I have been discussing. He does this by introducing the concept of 'pain-behaviour': 'Here is one possibility: words are connected with the primitive, the natural, expressions of sensation and used in their place. A child has hurt himself and he cries; and then adults talk to him and teach him exclamations and, later, sentences. They teach the child new pain-behaviour. "So you are saying that the word 'pain' really means crying?"—On the contrary: the verbal expression of pain replaces crying and does not describe it.'[1] The word 'sentences' in this quotation might mislead; Wittgenstein is not suggesting that the child is taught all the possible sentences in which the word 'pain' can occur but merely that the teaching process starts with substituting expressions which are almost parts of the language (my English-German dictionary gives 'ouch *int.* autsch!, au!'.) for the simple yells of the baby, and then proceeds to introduce proper words by means of full sentences. Here, as in other cases, the child is expected to be able to 'go on' to construct, e.g. if he has been

[1] *PI*, § 244.

taught to say that he has a pain in his leg and can also refer to his elbow, he is expected to be able to tell us that he has a pain in his elbow without further instruction.

Thus the statement 'I have a pain' is to be construed as a particular form of *pain-behaviour* rather than as an assertion that I 'have' a peculiar kind of object, a sensation. My statement about my own pain is on the same level as the pain-behaviour from which I deduce that you are in pain, or rather there is no need to talk of deduction or of any sort of inference here. It is only the analogy with other parts of our language that had held us captive and prevented us from seeing 'the way out of the fly-bottle'. There seem to be two sets of difficulties with this account. The first is that ably discussed by Roger Buck in his article 'Non-other Minds'.[1] He expresses his problem thus: 'If mental predicates have their criteria in behaviour, what of self-ascriptions of such predicates. Does one have to observe his own behaviour, listen to his own utterances, in order to find out that he is angry, has a toothache etc.?'[2] The second set of difficulties is connected with the kind of genetic account that Wittgenstein gives of this and other mental concepts, an account which, if hardened into dogma, seems to restrict unduly the possibilities of language.

To return to the first of these problems. To many of his readers Wittgenstein seems to be taking away something, to be denying the existence of inner sensations by reducing them to their outward expressions: 'And now it looks as if we had denied mental processes. And naturally we don't want to deny them.'[3] The upshot of his treatment might seem to be a kind of James-Lange theory of pain in which the expression of pain replaces the sensation. One caveat needs to be entered immediately; it is wholly foreign to Wittgenstein's method to try to produce a final account, a definite *solution* of any philosophic problem. He stresses in the Preface to *Philosophical Investigations* that 'The philosophical remarks in this book are, as it were, a number of sketches of landscapes which were made in the course of these long and involved journeyings.'[4] He is concerned with breaking the hold on our thought of certain pictures which have held us captive, not with producing a detailed map of the territory traversed. Hence it is always dangerous to talk of 'Wittgenstein's

---

[1] *Analytical Philosophy*, ed. R. J. Butler, Oxford, 1962, pp. 187–210.
[2] *Op. cit.*, p. 187.   [3] *PI*, § 308.   [4] *PI*, p. ix.

account of . . .' as if he had said all that was required. Often when such a claim is made it is the result of hardening a series of hints into a fully-fledged doctrine. William James was clear that he was putting forward a new *theory* of the emotions, one which corrected the accounts given previously. Wittgenstein is always saying 'Try looking at it in this way' to get a different perspective, though not necessarily a final and complete view, of something that we find puzzling. My remarks here are not for the purpose of confirming or refuting such a way of looking at things but rather an attempt to do the same kind of thing as Wittgenstein, assembling a series of reminders to help us find our way through a piece of confusing territory.

Buck agrees with Wittgenstein, or with his interpretation of Wittgenstein, that a verbal expression of pain is as good as a pre-verbal one in establishing that someone is in pain, but he seems to want something more than this. I quote the last sentences of his article: 'The fact that my linguistic behaviour in saying "My leg hurts" functions as a central criterion for my leg hurting does show that my so saying plays a rôle like that of groaning, limping, etc. But it does not show that my saying "My leg hurts" does not also play the other normal rôle of a straightforward autobiographical report.'[1] In one sense 'My leg hurts' is a standard instance of an 'autobiographical report'; what is peculiar here is the distinction between this and the rôle of the statement as a criterion of my being in pain. It seems almost as if Buck had failed to see the point of the whole argument, and the reason for this is perhaps his stress on the notion of 'criterion', which is out of place in this particular discussion. Certainly a statement of being in pain is normally a criterion for us to accept that the maker of the statement is in pain, but the important point for this discussion is why it should be, and the answer that Wittgenstein gives is that 'the verbal expression of pain replaces crying and does not describe it'. In this sense the notion of a 'report' is out of place; I can report on your pain but only express or evince my own, though given the functioning of the rest of language it is quite natural that we should talk of someone 'reporting his pain', and describe 'I have a pain in my leg' as a statement. The word 'criterion' is partly responsible for this trouble; Malcolm calls it a 'most difficult region in his (Wittgenstein's) philosophy'. But this is so only if it

[1] *Op. cit.*, p. 210.

is assumed that Wittgenstein had a fully worked out *doctrine* of criteria which has to be discovered from the scattered remarks in the *Investigations*. If instead it is treated merely as a useful way of expressing certain insights there is less danger of puzzlement.

This last point is connected with an excessive emphasis on the form of words 'I know I am in pain', on the incorrigibility of pain-utterances in general. It may lead to strange claims; for example, Feyerabend says of the certainty of statements about mental processes: 'It is their lack of content that is the source of their certainty.'[1] He contrasts this lack of content with the content of physical object statements. It seems odd that to say that 'There is a table in the room' has more content than 'I have a pain in my leg'. The latter is often a demand for immediate action and, in a context where doubt is possible, e.g. the consulting-room of an Army Medical Officer, far more difficult to verify. For one of the reasons for the 'incorrigibility' of pain expressions in their verbal form is, as Buck points out, that we are trained to be honest about them at the same time, or later, as we are taught the language-game. If the child tries to get out of some undesired obligation by feigning a pain, he soon learns that other, and to him undesirable, consequences also follow, such as not having ice-cream for lunch. And there are other means of reinforcing lessons of this type. Where there are strong reasons for lying, as in the Services in war-time, assertions about pain are certainly not taken as incorrigible. Many people will remember suffering from this doubt either as children or in the Army. As a child I once spent three days in considerable pain from a broken arm that a doctor had failed to diagnose. I was unable to convince my elders that I was in acute pain. It is situations like this that give force to statements of the form 'I know I'm in pain in a way you can't'.

In doubtful cases it is the discovery of the physical cause of the pain which tends to be decisive; in my own case as soon as another doctor diagnosed the fracture, everyone was overcome with sympathy. There are pains which are not accompanied by physical symptoms, but these are to some extent 'parasitic' on the primary cases where the physical evidence provides the final verification. Indeed this primacy of physical causes seems to be incorporated into the teaching of the 'new pain-behaviour'; the mother asks

---

[1] 'Problems of Empiricism', p. 191, in *Beyond the Edge of Certainty*, ed. R. G. Colodny, U.S.A., 1965.

to look at the painful limb, takes the child's temperature etc. and treats the results of these observations as decisive. One reason for the rarity of malingering is the efficiency of methods of detecting causes of pain. Mothers start making the distinction between genuine and fake pain-behaviour even before the stage at which language learning begins; if there appears to be no immediate physical cause for the baby to cry they may say that it is crying out of temper or for no reason at all. There are also further discriminations which are introduced into the teaching of pain-behaviour. The baby tends to cry for slight as well as for more serious pains, but the child is expected to pass over minor pains in silence, and the adult perhaps to keep quiet about most of his pains under normal circumstances. Of course communities differ in the extent to which they expect 'Spartan' behaviour, e.g. girls may burst into tears but not boys, but in all of them there is a restriction on the uninhibited expression of pain, whether verbally or pre-verbally. In fact all pain-behaviour is affected by the training received; I have already mentioned that ejaculations are in many cases conventional and differ from language to language. Clasping an injured limb may be a basic reaction, but when a man clasps his hurt knee this may be as much to indicate to others the source or severity of the pain as an 'instinctive' gesture. Lying or dissembling is as much a matter of behaviour in this area as of uttering untruths. Konrad Lorenz even claims that animals can pretend to be in pain. In *Man meets Dog* he has a chapter entitled 'Animals that Lie', in which he says 'I do not regard this inability to deceive as a sign of the cat's superiority, in fact, I regard it as a sign of the much higher intelligence of the dog that it is able to do so. There is no doubt that dogs can dissemble up to a certain point....'[1] This would seem to contradict Wittgenstein's remarks: 'Why can't a dog dissemble? Is he too honest? Could one teach a dog to simulate pain?'[2] He continues: 'Perhaps it is possible to teach him to howl on particular occasions as if he were in pain, even when he is not. But the surroundings which are necessary for this behaviour to be real simulation are missing.' In his descriptions Lorenz does provide the 'surroundings' which make it plausible so to describe the dog's behaviour, give the thing a context in which it is hard to say other than 'The dog was shamming when it limped'. When he rode his bicycle in the direction

---

[1] Penguin edition 1964, p. 167.　　　　[2] *PI*, § 250.

of the barracks, where the dog would have to remain all day, the dog limped, but if Lorenz turned round towards the country the limp was forgotten and the dog ran normally. Of course the dog wasn't *taught* to simulate pain, but then neither, in most cases, is the child; they both spontaneously cotton on to the advantages which have been gained in the past from genuine pains. 'Lying is a language-game which needs to be learned like any other one.'[1] But it is improbable that it is taught like any other language-game.

It might seem that this 'genetic' account of how pain-vocabulary comes to be acquired still left the door open for the problem of 'primacy', that the child is taught to substitute words for his primitive expressions of pain and so the words 'mean' or name *his* pain. It seems possible that what the adults thought was pain-behaviour was really an expression of pleasure so that the child was taught the language the 'wrong way round'. To put this point another way, we have got to be certain that *this* is pain-behaviour for the whole procedure to get off the ground. The child has to grasp what it is he has to substitute 'I've got a pain' for. Could he get it wrong? If someone were to challenge my statement that I was in pain with 'How do you know?' I think it would be in order to reply, as Wittgenstein did to a similar question, 'I have learnt English'.[2] A basic agreement in reactions is a presupposition of a common language, but this is something which is *shown* by the language, not something which can be expressed in it.[3] In this sense the proper answer to such questioning is 'shutting one's eyes' to these philosophical doubts. This answer may seem too cavalier a way of treating the problem; in the remainder of the paper I will offer some further remarks which will amplify and extend what I have just been saying.

The first question is that of what is to count as pain-behaviour. Here it is noteworthy that the question is rarely asked; we assume that we can tell, and this confidence goes beyond the human species. We are willing to assert that the dog is in pain on the grounds of his behaviour. (As distinct from saying he is in pain because of some obvious injury. Cf. 'The dog is in pain' and

---

[1] *PI*, § 249.

[2] *PI*, § 381. I have discussed this passage in 'Games and Family Resemblances' in *Philosophy*, Vol. XLII, No. 161. See especially pp. 221–5.

[3] 'What expresses *itself* in language, *we* cannot express by means of language.' *Tractatus* 4.121.

'The dog must be in pain'.) But in talking thus we do not mean that we could teach the dog the sophisticated form of pain-behaviour which is our pain-language. What then are we saying of him? The answer seems to be that he is in pain—or perhaps that this is pain-behaviour. We have expectations about future reactions and so on, but behind it lies the temptation to say that he is feeling a pain in the same kind of way as I do. Most contemporary Englishmen find no difficulty in attributing pain to dogs, cats and so on, in fact to members of the genus mammal; with reptiles there is room for some doubt, or perhaps for less concern; with lower forms of life the doubts become strong. 'A kindly grey-eyed fisherman assured me that the fish don't feel, as he cut open a sole.' Now it is not being denied that fish and other animals avoid certain things, that they wriggle when caught on hooks etc. It would seem that in spite of this people don't feel it necessary to talk of the fish feeling pain. And if someone claims that they do, how could the question be settled? There are no facts about the fish that could be appealed to; it is clear that messages pass along its nerves, and that these are more intense if there is a hook in its mouth than if its side has been lightly touched, and that its efforts to escape from the former would be stronger than those to escape from the latter. The facts are not in doubt, yet there would seem to be a difference between a person who asserts that the fish feels pain and one who denies it. The difference will be manifested in behaviour towards the fish, perhaps, but the reason for the difference seems to demand expression in terms of the fish 'feeling the same' (or something very like) what we feel when we feel pain. There seems to be room for a genuine difference between a person who says that fish feel and one who denies it, whereas if we came across people arguing whether a machine had feelings we would fail to understand them. 'Look at a stone and imagine it having sensations.—One says to oneself: How could one so much as get the idea of ascribing a *sensation* to a *thing*? One might as well ascribe it to a number!—And now look at a wriggling fly and at once these difficulties vanish and pain seems able to get a foothold here, where before everything was, so to speak, too smooth for it.'[1]

In the last paragraph I referred to 'most contemporary Englishmen' finding no difficulty in attributing pain to some animals;

[1] *PI*, § 284.

the caveat was entered because there is a disagreement among different peoples about the treatment of animals. Some are, to English eyes, completely indifferent to animal suffering or even take pleasure in it. (Compare the old English sports of bear- and bull-baiting.) Sometimes these differences in attitude to animals are coupled with differences in attitude to people; 'To behold suffering gives pleasure, but to cause another to suffer affords an even greater pleasure. This severe statement expresses an old, powerful, human, all too human sentiment. . . .'[1] It is said that among Red Indians the highest compliment to pay a prisoner was to give him the most painful death. There are, in fact, a variety of possible human attitudes to the pain of other creatures, just as there are a number of different attitudes inculcated to one's own pain (Spartan or anti-Spartan). What we might call 'cruelty to animals' does not involve a philosophic doubt about the feelings of dumb creatures; the peasant who ill-treats his donkey is indifferent to it. Because there is no single human attitude to pain, except perhaps at the very basic level of a mother's reaction to a child's cry, the differences must be accounted for by the training received in different societies. Hence it is now necessary to return to the process of learning pain-language.

Wittgenstein, when he talked of the replacement of the natural pain-behaviour, was concerned with the first steps in this procedure, not claiming that he had given a full and final account of it. For to have replaced crying with 'My knee hurts' is to have taken a step on the road to learning our pain-language, but it is by no means to have completed the process. Even quite early on the expressions of pain of others besides the learner are taken into consideration; these others include other children, adults and, in the case of England at least, animals. The child is taught that others' expressions of pain demand the same kind of sympathetic treatment as he demands for his own; he learns to imitate his mother's treatment of his injured leg when his sister injures hers and so on. It is made clear to the child that pulling the cat's ears causes the cat to feel the same as he does—'How would you like to have someone much bigger than you pull your ears?' It is not that we first learn the meaning of the word 'pain' and then, as a consequence of this learning, feel sympathy with someone when he says he is in pain; the sympathy is learnt with the learning of

[1] Nietzsche, *Genealogy of Morals*, Doubleday Anchor Books, 1956, p. 198.

the word. The sympathy may ultimately rest on unlearned responses to others' primitive pain-behaviour, but the distance to which this sympathy is extended depends on teaching; in our society animals (or at least the higher animals) are included, but they need not be. Nor need all human beings; certain 'enemy' groups may be left out. 'Only of a living human being and what resembles (behaves like) a human being can one say that it *has* pains.'[1] And what is to count as a human being (or as behaving like a human being) is not given by the facts but by the 'form of life' of the society in question.

For learning the new pain-behaviour is learning a whole form of life and one which is fairly central in any culture. Hence the great complexity of the process. The ability to use the word 'red' is simple in comparison, hence it is comparatively easy to say when a child has grasped the notion, even though there are no formal tests normally used for this purpose. Just as there are some children who cannot, because of physical factors, learn the use of 'red' so there are some who apparently fail to learn the full form of life associated with pain, who are unable to sympathize with others' pain, psychopathic personalities of some kind. (Whether this is due to some innate disability or to some fault in the teaching process is a subject of discussion among psychologists, e.g. discussions about the influence of early maternal deprivation on future character.) It was this involvement with a whole form of life that Wittgenstein was stressing, I think, when he said, 'You learned the *concept* of "pain" when you learned language.'[2] What I have been trying to bring out is the complexity of this particular piece of learning language; here the use of the word cannot be separated from a mass of other things which are necessarily involved in that use, for it is a whole concept and not a single word that is being learnt.

Hence it is not surprising that philosophers were puzzled over the word 'pain', or that Wittgenstein continually returns to the question of it, both for its own importance and as an instance of all talk about sensations. Our normal way of thinking about the relation between words and the world leads to insoluble puzzles when we try to apply it to 'pain'. So long as it is treated as a mere word no solution is possible. Wittgenstein was concerned first of all to break the hold of the private sensation language, which

[1] *PI*, § 283.   [2] *PI*, § 384.

seemed to make other people's assertions about pain unverifiable, and then to show that an alternative account could be developed, one which does justice to the complexity of our actual pain-language. I have been concerned to amplify this account and to show some directions in which it might be extended.

VII

WITTGENSTEIN'S FREUD

Frank Cioffi

INTRODUCTION

WITTGENSTEIN'S remarks on Freud do not form part of one
continuous exposition. Most of them were not intended for publi-
cation. Some are sketchy to the point of incomprehensibility,
others are apparently, and perhaps even ultimately, inconsistent.
Nevertheless, they seem to me to offer a more illuminating
characterization of Freud than any other and one of the few which
can be confronted with its subject without producing acute
feelings of incongruity.

There are three habits of mind which it is natural to refer to
Freud. One is the tendency to see a large segment of human life
as comprising the pursuit of ends of which the agent has no
cognizance, even to the point of seeing as instances of purposive
activity what would have formerly been considered happenings
and of re-drawing the customary boundary between what we
undertake and what we undergo. Another, the pursuit of hidden
meanings, the readiness to see a wide range of phenomena, from
dreams, errors and the symptoms of neurotics to works of art and
the anonymous productions of culture—like legend and myth—as
the distorted manifestation or symbolic gratification of unconscious impulses. (Everything is what it is *and* another thing.) Third,
the tendency to trace the personalities of adults, their interests,
attitudes, sexual proclivities and susceptibility to neurotic illness,
to the influence of infantile sexual vicissitudes.

In what follows I try to elicit and assess Wittgenstein's answer to the question of how the currency of these habits is to be accounted for, by examining two more determinate questions: What is Freud really up to when he proffers interpretations of symptoms, errors, dreams, etc? What is the character of the claim that these phenomena are 'mental acts', are motivated, are wish-fulfilments? Freud himself has more answers to these questions than he chooses to be aware of. However, all of them involve him in the claim that he is in some sort explaining these phenomena, that he is accounting for their occurrence. A proto-typical Freudian utterance would have the following features: It would assert of some phenomenon like a slip of the tongue, a lapse of memory, a reminiscence, a dream, a phobia, an hysterical symptom, or an obsessive thought, that though it might appear to be something which the patient had passively suffered, it was, nevertheless, motivated, purposive, and that by submitting the item to free association and/or translating it according to certain rules, a wish would be arrived at, often of an infantile sexual character, of which the patient may have been unaware but which had been secretly at work, waiting for an opportune moment to contrive its gratification. About such remarks Wittgenstein holds the following views: They are not hypotheses; their production is more a consummatory than an instrumental activity. Neither the wish-fulfilling and symbolic character of the events they purport to explain nor their connexion with sexuality are matters of evidence. If such remarks have come widely to be accepted and made models for still other remarks, this is not to be attributed to any explanatory use to which they can be put but to the appeal they exert, an appeal partly to be explained in terms of their invocation of the notion of hidden meaning and of sexuality.

In the *Introductory Lectures*, Freud refers to 'the displeasing proposition that mental processes are essentially unconscious' and says, 'By thus emphasizing the unconscious in mental life, we have called forth all the malevolence of humanity.' In the *New Introductory Lectures*, he speaks of 'the burdens under which we groan—the odium of infantile sexuality, the ludicrousness of symbolism'. In his 1925 paper on 'The Resistances to Psycho-analysis', he attributes these 'above all to the very important place in the mental life of human beings which psychoanalysis assigns to what are known as the sexual instincts'. And in accounting for the popularity of Adler he said: 'Humanity is ready to accept anything when tempted with ascendancy over sexuality as the bait.'

A succinct way of giving Wittgenstein's view of Freud is simply to state that he stands these propositions on their heads. In a letter to Norman Malcolm, he said of Freud: 'He always stresses what great forces in the mind, what strong prejudices work against the idea of psychoanalysis but he never says what an enormous charm this idea has for people just as it has for Freud himself.'[1] In the first of the conversations with Rush Rhees on Freud, he says of the notion of the unconscious: 'It is an idea which has a marked attraction.'[2] In the third of the lectures on Aesthetics, he says about Freud's sexual interpretation of a dream: 'The connexions he makes interest people immensely. They have a charm. It is charming to destroy prejudice. . . . It may be the fact that the explanation is extremely repellent that drives you to adopt it'; and of psychoanalytic explanations in general that many 'are adopted because they have a peculiar charm. The picture of people having unconscious thoughts has a charm. The idea of an underworld, a secret cellar. Something hidden, uncanny . . . A lot of things one is ready to believe because they are uncanny.'[3]

I

In what way are psychoanalytic explanations uncanny? Consider the protective, interest-serving relationship in which the unconscious so often stands to its possessor: Ferenczi's unconscious makes him forget a witticism which might have caused offence and embroiled him in controversy; Jones' causes him to mislay his pipe when he is suffering from the effects of over-smoking and to find it again when he has recovered; an engineer's (who has reluctantly agreed to work one evening) to put out of commission the equipment necessary for the task; a house physician's

---

[1] Norman Malcolm, *Ludwig Wittgenstein—A Memoir*, (London, 1958), p. 44. Freud was not always so disingenuous about this. In 1893 he wrote to his friend Fliess: 'The sexual business attracts people; they all go away impressed and convinced, after exclaiming: No one has ever asked me that before.' S. Freud, *Origins of Psychoanalysis* (New York, 1954), Letter 14.

[2] Cyril Barrett (Ed.), *Ludwig Wittgenstein—Lectures and Conversations* (Oxford, 1966), p. 43.

[3] Barrett, *Lectures and Conversations*, pp. 24–5.

to absent himself during duty hours without detection; a keen classicist's to present her with a coveted antique Roman medallion which she finds she has unwittingly packed among her belongings; that of girls with beautiful hair to 'manage their combs and hairpins in such a way that their hair comes down in the middle of a conversation'. Freud's unconscious permits him to forget to keep professional engagements which are not lucrative and to miss a train connexion while travelling to Manchester via Holland and thus fulfil a long-cherished with to see Rembrandt's paintings without defying his elder brother's request not to break his journey. On one occasion it admonished him before visiting a patient to take particular care not to repeat a diagnostic error.

It also assuages the sense of guilt by punishing moral breaches. In support of this view Freud cites a correspondent who informs him that he has observed how often men who turn round to look back at passing women in the street meet with minor accidents such as colliding with lamp-posts.

Along with this benevolence you must also consider the unconscious' superiority in performance as compared with that of the person whose unconscious it is. Freud freely acknowledged his inferiority to his unconscious in performing arithmetical calculations or aiming accurately. He relates that on one occasion when he received news that a seriously ill daughter had taken a turn for the better and his unconscious had decided that a sacrificial act of thanksgiving to fate was in order, he impulsively kicked a slipper at a little marble statue of Venus, knocking it to the ground, where it broke. The fact that he did not hit any of the objects which were closely grouped around it, he attributes to the superior aim of the unconscious mind. Freud gives another example of the superior dexterity of the unconscious: the manner in which he broke the marble cover of his inkpot. 'My sweeping movement was only apparently clumsy; in reality it was exceedingly adroit and well directed, and understood how to avoid damaging any of the more precious objects that stood around. It is my belief that we must accept this judgement for a whole series of seemingly accidental, clumsy movements . . . they prove to be governed by an intention and achieve their aim with a certainty which cannot in general be credited to our conscious voluntary movements.' (Elsewhere Freud speaks of the 'unconscious dexterity' with which objects are mislaid 'if the unconscious has a motive in doing so'.) Freud also informs us that 'apparently clumsy movements can be most cunningly used for sexual purposes'. One such which he relates 'was accomplished with the dexterity of a conjurer'. This was when Stekel, in extending his hand to greet his hostess, undid the bow of her gown without being aware of any dishonourable intention.

Rank, Freud reports, has provided evidence of the superior ability of the unconscious to see under unfavourable conditions: it enabled a girl, who coveted a cheap piece of jewellery, to find on the pavement, a note for exactly the amount required. 'Otherwise it would be impossible to explain how it was, that precisely this one person, out of many hundreds of passers-by—and with all the difficulties caused by poor street lighting and the dense crowds—was able to make the find.'

Don't these stories remind you of something? Don't they illustrate the degree to which the notion of the unconscious meets the same demands as those which produce the invisible companion phantasies of our childhood? Though we know what Freud would have said to this suggestion: that invisible companion phantasies are endopsychic perceptions of the operation of unconscious agencies.[1]

It may seem strange but it is undeniable that accounts in which the rôle assigned to the unconscious is a punishing rather than a benevolent one are found equally gratifying. In this connexion Freud writes of a class of patients whom he describes as 'those wrecked by success', people who fall mentally ill 'precisely because a deeply rooted and long-cherished wish has come to fulfilment'. He cites the case of a teacher who developed melancholia when offered promotion and of a woman who broke down when the obstacles to her marriage to the man she loved were

---

[1] In *The Red and the Black* Stendhal attributes this same relish in the masterfulness of the unconscious to his Mathilde de la Mole:

'As she made these reflections, Mathilde's pencil was tracing lines at random on a page of her album. One of the profiles she had just completed amazed and delighted her; it was strikingly like Julien. "It's the voice of Heaven! Here's one of the miracles of Love"! she cried in rapture. "Quite unconsciously I've drawn his portrait."

'She rushed off to her room, locked herself in, applied herself to her task, and tried hard to draw a portrait of Julien. But she could not do it; the profile sketched by accident still remained the best likeness. Mathilde was enchanted by this; she saw in it a clear proof of a grand passion.'

All the examples referred to on pages 186 to 188 are from *The Psychopathology of Everyday Life*. James Strachey's translation has an index of all the examples Freud uses.

removed.[1] The 'peculiar attraction' of such explanations can be illustrated by contrasting them with the case of the cricketer who was perfectly happy as long as he scored no runs, but broke into tears if he scored more than fifty. If this were all, one could have added him to Freud's list as a particularly striking case of self-punishment consequent on success, and predicted a great bibliographical future for him in the literature of psychoanalysis. But he was diagnosed as a diabetic whose distress was induced by the effect on his blood sugar level of the exertion of running between the wickets. When he was given glucose sweets to suck he was able to score a century without too much anguish. Don't we feel that by unimaginatively responding to so banal a form of treatment he forfeited his claim to our interest?—though we could restore this interest if we could be persuaded that, as Freud once remarked when he came upon an organic determinant of an illness, 'the neurosis had seized upon this chance event and made use of it for an utterance of its own'.[2]

This remark brings us to another characteristic of the unconscious; one which reinforces Wittgenstein's suggestion as to its affinities and the source of its appeal. It is alluded to rather cryptically in the *Introductory Lectures* in the remark that 'the neurosis of hysteria can create its symptoms in all systems of the body (circulatory, respiratory, etc.)'.[3] Though this could be construed as simply an allusion to the phenomenon of hypochondriacal conviction which does not involve any assumption of mental control over physical processes, there is reason to believe that Freud means more than this. In the case history of Dora, Freud explains how Dora was able to make use of an organically based disorder of the throat, which induced coughing and aphonia, to express symbolically her unconscious love for a man by falling ill when he was away and recovering when he returned. That the periods did not invariably coincide is attributed by Freud to the fact that 'it became necessary to obscure the coincidence between her attacks of illness and the absence of the man she secretly loved, lest its regularity should betray her secret'.[4]

[1] Sigmund Freud, 'Some Character Types met with in Psychoanalytic Work (1915), *Collected Papers*, Vol. IV (London 1956), pp. 324–5.
[2] Sigmund Freud, 'Fragments of an Analysis of a Case of Hysteria' (1905), *Collected Papers*, Vol. III (London, 1925), p. 123.
[3] Sigmund Freud, *Introductory Lectures on Psychoanalysis* (1915–17), (London, 1922), p. 259.   [4] Freud, *Collected Papers*, III, p. 49.

Unlike Kitty Bennett, Dora had complete discretion in her coughs and timed them beautifully.

Since Freud isn't clear as to whether the wish produces, or merely exploits the catarrh, this example might seem open to an alternative construction. More conclusive evidence of his proclivity for this mode of thought, along with a suggestion that he was nervous about making it too explicit, is contained in a letter to Groddeck: '. . . it is not necessary to extend the concept of the unconscious in order to include your experience with organic disorders. In my article about the unconscious which you mention, you will find a small footnote: "We shall save for mention in another connexion a further important prerogative of the unconscious." I shall tell you what I kept back there, namely the assertion that acts of the unconscious have intense plastic effects on somatic processes in a manner impossible to achieve by conscious acts.'[1] Further evidence on this point is to be found in Ernest Jones' biography, where we are told that at the end of 1916 Freud was considering writing a book, the essential content of which was 'that the omnipotence of thoughts was once a reality. Our intention is to show that Lamarck's conception of need which creates and modifies organs is nothing else than the power unconscious ideas have over the body, of which we see the remains in hysteria—in short, "the omnipotence of thoughts".'[2]

We can account both for this conviction of Freud's and for our readiness to be convinced by varying slightly his judgement on Adler: 'There is nothing humanity won't accept with ascendancy over matter as the bait.'

---

[1] Ernst Freud (Ed.), *Letters of Sigmund Freud* (London, 1961), Letter 176.

[2] Ernest Jones, *Sigmund Freud—Life and Work* (London, 1957), Vol. III, p. 335. Freud explicitly endorses the felicity of Wittgenstein's term 'uncanny'. In his account of 'the peculiar quality . . . which arouses in us the feeling of uncanniness' (*Collected Papers*, IV, pp. 368–9), Freud invokes just those features which we have seen to characterize his notion of the unconscious. See also the essay 'Animism, Magic and the Omnipotence of Thought' in *Totem and Taboo* (Footnote 25, Strachey Translation: '. . . we invest with a feeling of uncanniness those impressions which lend support to a belief in the omnipotence of thoughts'. It is as if he were constructing his explanations to a formula.

II

But what is noteworthy in Freud is not the credulity he evinces, and evokes, towards the outlandish but the tendentious way in which he describes the commonplace. This brings us to another of Wittgenstein's theses: that in Freud's hands the notions of unconscious mental acts and of wish-fulfilment are notations. Among the most reliable stigmata of a notation is the advancing of a thesis in the company of its own counter-examples. The principle at work is that all putative counter-instances are to be considered clandestine specimens of confirmatory instances. If we examine Freud's investigation of errors of which he said that it was 'the prototype of every psychoanalytic investigation' and that it was 'better calculated than any other to stimulate a belief in the existence of unconscious mental acts', we see how great is the notational component in the claim that 'acts of a mental nature, and often very complicated ones, can take place in you . . . of which you know nothing'. Less than a quarter of the 250 or so examples which *The Psychopathology of Everyday Life* came to contain are even apparently illustrations of the phenomena they are said to exemplify, 'of a will striving for a definite aim'.

Consider those cases of forgetting which Freud describes as 'forgetting from a motive of avoiding unpleasure'. Let us suppose that the empirical facts are not in question, i.e. that there is a tendency for names or words or intentions with unpleasant associations to be forgotten. Is there anything in this fact which demands description in terms of the behaviour of an unconscious agency which censors the thoughts of the subject in the interests of his peace of mind? Freud says of these cases 'the motive of forgetting actuates a counter-will'. But he also compares them with the flight reflex in the presence of painful stimuli. Why then do they demand description in terms of an unconscious agency any more than this does? Is my inability to hold my hands above my head for an indefinite period to be ascribed to the victory of a counter-will to lower them? 'Couldn't the whole thing have been differently treated?'[1] Considerations like these suggest that what Freud often sees as instances of the operation of unconscious agencies really register his determination to describe familiar facts in a novel and congenial idiom.

[1] Barrett, *Lectures and Conversations*, p. 45.

In *Zettel*, § 444, Wittgenstein compares Freud's theory that all dreams are wish-fulfilments with the thesis that every proposition is a picture. '. . . it is the characteristic thing about such a theory that it looks at a special, clearly intuitive case and says: that shows how things are in every case. This case is the exemplar of all cases.'[1] And in the 'Conversations on Freud', he says of this theory of Freud's, 'it is not a matter of evidence' but 'is the sort of explanation we are inclined to accept . . .[2] Some dreams obviously are wish fulfilments: such as the sexual dreams of adults for instance. But it seems muddled to say that all dreams are hallucinated wish-fulfilments.'[3]

Even those dreams which are incontestably wish-fulfilments don't justify the inferences which Freud draws from them. Consider Freud's anchovy dream. On nights on which he has eaten anchovies he wakes thirsty, but not before he has dreamt of gulping down draughts of cold water. This is certainly an instance of wish-fulfilment. As is the case of the hungry dreamer who dreams of a delicious meal. But Freud goes on to say of this last example: 'The choice was up to him of either waking up and eating something or of continuing sleep. He decided in favour of the latter.'[4] What is there in these examples to justify the assumption of a supervisory agency accompanying the phenomena and regulating their manifestations? If I succeed in waking at a predetermined hour, must I assume that some delegate of myself has kept vigil through the night? 'Unconscious mental acts', 'choice', 'decision': If it were a matter of Penelope unravelling her web in a nocturnal trance, or Lady Dedlock sleep-walking her way to Captain Hawdon's grave, there might then be some justification for the suggestiveness of these idioms.

Freud has various devices for dealing with counter-examples. The most notorious occurs in Chapter 4 of *The Interpretation of Dreams*. A patient recounted a dream in which something she wished to avoid was represented as fulfilled. Freud comments:

---

[1] In his autobiography Freud neatly exemplifies this habit of mind. 'The state of things which he (Breuer) had discovered, seemed to me, to be of so fundamental a nature, that I could not believe it could fail to be present in any case of hysteria if it had proved to occur in a single one.' (*An Autobiographical Study*, Hogarth Press, 1950, p. 36.)

[2] Barrett, *Lectures and Conversations*, p. 42.

[3] *Ibid.*, p. 47.

[4] Sigmund Freud, *An Outline of Psychoanalysis* (London, 1949), p. 36.

'Was not this in sharpest opposition to my theory that in dreams wishes are fulfilled? No doubt . . . the dream showed that I was wrong. *Thus it was her wish that I might be wrong, and her dream showed that wish fulfilled.*'[1] (Freud's italics.) Nor is he timid about generalizing this solution. 'Indeed it is to be expected that the same thing will happen to some of the readers of the present book: they will be quite ready to have one of their wishes frustrated in a dream if only their wish that I may be wrong can be fulfilled.'[2] Anxiety dreams are dealt with either by invoking the masochistic wish for pain or the super-ego's satisfaction in inflicting punishment on the ego.

The problem that most dreams have a neutral or indifferent content is dealt with by means of the distinction between the latent and the manifest content of the dream. It is the latent content which constitutes the fulfilment of the wish, the manifest content being a consequence of distortion.

Wittgenstein comments on this in the second conversation: 'The majority of dreams Freud considers have to be regarded as camouflaged wish-fulfilments and in that case they simply don't fulfil the wish. *Ex hypothesi*, the wish is not allowed to be fulfilled and something else is hallucinated instead. If the wish is cheated in this way, then the dream can hardly be called a fulfilment of it. Also it becomes impossible to say whether it is the wish or the censor that is cheated. Apparently both are, and the result is that neither is satisfied. So that the dream is not an hallucinated satisfaction of anything.'[3]

The applicability of these remarks is not confined to the dream theory but extends to Freud's account of the neuroses, where one is often equally at a loss to see the grounds for Freud's insistence that the symptoms of the disorder represent the fulfilment of a wish, or of the wish to frustrate the wish, or both.

Consider his explanation of epileptoid attacks like those from which Dostoevsky suffered in his youth. Deathlike seizures of this kind 'signify an identification with a dead person, either with someone who was really dead or with someone who was still alive and whom the subject wished dead', in which case the attack has the significance of a punishment. 'One has wished another

---

[1] Sigmund Freud, *The Interpretation of Dreams* (London, 1954), p. 151.
[2] Freud, *The Interpretation of Dreams*, p. 158.
[3] Barrett, *Lectures and Conversations*, p. 47.

person dead and now one is this other person and is dead oneself
...' Thus Dostoevsky's 'early symptoms of deathlike seizures can
be understood as a father-identification on the part of his ego,
permitted by his super-ego as a punishment. "You wanted to kill
your father in order to be your father yourself. Now you *are* your
father, but a dead father ... now your father is killing *you*." '¹ And
this is how Freud derives a wish-fulfilment from a young girl's
attempt at suicide: She was simultaneously punishing herself for
a death-wish against her mother and gratifying it since 'the girl's
identification of herself with her mother makes this "punishment-
fulfilment" again into a wish-fulfilment'. I.e. if I *am* my mother
and I kill *myself*, I kill my mother and my mother's murderer.²

Interpretations like these are the conceptual equivalents of
impossible objects. But to speak of Freud's conceptual confusion
in this context is to slight his grammatical genius, his ingenuity
in devising unconstruable idioms. It is as if one were to attribute
the self-contradictory structures in M. C. Escher's prints to his
inability to draw.

(We tend to be diffident about characterizing explanations like
these because it is so difficult to be sure one has got hold of them.
But why shouldn't this resistance to paraphrase be the most
important thing about them? Why shouldn't it be the essence of
the matter? What a psychoanalytic explanation tells us is itself.)

Though 'the peculiar attraction' of the uncanny goes far
towards explaining the appeal of the idioms in which psychoanalytic explanations are couched it is inadequate as an account of
why Freud employs them. In the *Blue Book* Wittgenstein says of
the thesis that there exist unconscious thoughts: '... it is just a
new terminology and can at any time be translated into ordinary
language'.³ Later, after remarking on how we may be 'irresistibly
attracted or repelled by a notation', he says: 'The idea of there
being unconscious thoughts has revolted many people. ... The
objectors to unconscious thoughts did not see that they were not
objecting to the newly discovered psychological reactions, but to
the way in which they were described. The psychoanalysts, on the
other hand, were misled by their own way of expression into

¹ Sigmund Freud, 'Dostoevsky and Parricide' (1928), *Collected Papers*, Vol. V
(London, 1957), pp. 229 and 232.
² Sigmund Freud, 'The Psychogenesis of a Case of Homosexuality in a Woman'
(1920), *Collected Papers*, Vol. II (London, 1948), p. 220.
³ Ludwig Wittgenstein, *The Blue and The Brown Books* (Oxford, 1958), p. 23.

thinking that they had done more than discover new psychological reactions: that they had in a sense discovered conscious thoughts which were unconscious.'[1] These remarks seem to me mistaken in seeing in the notion of unconscious thoughts a disinterested notational compulsion and in thinking that they merely record 'newly discovered psychological reactions' which 'can at any time be translated into ordinary language'. The notion of unconscious thoughts is not a detachable excrescence which can be removed leaving a neutral core of 'phenomena and connexions not previously known'.[2] Its function is to give a self-authenticating character to psychoanalytic method.

When Freud says 'we call a process unconscious when . . . it was active at a certain time although at that time we knew nothing about it',[3] he is not merely succumbing to the appeal of a notation, not just adopting a form of description which 'adds nothing to what we know but only suggests a different form of words to describe it'.[4] For what other manner of speaking would enable him to insist on the irrelevance of any doubts as to the existence of such connexions not based on the use of a specialized method of introspection? What has been taken for conceptual audacity was really prudence.

Making the reference of his claims an imperceptible process, contemporary with the 'act' it is supposed to explain, enables Freud to combine the compatibility with an agent's candid disavowal of a hypothesis about the causes of his behaviour, with the invulnerability to counter-example of Collingwood-type reconstructions of an historical agent's grounds for his action. The objection to speaking in this connexion of the 'abominable mess' made by Freud's disciples in confusing cause and reason,[5] is that it represents the state of affairs too much as one of helpless confusion and overlooks the way in which the confusion is ingeniously exploited in the interests of the theory. In the notion of reasons which are causes there is more grammatical flair than grammatical muddle.

By encapsulating the thought inside the agent's head, Freud is enabled to dispense with the surroundings and by making it

[1] Wittgenstein, *The Blue and The Brown Books*, p. 51.
[2] G. E. Moore, 'Wittgenstein Lectures in 1930–1933', *Mind*, Vol. 64 (1955), p. 15.
[3] Sigmund Freud, *New Introductory Lectures* (London, 1949), p. 95.
[4] Wittgenstein, *The Blue and The Brown Books*, p. 136.
[5] Moore, *Mind*, Vol. 64 (1955), p. 20.

unconscious to dispense with the agent's assent as well. Once we grasp that it is not the hypothesis of the existence of unconscious wishes which gives Freud's theory its distinctive character but the assumption that psychoanalytic method affords a unique access to them, many puzzles surrounding psychoanalytic claims are dissipated.

III

Wittgenstein thinks psychoanalytic explanations are like aesthetic explanations; but it doesn't help us to know this unless we know what he thinks aesthetic explanations are like. All that is certain is that he thinks they are unlike explanations in terms of brain mechanisms. But though, when he says that the giving of a cause cannot resolve our puzzlement over an aesthetic impression, he sometimes means that the giving of the physical substrate of the impression cannot answer our question (e.g. an account of the state of the olfactory nerve while we are smelling a rose doesn't shed light on the aesthetic question why it smells pleasant),[1] he doesn't always mean only this.

In his remarks on Frazer in the same series of lectures something else is in view. According to Moore, 'He said that it was a mistake to suppose that why, e.g. the account of the Beltane festival "impresses us so much" is because it has "developed from a festival in which a real man was burnt" . . . Our puzzlement as to why it impresses us' (which Wittgenstein said was an aesthetic question), 'is not diminished by giving the causes from which the festival arose, but is diminished by finding other similar festivals: to find these may make it seem "natural", whereas to give the causes from which it arose cannot do this.'

Darwin is taxed with a similar mistake in supposing that 'because our ancestors when angry wanted to bite' is a sufficient explanation of why 'we show our teeth when angry'. I am not sure of the force of 'sufficient' here and not sure how the question why we show our teeth when angry is like the question why the account of the Beltane festival impresses us. And there are other puzzles connected with these remarks. The question to which Frazer is supposed to have given a mistaken reply is never raised

---

[1] Moore, *Mind*, Vol. 64 (1955), p. 18.

by Frazer, whose main interest (in Balder the Beautiful) seems to be whether the point of Fire festivals is to reinforce the sun's heat by sympathetic magic or to destroy evil and threatening things. Also, the method recommended by Wittgenstein to relieve us of our puzzlement as to why we are impressed—'. . . finding other similar festivals'—sounds like a description of what Frazer is doing a good deal of the time: 'Bonfires at the Ponggol festival in Southern India . . . bonfires at the Holi festival in Northern India . . . the fire walk in China . . . the fire walk at the Hindu festival . . . the fire walk among the Badagas . . . the fire walk in Japan etc., etc.' I have said enough to show why it is difficult to have much confidence in the construction one puts on these remarks. Nevertheless, it is hard not to feel, at some points, an almost Spenglerian disdain for causal inquiry at work; that, e.g., Wittgenstein hasn't misremembered the question that Frazer set himself but just feels that his own is more interesting and Frazer's an error of sensibility. But there is an alternative and plausible construction that might be put on these remarks which fall short of attributing to Wittgenstein an antipathy to causal questions. Wittgenstein may just be calling attention to an error which there is a natural tendency to make. The error in question might be described as looking for consummation in the wrong place; an instance of which is asking for the etiology of a phenomenon where what we really want is an analysis of the impression produced on us by the phenomenon. For example, we often think we are interested in the past when it is really the experience of pastness which absorbs us. We forget that the peculiar impression ruins make on us is not accounted for by discovering how they came to be in that condition. Someone who embarked on a course of astronomical study in the vague hope of shedding light on the nature of the impression made on him by the night sky when the stars are out is also making this kind of mistake. Again, the peculiar impression made on us by the distinctive movements of achondroplastics ('a friendliness was in the air as of dwarfs shaking hands') is not elucidated by an account of the endocrinology of the condition. And yet when Wittgenstein speaks of 'the sort of explanation one longs for when one talks of an aesthetic impression' one doesn't feel that it is the analysis of an impression that he wants: it is still too much like a hypo-thesis.

A clue to what he does have in mind is provided by a comparison he makes in the second lecture on Aesthetics between aesthetic remarks and expressions like 'What is it I wanted to say?' and 'What people really want to say is so and so'.[1] In *Philosophical Investigations*, § 334, of the expression 'So you really wanted to say . . .', Wittgenstein says 'We use this phrase in order to lead someone from one form of expression to another'. This suggests to me that the kind of remark which Wittgenstein thinks aesthetic puzzlement calls for is one which, though it may seem to be describing or explaining a certain past state of mind, is really prolonging an experience in a particular direction; like the angle-trisector who, when shown the proof that what he was attempting to do was impossible, says 'That this was the very thing he was trying to do, though what he had been trying to do was really different', or the regular pentagon-constructor who, in similar circumstances, says ' "That's what I was really trying to do" because his idea had shifted on a rail on which he was ready to shift it'.[2] Perhaps the remarks of William James' Mr. Ballard are another instance of this. The Egyptian intellectuals of the twenties, who declared that their countrymen were Arabs, exemplify a related phenomenon, as do the estranged couple who say they never loved one another: statements which, though apparently descriptive of the past, really serve to orient their utterers to a projected future; and like some interpretations of the analyst 'make it easier for them to go certain ways . . . make certain ways of behaving and thinking natural for them'.[3]

Often these remarks take the form of an analogy; the finding of something to which we feel we stand in a similar relation as to that which puzzles or impresses us.

In Moore's notes Wittgenstein speaks of Aesthetics as a matter of 'giving a good simile' and of 'putting things side by side'. And in the third lecture on Aesthetics he speaks of 'the explanation we should like to have when we are puzzled about aesthetic impressions. . . . As far as one can see, the puzzlement I am talking about can only be cured by peculiar kinds of comparison . . .'.[4] In the second conversation he says: 'When a

---

[1] Barrett, *Lectures and Conversations*, p. 37.
[2] Moore, *Mind*, Vol. 64 (1955), pp. 9–10.
[3] Barrett, *Lectures and Conversations*, pp. 44–5.
[4] *Ibid.*, p. 20.

dream is interpreted it is fitted into a context in which it ceases to be puzzling. In a sense, the dreamer re-dreams his dream in surroundings such that its aspect changes.'[1] In the *Brown Book*, in discussing what an explanation in Aesthetics is like, he says: '. . . it may consist in finding a form of verbal expression which I conceive as the verbal counterpart of the theme . . . the word which seemed to sum it up'. There is some inadvertent testimony from Wittels that psychoanalytic explanation may also be a matter of 'the word which seemed to sum it up'.[2] He speaks of '. . . neurotic patients who were peculiarly ready to adopt the use of the word "castration" as soon as they heard me employ it. Their reminiscences then tended to assume some such form as the following: "My mother castrated me when I was a little boy. But the one who especially castrated me was my paternal grandfather. Yesterday my mistress castrated me." '[3] Freud gives a sexual explanation of obsessive thinking. He speaks of the tendency to 'sexualize thinking and to colour intellectual oper-ations with the pleasure and anxiety which belong to sexual processes proper . . . investigations become a sexual activity . . . the thought process itself becomes sexualized . . . the gratification derived from reaching the conclusion of a line of thought is experienced as sexual gratification . . . (the feeling that comes from settling things in one's mind and explaining them replaces sexual satisfaction)'.[4] We can easily imagine that someone on reading these words might have a delighted feeling of recognition and be moved to assent. But would it follow that they constitute a hypothesis? When in this connexion Karl Abraham points out that 'In Biblical Hebrew the word to "know" is used for the sexual act. A man is said to know his wife', and that 'the com-parison of mental and sexual acts is not uncommon. We speak for instance of the conception of a poetical work'; or when Freud says of Leonardo 'He had merely converted his passion into a thirst for knowledge . . . at the climax of intellectual labour, when knowledge had been won, he allowed the long restrained affect to break loose and flow away freely . . .', aren't these once again

---

[1] Barrett, *Lectures and Conversations*, p. 45.

[2] Wittgenstein, *The Blue and The Brown Books*, pp. 166–7.

[3] Fritz Wittels, *Sigmund Freud* (London, 1924), pp. 160–1.

[4] This passage is an amalgam of remarks in Freud's *Leonardo da Vinci* (London, 1963), p. 114 and in his 'Notes upon a Case of Obsessional Neurosis' (1909), *Collected Papers*, III, p. 380.

simply a matter of 'giving a good simile', of 'placing things side by side'? And even if some sequaceous patient testified to an irresistible compulsion to shout "Eureka" whenever he achieved orgasm wouldn't this just be another copy of the same newspaper?

Consider Baudelaire's comparison of the act of love to an application of torture—'. . . these sighs, these groans, these screams, these rattling gasps. . . . What worse sights can you see at any inquisition? These eyes rolled back like sleep-walkers, these limbs whose muscles burst and stiffen as though subject to the action of a galvanic battery, etc., etc.' Contrast our state of mind as we read these words with that in which we take in Freud's observations on the sadistic nature of coitus, or his characterization of sexual consummation as a minor form of epilepsy ('a mitigation and adaptation of the epileptic method of discharging stimuli').[1] No one would confuse his gratitude to Baudelaire for momentary relief from the burden of being high-spirited about his sexuality with the appreciation of a discovery or the consideration of a hypothesis, but with Freud this is happening all the time.

'The attraction of certain kinds of explanation is overwhelming. At a given time the attraction of a certain kind of explanation is greater than you can conceive. In particular, explanations of the kind "this is really only this". ' This remark of Wittgenstein's brings out what most discussions of Freud, even when they are critical, miss—the compulsive quality of Freud's interpretations. 'There is a strong tendency to say: "We can't get round the fact that this dream is really such and such" . . . If someone says: "Why do you say it is really this. Obviously it is not this at all", it is in fact even difficult to see it as something else.'[2] Try telling someone who is psychoanalytically oriented that Van Gogh's mutilation of his ear may have had no connexion with castration, or that Oedipus' blinding of himself was not a castration-substitute and you meet not so much with incredulity as bewilderment. He will have difficulty in giving your statement sense. He behaves as if he had learned the expression 'castration-symbol' ostensively. This is simply what castration-substitute *means*. 'The correct analogy is the accepted one.'

[1] Freud, 'Dostoevsky and Parricide', *Collected Papers*, V, p. 226.
[2] Barrett, *Lectures and Conversations*, p. 46.

IV

In Moore's account of the 1933 lectures Wittgenstein is reported as saying 'that Freud did not in fact find any method of analysing dreams which is analogous to the rules which will tell you what are the causes of stomach ache'.[1] But aren't repressed thoughts the green apples of Freudian psychopathology? We might ask how Freud manages to detect allusions to castration, defloration, birth, intercourse, menstruation, masturbation, etc., etc., on so many occasions if he has not discovered rules analogous to those 'which will tell you what are the causes of stomach ache'. And in the second conversation, in contrasting the real character of psychoanalytic interpretations with their apparent character, Wittgenstein describes what 'might be called a scientific treatment of the dream ... one might form a hypothesis. On reading the report of the dream, one might predict that the dreamer can be brought to recall such and such memories. And this hypothesis might or might not be verified.'[2] But isn't this what Freud does? Doesn't Freud produce instances where the interpretation is tied to some independently authenticatable event? But before we accept this argument we must look more closely at Freud's reconstructive achievements. When we do, we find that they are almost invariably inconclusive in one of the following ways: either the inferred event is ubiquitous, or it was known independently of the procedure which ostensibly inferred it. In either case the reality of the inferred event wouldn't, in itself, show the validity of the means by which it was arrived at.

If we doubt this and consult the case histories to reassure ourselves on the point, we find that either the events or scenes reconstructed have too great an independent probability to support the validity of the interpretative technique (as with Dora's urinary incontinence), or were known independently of the analysis (as with the severe beating Paul had from his father and the castration threats to which Little Hans was exposed). The apparent exception to this is, what is often regarded as Freud's greatest reconstructive achievement, his discovery that a patient, at the age of 18 months, saw his parents engage in 'a coitus a

---

[1] Moore, *Mind*, Vol. 64, p. 20.
[2] Barrett, *Lectures and Conversations*, p. 46.

tergo, thrice repeated',[1] at five in the afternoon. This certainly doesn't lack circumstantiality. What it lacks is corroboration. Freud is aware of this and falls back on a coherence argument.

It might be felt that even if these objections hold of the cases Freud reported at length, he does assure us that he has produced reconstructions to which these objections do not apply; where the reconstructed events were not known in advance and were independently authenticated through 'lucky accidents' as, for example, Marie Bonaparte's servants confirming Freud's suspicion that she had witnessed intercourse before the age of one.[2] But for this to count in favour of the claim that Freud discovered the laws according to which repressed memories are distorted, we should have to know how often Freud gave reconstructions which contained primal scenes; and we have reason to believe that it was very often. That he should have failed to report those which were not corroborated doesn't involve attributing to him any improbable degree of disingenuousness, since he himself tells us that he attached no importance to this kind of authentication, convinced as he was that his reconstructions must have been essentially true in any case:

> I should myself be glad to know whether the primal scene in my present patient's case was a phantasy or a real experience; but taking other similar cases into account I must admit that the answer to this question is not in reality a matter of very great importance. These scenes of observing parental intercourse, of being seduced in childhood, and of being threatened with castration are unquestionably an inherited endowment, a phylogenetic inheritance. . . .[3]
>
> If they can be found in real events, well and good; but if reality has not supplied them, they will be evolved out of hints and elaborated by phantasy. The effect is the same, and even today we have not succeeded in tracing any variation in the results according as phantasy, or reality, plays the greater part in these experiences.[4]

With phylogenetic inheritance to fall back on Freud deprives himself of any way of discovering that his reconstructions are mistaken and his principles of interpretation invalid, which means that he deprives himself of any reason for believing that they are

[1] Freud, 'From the History of an Infantile Neurosis' (1918), *Collected Papers*, III, p. 508.
[2] Jones, *Freud—Life and Work*, Vol. III, p. 129.
[3] Freud, 'History of an Infantile Neurosis', *Collected Papers*, III, p. 576.
[4] Freud, *Introductory Lectures*, p. 310.

not. He fails to see this because he exploits an unconscious presumption that the complexity of an interpretation, the number of cross-references it contains to incidents in the life of the patient, '. . . the long thread of connexions that spun itself out between a symptom of the disease and a pathogenic idea', is an index of its truth. We underestimate enormously the possibility of producing such an appearance of intricate coherence where the items are not genuinely related. (Isn't this the real moral of the discovery of the falsity of so many of the assumptions on which the Leonardo essay was based?)

In justifying his conviction as to the reality of a primal scene Freud said: 'Everything seemed to converge upon it . . . the most various and remarkable results radiated out from it [and] not only the large problems but the smallest peculiarities in the history of the case were cleared up by this single assumption . . . [the analyst] will disclaim the possession of the amount of ingenuity necessary for the concoction of an occurrence which can fulfil these demands.'[1]

Wittgenstein doubts this: 'Freud remarks on how after the analysis of it, the dream appears so very logical. And of course it does. You could start with any of the objects on this table—which certainly were not put there by your dream activity—and you could find that they all could be connected in a pattern like that, and the pattern would be logical in the same way.'[2]

Either Wittgenstein's table was more cluttered than mine or he shared Freud's genius for constructing associative links between any two points, for I have not been able to produce patterns anywhere near as convincing as Freud's. But the force of this consideration is weakened if we remember that Freud lays his own table: 'The material belonging to a single subject can only be collected piece by piece at various times and in various connexions.'

But it is the elasticity and multiplicity of the rules which do most to reduce the *a priori* improbability of producing associative links to and between his patients' dreams, symptoms, reminiscences, etc, where there are really none. The link between the unconscious thought and its manifestation is often simply that in both something is inside something, or something is going

---

[1] Freud, 'History of an Infantile Neurosis', *Collected Papers*, III, p. 256.
[2] Barrett, *Lectures and Conversations*, p. 51.

into something, or something is coming out of something, or something is being detached from something, etc., etc.

It is this which enables Freud to see an allusion to castration anxiety in a symptom of obsessional neurotics 'by means of which they manage to ensure themselves continual torment. When they are in the street they are constantly watching to see whether some acquaintance will salute them first, by taking off his hat, or whether he seems to wait for their salute; and they give up a number of their acquaintances who they imagine no longer salute them or do not return their salute properly ... the source of this excess of feeling can easily be found in relation to the castration complex.'[1] (Something is being detached from something.)

And to an incestuous desire for his mother in 'Little Hans'' inability to venture out of doors. This phobia involved a 'restriction on his freedom of movement. ... It was, therefore, a powerful reaction against the obscure impulses to movement which were especially directed against his mother.' That a horse should have been the object of his phobia lends itself to the same construction. 'For Hans, horses had always typified pleasure in movement ... but since this pleasure in movement included the impulse to copulate, the neurosis imposed a restriction on it and exalted the horse into an emblem of terror.'[2] (Something is moving.)

And to defloration in the following example: 'Do you know why our old friend E. turns red and sweats whenever he sees a certain class of acquaintance. ... He is ashamed, no doubt; but of what? Of a phantasy in which he figures as the deflowerer of every person he comes across. He sweats as he deflowers because it is hard work. ... Moreover, he can never get over the fact that at the university he failed to get through in Botany so he carries on with it now as a "deflowerer".'[3]

'It is all excellent similes.' Freud turns his patient into a walking rebus.

Though the interpretations tell their own story there is some interesting testimony on this point from an American psychiatrist who underwent a training analysis with Freud: 'I would often give a whole series of associations to a dream symbol and he would

[1] Freud, 'Connection between a Symbol and a Symptom' (1916), *Collected Papers*, II, p. 163.

[2] Freud, 'Analysis of a Phobia in a Five Year Old Boy' (1909), *Collected Papers*, III, p. 280.

[3] Sigmund Freud, *Origins of Psychoanalysis* (New York, 1954), Letter 105.

wait until he found an association which would fit into his scheme of interpretation and pick it up like a detective at a line-up who waits until he sees his man.'[1]

It seems that Freud stood to his patients' associations, dreams, symptoms, reminiscences and errors more as the painter to his pigments than as the sleuth to his traces of mud and cigar ash.

The implications of this are that instead of seeing in 'condensation', 'displacement', 'representation by the opposite', etc., etc., laws governing unconscious processes, we recognize them as recipes for the construction of associative chains to preselected termini; not mechanisms by whose operation the symptom, dream, etc, was constructed, but rules for 'working a piece of fancy into it'.

v

As to the thesis that infantile experience determines adult character, e.g. the rôle of primal scenes, Wittgenstein once again locates its persuasive power in its attractiveness, 'the attractiveness of a mythology', of 'explanations which say this is all a repetition of something which has happened before', thus 'giving a sort of tragic pattern to one's life. . . . Like a tragic figure carrying out the decrees under which the Fates had placed him at birth.'[2]

An objection which might be brought against Wittgenstein here is that he comes to this conclusion while discussing no topic other than interpretation. What of the evidence for the pathogenic power of infantile sexual occurrences and the developmental claims about infantile sexuality? Surely these provide a sufficient explanation of how the themes of infancy and sexuality came to figure so prominently in psychoanalysis, without the necessity of invoking 'charm' or the appeal of the repellent?

Wittgenstein's failure to mention these topics might lend some credence to Professor Wollheim's suggestion that his view of Freud is to be put down to a combination of ignorance and envy. On the other hand, perhaps Wittgenstein noticed something which Professor Wollheim missed. If, undisheartened by the extravagance of this supposition, we re-examine Freud to see what basis there might be for it, we find that far from constituting an

[1] J. Wortis, *American Journal of Orthopsychiatry*, Vol. X, 1940, pp. 844–5.
[2] Barrett, *Lectures and Conversations*, p. 51.

objection to Wittgenstein, his implicit dismissal of Freud's etiological and developmental claims alerts us to a certain peculiarity of psychoanalytic discourse which has gone largely unnoticed: the extent to which Freud dehistoricized his theory so that the etiological and developmental claims, which ostensibly underpinned his interpretations, were actually derived from them.

When we re-read Freud in the light of Wittgenstein's remarks the conviction forces itself on us that the end of analysis, to serve which the rest of the theory exists, is the construction and emission of interpretations; that it is this activity which must at all costs be sustained; that if Freud had come to the conclusion that his views as to infantile sexual life were mistaken the stream of interpretations would not on that account have been halted.

This might seem an idle speculation which there is no way of checking and which is in any case extremely implausible. It is therefore worth mentioning that Freud himself once discussed the possibility that 'what analysts put forward as being forgotten experiences of childhood ... may on the contrary be based on phantasies brought about on occasions occurring in later life'. This is his comment: 'And if this interpretation of the scenes from infancy were the right one ... The analysis would have to run precisely the same course as one which had a naïve faith in the truth of the phantasies ... A correct procedure, therefore, would make no alterations in the technique of analysis, whatever estimate might be formed of these scenes from infancy.'[1]

But, if interpretations containing allusions to infantile sexuality are to be advanced in spite of a disbelief in the occurrence of infantile sexual phantasies, Freud's convictions as to the rôle of infantile sexuality in the etiology of the neuroses cannot be his ground, but only his pretext, for interpreting symptoms in infantile sexual terms.

Just as often as Freud tells us that the psychoanalytic theory of infantile sexual development has been or could be confirmed by the direct observation of children, just so often does he imply that we are to expect nothing of the kind. '... Direct observation

[1] Freud, 'History of an Infantile Neurosis', *Collected Papers*, III, p. 522.
   In these remarks Freud is anticipating a contingency very like that which overtook him in 1897 when he concluded that in many cases the sexual interference which he had stated was the specific cause of hysteria had not taken place and which he met by assigning to infantile sexual phantasies the pathogenic role vacated by infantile seductions. And he is meeting it with the same tenacity.

has fully confirmed the conclusions drawn from psychoanalytic investigation and thus furnished good evidence for the reliability of the latter method of investigation.'[1] But elsewhere it is psychoanalytic investigation which confirms the reliability of our observation of infantile sexual life: '. . . we call the doubtful and indefinable activities of earliest infancy towards pleasure sexual because, in the course of analysing symptoms, we reach them by way of material which is undeniably sexual';[2] 'But those phases of the sexual development . . . which are of the greatest interest theoretically (are) gone through so rapidly that direct observation alone would perhaps never have succeeded in determining (their) fleeting forms. Only by the help of psychoanalytic investigation of the neuroses has it become possible to penetrate so far back . . .';[3] and of observations on small children: 'They do not carry such complete conviction as is forced upon the physician by psychoanalyses of adult neurotics.'[4] His account of his grounds for the conviction that the key to the neuroses is to be found in infantile sexual life is infected with the same ambivalence. 'If anyone should enquire where he is to look for an incontestable proof of the etiological importance of sexual factors in psychoneuroses— since . . . a specific etiology in the form of particular infantile experiences is not forthcoming—then I would indicate psychoanalytic investigation of neurotics as the source from whence the disputed conviction springs.'[5] It has not generally been realized how often Freud implies (what his practice confirms) that the character of a child's infantile sexual life is to be determined by waiting until he is an adult and then psychoanalysing him.[6]

---

[1] Sigmund Freud, 'Three Contributions to the Theory of Sex', *The Basic Writings of Sigmund Freud* (New York, 1938), p. 594.

[2] Freud, *Introductory Lectures*, p. 273.   [3] Freud, *Introductory Lectures*, p. 274-5.

[4] Freud, *The Interpretation of Dreams*, p. 258.

[5] Sigmund Freud, 'My Views on the Part Played by Sexuality in the Etiology of the Neuroses' (1905), *Collected Papers*, Vol. I (London, 1948), p. 281.

[6] 'An analysis which is conducted on a neurotic child . . . cannot be very rich in material; too many words and thoughts have to be lent to the child and even so the deepest strata may turn out to be impenetrable to consciousness. An analysis of childhood disorder through the medium of recollection in an intellectually mature adult is free from these limitations.' ('From the History of an Infantile Neurosis', *Collected Papers*, III, p. 475.)

See also Freud's explanation of why 'we know less about the sexual life of little girls than of boys'. Because 'the sexual life of adult women is "a dark continent" for psychology'. (S. Freud, 'The Question of Lay Analysis' (1926), *Standard Edition* Vol. XIX, p. 243.)

But the character of Freud's claims concerning infantile life is often such that even the patient's acquiescence cannot assuage our doubts; it merely raises the Ballard problem of *Philosophical Investigations*, § 342, and *Zettel*, § 109, in a more acute form. If it is a matter of 'dim impulses which it is impossible for the child to grasp psychically at the time',[1] if we are to 'consider how little the child is able to give expression to its sexual wishes and how little it can communicate them',[2] aren't we justified in treating the patient's assent as Wittgenstein treats Ballard's reminiscence of the period before he knew language? 'Are you sure—one would like to ask—that this is the correct translation of your wordless thoughts into words? . . . These recollections are a queer memory phenomenon, and I do not know what conclusions one can draw from them about the past of the man who recounts them.'[3]

When Freud says of the influence of infantile castration fears that 'psychoanalytic experience' has put it 'beyond the reach of doubt',[4] this is not hyperbole. He means it. What allows him to mean it is his intermittent conviction that his achievement consists in having defeated the malice of nature in compelling men to observe each other's minds through so opaque a medium as a human skull by providing access to the thing itself.[5] ('Off, you lendings!') Wittgenstein has brought us to feel that this is an ambition which not even God could reasonably entertain.

The behaviour of patients under analysis, which began as evidence of the vicissitudes through which they had passed, gradually became criteria for the ascription of these vicissitudes. To say of a patient that he had entertained such and such wishes, or had repressed such and such phantasies, is to say that he now behaves towards the analyst in such and such a way, responds to the proffered interpretations in such and such a manner. Interpretation has been dehistoricized. The notion of truthfulness has replaced that of truth. The narration of infantile reminiscences has been assimilated (incoherently) to the narration of dreams.

---

[1] Freud, 'Female Sexuality' (1931), *Collected Papers*, V, p. 265.

[2] Freud, *New Introductory Lectures*, p. 155.

[3] Ludwig Wittgenstein, *Philosophical Investigations* (Oxford, 1953), Section 342.

[4] Freud, 'Dostoevsky and Parricide', *Collected Papers*, V, p. 231.

[5] 'The unconscious is the true psychical reality.' (Freud, *The Interpretation of Dreams*, p. 613.)

CONCLUSION

When, in Moore's notes, Wittgenstein speaks of Freud as giving accounts which sound like science when, in fact, they are only 'a wonderful representation',[1] he may be referring to the extent to which the world, conceived of psychoanalytically, is just the everyday world taken over again with an altered expression. An illustration: in the grammatical phantasies which constitute the libido theory we can see the operation of a typically metaphysical motive in the way in which the quotidian world disappears from view behind the permutations of the libido, e.g. the meta-psychological account of why we mourn our dead; of why, as Freud puts it, 'the ego never abandons a libido-position willingly'. If this fact is perplexing, by reference to what is it to be rendered intelligible? '. . . the adhesiveness of the libido'; 'cathetic fidelity'; 'the economic conditions of mental pain'. It seems that a Freud-person would have no difficulty in feeling grief—'that pattern in the weave of our lives'—for a second, or, if he did, it would be from the same causes which make it difficult to empty a bath tub or a bottle of glue in a second. But Freud is sometimes in the position of the impressionistic painter of *Philosophical Investigations*, § 368: 'I describe a room to someone, and then get him to paint an impressionistic picture from this description, to show that he has understood it. Now he paints the chairs which I described as green, dark red; where I said yellow he paints blue—that is the impression which he got of that room. And now I say: "Quite right! That's what it's like." '

I think it is this sort of thing which Wittgenstein was referring to when he said that Freud had genius and therefore might 'find out the reason of a dream',[2] even though 'if you are led by psychoanalysis to say that really you thought so and so, or that really your motive was so and so, this is not a matter of discovery but of persuasion',[3] and that 'there is no way of showing that the whole result of analysis may not be "delusion" '.[4]

Freud certainly produced statements to which an enormous number of people have said 'yes', but there are good grounds for assimilating his achievement to that of the anonymous geniuses

[1] Moore, *Mind*, Vol. 64, p. 20.   [2] *Ibid*.
[3] Barrett, *Lectures and Conversations*, p. 27.   [4] *Ibid*., p. 24.

to whom it first occurred that Tuesday is lean and Wednesday fat, the low notes on the piano dark and the high notes light. Except that instead of words, notes and shades, we have scenes from human life.

In this paper I have tried to demonstrate the impossibility of accounting for Freud's preoccupations, or our preoccupation with Freud, without invoking what Wittgenstein called 'charm'. We were caused to re-dream our life in surroundings such that its aspect changed—and it was the charm that made us do it.

International Library of Philosophy & Scientific Method

Editor: Te

(Demy 8vo

Allen, R. E.
    Plato's   70.
Allen, R. E. and Furley, David J. (Eds.), Studies in Presocratic Philosophy
    326 pp. 1970.
Armstrong, D.M., **Perception and the Physical World** 208 pp. 1961.
    A Materialist Theory of the Mind 376 pp. 1967.
Bambrough, Renford (Ed.), **New Essays on Plato and Aristotle**
    184 pp. 1965.
Barry, Brian, **Political Argument** 382 pp. 1965.
Bird, Graham, **Kant's Theory of Knowledge** 220 pp. 1962.
Broad, C. D., **Lectures on Psychical Research** 461 pp. 1962.
    (2nd Impression 1966.)
Crombie, I. M., **An Examination of Plato's Doctrine**
    I. Plato on Man and Society 408 pp. 1962.
    II. Plato on Knowledge and Reality 583 pp. 1963.
Day, John Patrick, **Inductive Probability** 352 pp. 1961.
Dennett, D. C., **Content and Consciousness** 202 pp. 1969.
Dretske, Fred I., **Seeing and Knowing** 270 pp. 1969.
Ducasse, C. J., **Truth, Knowledge and Causation** 263 pp. 1969.
Edel, Abraham, **Method in Ethical Theory** 379 pp. 1963.
Farm, K. T. (Ed.), **Symposium on J. L. Austin** 512 pp. 1969.
Flew, Anthony, **Hume's Philosophy of Belief** 296 pp. 1961.
Fogelin, Robert J., **Evidence and Meaning** 200 pp. 1967.
Franklin, R., **Freewill and Determinism** 353 pp. 1968.
Gale, Richard, **The Language of Time** 256 pp. 1967.
Glover, Jonathan, **Responsibility** 212 pp. 1970.
Goldman, Lucien, **The Hidden God** 424 pp. 1964.
Hamlyn, D. W., **Sensation and Perception** 222 pp. 1961.
    (3rd Impression 1967.)
Husserl, Edmund, **Logical Investigations** Vol. I: 456 pp. Vol. II: 464 pp.
Kemp, J., **Reason, Action and Morality** 216 pp. 1964.
Körner, Stephan, **Experience and Theory** 272 pp. 1966.
Lazerowitz, Morris, **Studies in Metaphilosophy** 276 pp. 1964.
Linsky, Leonard, **Referring** 152 pp. 1967.
MacIntosh, J. J. and Coval, S. C. (Eds.), **Business of Reason** 280 pp. 1969.
Meiland, Jack W., **Talking About Particulars** 192 pp. 1970.
Merleau-Ponty, M., **Phenomenology of Perception** 487 pp. 1962.
Naess, Arne, **Scepticism** 176 pp. 1969.
Perelman, Chaim, **The Idea of Justice and the Problem of Argument**
    224 pp. 1963.
Ross, Alf, **Directives, Norms and their Logic** 192 pp. 1967.
Schlesinger, G., **Method in the Physical Sciences** 148 pp. 1963.
Sellars, W. F., **Science and Metaphysics** 248 pp. 1968.
    Science, Perception and Reality 374 pp. 1963.
Shwayder, D. S., **The Stratification of Behaviour** 428 pp. 1965.
Skolimowski, Henryk, **Polish Analytical Philosophy** 288 pp. 1967.